SOLVED BY WALKING
PARADOX AND RESOLUTION IN THE LABYRINTH

MARY HACKWORTH

DEDICATION

For My Family

CONTENTS

ACKNOWLEDGMENTS

Many thanks to Elizabeth Terzian, Victor Faessel, and Robert Rabel for their suggestions and encouragement.

Chapter 1
What Is a Labyrinth?

Bent is the path of eternity.

— Friedrich Nietzsche, *Thus Spoke Zarathustra*

Introduction

As a metaphor for epistemology in Western culture, the labyrinth has a long history, although the concept of "labyrinth" is likely rooted not in philosophy, or even in myth, but rather in ritual dance dating back to Neolithic times. Any exploration of this vast terrain is daunting, as the history of the subject is itself labyrinthine, proceeding in several enticing directions at once and affording just as many ways to get lost as there are possibilities for understanding. Five thousand years (or more) of history provide many forking paths and byways in which to wander while chasing the essence of the labyrinth.

Grasping the essential meaning of the labyrinth is as difficult as trying to navigate one. The labyrinth has so many possible interpretations that it is difficult to catalog them all. The origins of the word itself are in doubt, and its evolution from ritual to myth is not clearly understood. The symbol comprises multiple meanings—it is a metaphor for life, for truth, for moral conduct, and for philosophy. Even if one considers the labyrinth only as a literal structure, it contains two distinct possibilities: unicursal and multicursal. As depicted in medieval churches from Chartres to Amiens

1

(and in today's labyrinth revival), whether inscribed on the floor, the wall, or the doorposts of a building or laid out in brick or stone, the labyrinth, despite many twists and turns, highlights a single (unicursal) path. Proceeding by the greatest amount of digression possible toward the center, it is by no means a straight path, but there is nonetheless only one way in; the only choices are whether to enter and whether to continue. Moreover, the way in, with few exceptions, is the way out. One simply reverses one's steps to emerge from the labyrinth.

In contrast to the unicursal is the multicursal labyrinth, or maze. It has many possible paths, some of which are dead ends. There may be more than one entrance and exit. Depending on the maze's complexity, there may be a single (though difficult to discern) path to the center, or there may be multiple ways to get there. In a particularly fiendish maze, every available path may bypass the center altogether; there may not even be a center! The hallmarks of the multicursal labyrinth are confusion, choice, and an element of hazard or danger, since it is possible to lose one's way. One must adopt a strategy to navigate a maze, whereas little thinking (but a great deal of perseverance) is required to reach the center of a unicursal labyrinth. The path may appear convoluted, but it is in fact single and not multiple, although this may not be apparent until one has entered and gone some distance.

The labyrinth's forms are numerous: from dance to visual design; from a physical building or structure to a literary motif; from forest to castle, from dream to underworld; from centering device to well of confusion; from the human body to the manufactured city; from the form of writing to narrative form. Not surprisingly, it is easy to lose one's way in all the possibilities.

I am arguing that the particular form the labyrinth takes in literature and culture over time is a projection of the way the Western mind sees itself in relation to the world. In particular, the two forms of the labyrinth, unicursal and multicursal, represent distinctly different philosophical positions on what can be known and the ultimate source of that knowledge. Generally, the unicursal labyrinth is associated with a mythic or religious worldview with established beliefs, practices, and a version of "truth"; its rituals, teachings, and priests provide access to this truth. This style of thinking usually assumes there is a known basis for knowledge, and that one approaches it by approaching the gods (or God) in a prescribed manner. The multicursal labyrinth, or maze, symbolizes the loss of certainty regarding a sacred source of knowledge, or at the very least an unwillingness to approach it uncritically or in a predetermined manner. From this point of view, knowledge is acquired through rational thinking and personal experience; "truth" may be either unknowable or relative, but in any case there are many ways to access or test it. There may or may not be any "ultimate meaning," and the source of authority shifts from a priest or shaman in the first case to the individual in the second. In essence, then, the labyrinth illustrates two different approaches to reality, and whether this approach is a religious, experiential, philosophical, or scientific one (or all at once) depends on the individual's point of view.

Many modern writers on the labyrinth tend to catalog its history and not necessarily its philosophical dimensions. A few have examined the labyrinth's meaning in particular periods—for example, the Middle Ages or the Renaissance—or have looked at it from a literary, religious, or artistic point of view, but few have investigated its entire history in order to connect it to epistemology. Although others have, indeed, discussed the differences between the forms of the labyrinth and theorized on their meaning, this study analyzes the epistemological implications of those differences using a depth psychological lens. I have not concerned myself with literary analysis alone, or with visual representations, or with the intriguing and suggestive history of the labyrinth as dance but rather with all of them at once. I have included an examination of the labyrinth as a physical structure along with its appearance as a metaphor. It is the *concept* of the labyrinth that concerns me, and I have noted the clear distinction between the two types of labyrinths while offering an understanding of the way their meanings complement one another.

Tracking the transformation of the labyrinth across time is difficult, since even the etymology of the word is uncertain, and its history is woven of at least three separate strands. The labyrinth means two different things—single path and maze. Since the term is used interchangeably for both, a sense of uncertainty arises whenever the word appears—which kind of labyrinth is meant? Customs relating to the labyrinth, including the walking of the medieval-style labyrinths common today in churches across the United States, may seem to point to one provenance but actually involve more than one. Thus, for example, the modern labyrinth movement was inspired by the cathedral labyrinth at Chartres, but the element of ritual dance, a decidedly pre-Christian custom, also permeates the phenomenon. Most modern labyrinths, like Nancy Sinatra's boots, are made for walking (or skipping, or running), and many churches and other institutions provide labyrinth guides designed to instruct a newcomer in how to do this. Someone approaching a labyrinth for the first time sees centuries of history condensed into an elegant, stylized, somewhat abstract design laid out on grass, pavement, or flooring that rarely exceeds 40 feet in diameter and gives little hint of its storied past.

Two Labyrinths in One

The earliest depictions of the labyrinth go back at least five thousand years. The labyrinth has been scratched on rocks and cave walls, and stories about it appear in not only Greek and Roman but also Egyptian and Indian mythology and folklore. It appears in the mythology of the American Southwest, too, along with etchings of a labyrinth design identical to that found in the Greco-Roman world. Claims that the labyrinth symbol appears in all cultures cannot be substantiated, however; some versions resemble meanders or mazes more than the regular seven or eleven circuits of the "classical" labyrinth (I will elaborate on the "classical" form in Chapter 3). Although forms of the labyrinth appear in non-Western cultures, this study is primarily concerned with the labyrinth's significance in Western history.

A labyrinth can be seen as a diagram of the way life is experienced: as a series of unfolding events that are difficult to anticipate, in which perspective constantly shifts. One rarely attains wisdom merely by moving as fast as possible from point A to point B; successive layers of experience, trial, and error lead to deeper and more lasting knowledge. Only after the labyrinth has been completely traversed can one sense the whole pattern, which may not have been apparent before. When the labyrinth is a maze, the emphasis is on the individual's chosen path, with all its idiosyncratic detours, not the universal path. Perhaps unicursal and multicursal are two ways of looking at the same thing, the macroscopic or the microscopic: what you see depends on whether you are looking through a telescope, with its wide view of the cosmos, or a microscope, with its close-up view of a very specific piece of it (Doniger 7-9). Perhaps they also correspond to a

Platonic versus an Aristotelian view of the world; the emphasis may be on a transcendent source of knowledge and ultimate reality or on immanence and a physical world to be discovered.

What about the common tendency to confuse the two forms of the labyrinth? It appears that separate strands of meaning gradually became so intertwined that after many centuries it was difficult to remember that a labyrinth was originally a dance or else a pattern on the dancing surface that guided the dancers in their performance. It simply became a byword for complexity and difficulty. As Hermann Kern explains, evidence is dismayingly scanty, but signs point toward an ancient fertility or solar ritual intended to ensure fecundity and the regular progression of the seasons (33). It appears that something very basic, no less profound than the renewal of life, was bound up in this ritual; its choreographed steps and convoluted but careful progression indicate a communal and mediated approach to the sacred. Even when the word "labyrinth" was applied to other things—buildings, underground networks, cities, tombs—it retained the cachet of the old mystery and its urgency, so that it eventually became synonymous with a structure guarding a powerful secret.

The classical labyrinth design was found on a pitcher at Tragliatella, Italy (c. 620 BCE), with the designation "Truia" (taken by many scholars to indicate "Troy," a meaning Virgil develops in his description of the "Trojan Ride" performed at Anchises's funeral games in Book 5 of the *Aeneid*). This design (and variations thereof) was also found in medieval Hebraic manuscript references to Jericho, fabled city of difficult access, though Kern places the origins of the Jericho labyrinth tradition much earlier, at the time of the Diaspora in the first century CE (130); Jerusalem was also associated with the labyrinth. This evidence shows that the tradition of the labyrinth as a protective device guarding something valuable, a city or a treasure, was well established and widespread in the ancient world. Kern believes that the Tragliatella pitcher, of Etruscan design, may in fact depict the labyrinth as it was changing from a dance performed on foot to a dance performed on horseback (Kern 26-27, 30). The depiction of two copulating couples next to the labyrinth may be the link to the ancient fertility rite enacted in a communal dance, a performance that in more settled times became associated with protection of the city or fortress.

Even in the myth of Theseus, remnants of the labyrinth's ritual origins are suggested by the fact that Theseus and his companions dance a celebratory "Crane Dance" after escaping the labyrinth; vase illustrations depict them in the triumphant execution of this dance. Homer describes its appearance on Achilles's shield in Book 18 of the *Iliad*; in the next to last decorative ring on this shield, youths and maidens are shown dancing. Robert Rabel notes that Plutarch's account of the dance describes circling motions that commemorate the labyrinth; he also notes an element of eroticism in the dance and mentions the delight of the audience, also depicted on the shield, in its skillful performance (Rabel 176-78).

A key development in the myth is the attitude toward what is in the center of the labyrinth, which has shifted from worshipful to fearful in the story of Theseus: the dance has been transformed into a celebration of the defeat of a monster, although rebirth—or at least triumph over death—is still part of the story. Whether life or death is emphasized in the labyrinth myth, and whether the center contains monster, devil, angel, white whale, God, or something else correlates with a given period's view of philosophy and cosmology.

The labyrinth's most celebrated appearance in mythology is in the Greek myth of Theseus, in which the Athenian hero slays the Minotaur and emerges from the Cretan labyrinth victorious. The symbols of labyrinth and Minotaur form a basic pattern that appears under different guises throughout Western literature as an archetype for an encounter with a deeper layer of consciousness or source of knowledge. A guiding belief about the proper conduct of a life—by strict adherence to doctrine or by personal quest—is expressed in this archetypal story. The pattern of the myth is repeated in literary works from the *Queste del Saint Graal* to *Moby-Dick* to *The Name of the Rose*, all of which employ a labyrinthine journey full of hazards toward a powerfully compelling but elusive goal.

A journey through the labyrinth resembles the liminal stage in Arnold Van Gennep's three-part initiation ritual, the stage at which transformation occurs, a transformation that corresponds to knowledge and a newly acquired understanding (Van Gennep 18, 20). In the best-case scenario, one enters the labyrinth seeking knowledge or a transforming experience and leaves (when it is possible to leave) having achieved enlightenment or insight. There is also the possibility of wandering endlessly, without achieving anything, or worse, of entering a labyrinth that leads to a bad end. Jorge Luis Borges envisions these latter possibilities in his short story "The Library of Babel," as do medieval Christian writers who equate the labyrinth with heresy or sin. Dante's pilgrim in *The Divine Comedy* experiences this maze of sin and error as he wanders in the dark woods, although he ultimately finds the right path with the help of guides who lead him to an understanding of God's will and a steady unicursal progress toward Paradise.

Although the mythical labyrinth of Crete is a precursor to the labyrinths of the medieval churches with their distinct and regular seven- or eleven-circuit design, the transformation of the symbol to fit Christian teachings means the labyrinth Theseus braved is not the same one contemplated by early Christians. To begin with, the Cretan labyrinth, as represented in the myth, was multicursal, precisely what today we would call a maze. Obviously, since Daedalus's construction was built to imprison the dangerous Minotaur and keep him hidden from the world, this labyrinth would of necessity have involved a highly complex warren of passages. The depiction of a unicursal labyrinth in early Christian and medieval illustrations of the myth of Theseus is, I believe, an intentionally simplified schema that leaves out all "improper" choices to highlight the existence of the "one true path." Medieval Christianity adopted the classical myth (and the "classical" labyrinth design) for its own purposes, replacing Theseus with Christ and the Minotaur with Satan, as Craig Wright (in *The Maze and the Warrior*), Penelope Doob (*The Idea of the Labyrinth*), and Hermann Kern (*Through the Labyrinth*) have demonstrated. The dramatis personae are the same in each case; only the names change over time.

It is undoubtedly significant that the difference between the two forms of the labyrinth was glossed over, not only by the medieval Christian writers and architects but also by those who worked the "classical" unicursal design into coins, pottery, jewelry, and mosaics throughout the Greco-Roman world well before the advent of Christianity. The tendency to reduce the labyrinth to a single path may reflect origins in the primitive geometry of a related motif, the spiral, but I contend that it also reflects a worldview emphasizing the containment of the quest for truth within the prescribed boundaries of religion and accepted wisdom. The labyrinth reflects the specific preoccupations of time and place. There is a universalizing vision at work in both late classical and early medieval times that emphasizes a standard approach and a single source of truth, a vision expressed in an established, uniform path.

For classical writers since the time of Plato, philosophy is a path that leads to truth, and the maze of error is to be avoided by clear thinking (*Euthydemus* 447). For a Christian, likewise, there is but a single path, and Christ's triumph over the devil is the important truth revealed in the center of the labyrinth. Innovation and striking out on one's own, in either case, is neither necessary nor encouraged. Theseus, as the hero and king, defies the status quo to take on the tortuous labyrinth. His exceptional qualities give him a stature above and beyond that of other men and make it incumbent on him to defy tradition and put an end to the terrible tribute demanded by Minos, just as Christ accomplished the harrowing of hell.

The Greek myth has been endlessly re-envisioned from classical times to the present. The labyrinth and/or its characters were adopted from the classics by early Christian writers, appeared in the writings of Dante and Chaucer, shaped Shakespeare's *A Midsummer Night's Dream*, surfaced in *Moby-Dick*, inspired Pablo Picasso's *Minotauromachy*, received a nod from James Joyce, and continue to inspire postmodern thinkers and writers from Umberto Eco to J. Hillis Miller, who use Ariadne's thread as a metaphor for narrative and consciousness. A recent blockbuster film, *Inception* (2010), featured the motif of the maze as a basis of dream architecture requiring the design and navigation skills of a young Ariadne.

The Greek original, inspiration for so many later imaginings, is a treasure house of myths-within-the myth, with Theseus and the Minotaur,

Ariadne and Dionysus, Minos and Pasiphaë, and Daedalus and Icarus all playing a part. Complicating matters even further, the Greek myth has a subtext. In addition to being a heroic saga (see, for example, Mark P. O. Morford and Robert J. Lenardon's *Classical Mythology* [601], in which Theseus is described as "the great national hero of Attica"), the story contains strong intimations of its own shadow.

For Theseus, a warrior's virtues, along with Ariadne's favor, enable him to defeat a dangerous foe and escape the tortuous labyrinth. His courage and Ariadne's thread allow him to succeed where others have fallen. In all of this, the Minotaur is generally portrayed as a monster with no redeeming features. But if the unconscious, whether collective or personal, is, as C. G. Jung defined it, simply the unknown or the neglected, and the journey into the labyrinth is viewed not as a monster-slaying expedition but as an epistemological journey, the Minotaur suddenly appears in a different light.

In legend, killing a monster is often an initiatory adventure, in which the beast is the guardian of a treasure or the representation of some aspect of the hero himself, but it is not clear that this killing is always efficacious or appropriate. In this case, the Minotaur, according to Lima de Freitas, writing in the *Encyclopedia of Religion*, is more than it appears to be in a conventional reading. It is "the symbol of the repressed part of human nature, prerational and vital, which the new city hero wants to subdue . . .

But this is a fatal mistake on the part of the hero, for the Minotaur is also the hidden source of his own energy and power; killing the monster brings tragic forgetfulness, loss of purpose, decay, and disaster" (5278). Here, Freitas refers to Theseus's subsequent career, which includes abandoning Ariadne, causing the death of his father through carelessness, suffering through a family scandal, killing his own son, and dying in exile. Thus, the myth expresses conventional, "heroic" values along with a sense of what is missing in the conscious attitude or what may have been suppressed in pursuit of those values.

Some scholars, including Carl Kerényi, believe the Minotaur's name is Asterion, or "king of the stars" (*Gods of the Greeks* 110); he is so named in Borges's short story, "The House of Asterion." The name suggests that the Minotaur may be a distorted rendering of a primordial sun god. The Minotaur and the labyrinth represent primordial nature mysteries that—to a warrior age—may be terrifying (or inconvenient), but in an earlier time may have been approached with awe through rituals celebrating the sun as the source of life, "bodily movement being the primal, most direct form of expression—as verified by anthropology and ethnology" (Kern 27). Failing to recognize the Minotaur as his shadow—the instinctual, animal part of himself that is dangerous but vital—Theseus, from this perspective, fails the test of the labyrinth, even though he has succeeded on the conscious level. Finding his way out only with Ariadne's help (*Ariadne* = "most holy,"

Greek) (Kerényi, *Gods of the Greeks* 269), he leaves wisdom of a more primitive kind lying unrecognized in the depths of the maze. Theseus sets himself in opposition to nature, including his own inner nature, believing that he can overcome the beast with brute male strength. While Ariadne, daughter of Pasiphaë—"she who shines for all" in Greek (Kerényi, *Dionysos* 116)—and granddaughter of Helios (the sun god), provides the possibility of "shedding light" on the origins of human experience and the true nature of the labyrinth as the road that leads to birth, death, and rebirth, Theseus rejects the opportunity, emerging heroic but no wiser.

Other stories of the labyrinth in Western culture present their own versions of the quest for truth colored by the circumstances of their particular place and time. In each case, the underlying pattern is the same, but the view of the labyrinth differs. Aeneas, in the mold of heroic founder of cities, seeks to learn his destiny and establish a new kingdom after the fall of Troy; he pauses to look at the gates of Apollo's temple, carved by Daedalus to commemorate the labyrinth—"the house of toil" (Mandelbaum, *The Aeneid of Virgil* 6.39)—before consulting the Sibyl. Daedalus's labyrinth prefigures Aeneas's own tribulations. Centuries later, the Grail hero seeks a mystical union with God through the Holy Grail (the Minotaur transformed!); Ishmael and Ahab chase the white whale, symbol of nature and the encounter with the great unknown; and William of Baskerville tests his faith in the value of empirical reasoning to uncover the truth in a series of murders in *The Name of the Rose*. All include long and wearying trials (usually in the form of a journey), sudden reversals, and the characteristic labyrinthine experience of having the goal slip through the fingers when it seems most within reach.

The distinction between the two forms of the labyrinth is critical throughout: its multicursal or mazelike form, reflected in the journey taken by the Grail knights, Childe Roland, the crew of the Pequod, and William of Baskerville, and its unicursal form, depicted in Dante's *The Divine Comedy*, John Bunyan's *The Pilgrims Progress*, and most cathedral labyrinths, typify the two types of experience I have been discussing. The former reflects an unguided trip into *terra incognita* (in which anything can happen) and individual choice is essential, while the latter represents a guided journey through the well-mapped territory of established belief (in these examples, Christian belief). Both variations map a search for meaning and a quest for truth but suggest diverging strategies, one rooted in individual experience and the other in tradition or doctrine. The polarities here are similar to those engaged by religious studies scholar Mark C. Taylor, who points to the difference between structure and creative emergence and the continual "oscillation" between them (*Erring* 109-10).

Tracing the treatment of the literary labyrinth forward from classical times, we see the multicursal "maze" of Plutarch, Virgil, and Ovid, the test of a hero's mettle and ability to triumph over death, split into two different formulations, both employed by Christian writers. The multicursal maze, in the Grail Quest, is the symbol of the individual's mystical journey toward God, fraught with the possibility of failure and error but guided by character and choice. The predominance of the unicursal labyrinth in Dante does not shut out the presence of multiple paths but presents them in a generally negative light, since the approach to God through Christ is a difficult but sure path that leads to the goal if one continues to follow it. The path itself is the thread, and Christ is the guide. If one chooses the labyrinth of sin, on the other hand, it leads, just as inexorably, to hell and damnation.

Thus, there are two attitudes toward the maze in the Middle Ages, one positive and one negative. In most writers, including Dante, the multicursal maze is the sign of error and is to be avoided as an entanglement in sin. In the Grail legends, the way is labyrinthine and involves much error and delay, but the error is not only unavoidable (unless one is as pristine as Sir Galahad) but also pedagogical. Each knight takes a different tack, and each advances or falls back according to his ability. The individual is aided by God but still seeks his own path and learns by his own experience, though guides may appear to help him along the way.

The multicursal labyrinth, long present as a literary motif but not as a physical structure (except in the legendary past), began to appear as a landscape feature just when the Middle Ages and the hegemony of otherworldly Christianity in Europe were both drawing to a close. This might seem coincidental were it not for the fact that the maze was presented as an amusement or a curiosity and appeared in non-religious settings such as gardens or parks. It was never used in a religious or ritualistic context and was intended as a frivolous amusement for a solitary walker, or perhaps a couple. Its nearest antecedents were the labyrinths of love so popular as a poetic conceit in late medieval poetry and in actual (unicursal) garden labyrinths in France and other countries in the sixteenth and seventeenth centuries.

The use of the labyrinth by Petrarch in *Canzionere* in 1366 marks, in André Peyronie's view, nothing less than the transition from a religious world to a non-religious world; in this work, Petrarch envisions the maze as a "labyrinth of love" containing, not a Minotaur, but his beloved. Boccaccio also wrote of the labyrinth of love, and he and Petrarch are credited with freeing the labyrinth from its classical connections to Theseus, although Boccaccio certainly alluded to Theseus in some of his work (Peyronie, "The Labyrinth" 692). The literary "labyrinth of love" in Italian literature was a fresh interpretation of the symbol, liberated from the context of the Greek myth, though references to the Cretan labyrinth continued to appear in other works. This new conception of the maze reflects an increasingly worldly, humanistic orientation in keeping with the spirit of the Renaissance. There is a belief in God at the heart of science, geographic exploration, and other human enterprises, but the emphasis shifts to human initiative in discovering God's world.

Many of the later literary works I will focus on embody the solitary quest for knowledge and the emphasis on individual initiative playfully foreshadowed in these hedge and garden mazes and their appearance in a non-religious context, although negative attitudes toward the labyrinth as a snare and deception continue to appear throughout the Enlightenment, particularly in those thinkers, such as John Bunyan, who look toward a transcendent God for truth.

The scientific discoveries of Charles Darwin and other developments of the nineteenth century struck a blow to religious faith from which it never fully recovered, and depictions of the labyrinth in literature reflect a sense of this disorientation. While faith in reason as a path to understanding is evidenced in such literature as the detective novel, a sense of the loss of the center is evident in other works, such as Robert Browning's "Childe Roland to the Dark Tower Came," in which the labyrinth is not only inescapable but meaningless. Herman Melville's *Moby-Dick*, on the other hand, acknowledges the terror and the mystery of existence but recognizes that the separation of humanity from nature and human attempts to conquer nature are the wrong epistemological approach. While the crew of the Pequod endures a mazelike journey in search of the great whale, an abundance of spirals and spiral-like images suggests that a center still exists, although the way to approach it is not by domination. Traditional beliefs in God (or the gods) may be falling apart, but *Moby-Dick* suggests that wisdom lies in nature and the lost art of connecting and being at one with the other-than-human world. Thus, Melville returns us to the unspoken lesson of the myth of Theseus while anticipating our contemporary attempts to reconcile ourselves with nature.

Eventually, postmodern literature will torque the labyrinth idea to its utmost limits, exploring the ramifications of the maze from a subjectivist perspective in which the center may be nonexistent (or created anew by each individual). In the postmodern world, the predominant intellectual stance is an openness that recognizes complexity and multiple points of view. The multicursal labyrinth, or maze, is the fitting symbol for this complexity and for the process of individuation, which Jung saw as the new spiritual path for Westerners no longer satisfied, spiritually or intellectually, by Christian religion.

Postmodern examples of the labyrinth, in the fiction of Jorge Luis Borges, Lawrence Durrell, John Barth, and Umberto Eco, demonstrate that it remains an enduring symbol of the quest for knowledge and meaning that is subject to reinvention in fresh and surprising ways. What happens, for example, when a labyrinth no longer has a center? Centeredness is a quality that, while taken for granted in earlier versions of the myth, is frequently missing from postmodern literary labyrinths. I assert that the issue of the center is at the heart of the myth, separating those who believe in a shared (if mysterious) ground of meaning from those on the other side of the existential question who seek something other than ultimate meaning. The two camps may be roughly characterized as spiritual and "secular," although the terms themselves are slippery and tend to shade into one another. A multicursal maze can embody a spiritual quest, as we saw in the Middle Ages, but today it generally displays overtones of gamesmanship or intellectual challenge.

The maze may predominate in postmodern literature, but there are now more walking labyrinths than ever before. Physical mazes and labyrinths are both popular today, but as was true in the past, mazes tend to appear in non-religious settings and labyrinths in contemplative settings, usually in connection with churches, hospitals, or meditation centers. I believe this points to two tendencies that are not necessarily opposed in modern thinking: an emphasis on the individual freedom to pursue knowledge unfettered by doctrine *and* a deep-felt wish for a connection to an immovable center. Looked at another way, the maze corresponds more closely to the rational, problem-solving mind (which certainly has its advantages), and the labyrinth, with its element of ritual movement, to the wisdom of the body and the instinctual, animal life shared by all humans.

Images and symbols change over time. What was once a ritual may be transformed into a myth; an actual occurrence may become the basis of legend or live on in a ritual whose origins are no longer clear. What is most striking about the labyrinth (and the maze) is its persistence across time and cultures. The different interpretations applied to the symbols may tell us much about the preoccupations and epistemological stances of the various times and places; the symbol itself remains a constant, reflecting (I argue) a deeper structure of the mind that picks up the colorations of the times and places through which it passes. This deeper, archetypal structure is the concern of this study. I am interested in the transformations the symbol has undergone in the popular imagination across time and the uses to which it has been put. In particular, I am focusing on labyrinths in myth and literature but concomitant with that is the treatment of the symbol in the wider culture, whether classical, medieval, Renaissance, Enlightenment, Victorian, modern, or postmodern. I will demonstrate how the literary labyrinth (and/or the labyrinth as structure or artistic form) mirrors changing approaches and attitudes toward knowledge.

Review of the Literature

The most comprehensive and authoritative catalog of the labyrinth in all its forms is the monumental *Through the Labyrinth: Designs and Meanings Over 5,000 Years* by Hermann Kern. I rely on Kern for the facts of the labyrinth's history and include some of his speculations on its origins. He, Carl Kerényi, and Thomas M. Greene ("Labyrinth Dances in the French and English Renaissance") are especially helpful in tracing what is known of the labyrinth's possible beginnings in ritual dance and support the theory that the labyrinth represents, in its most primitive form, a ritual approach to the mystery of birth, death, and the origins of life. To a lesser extent, I have relied on the findings of W. H. Matthews, an expert on the labyrinth as structure and mythic motif universally acknowledged by latter-day scholars as having paved the way in historical labyrinth research. Also helpful is Jeff Saward, an editor of Kern's work, whose *Labyrinths & Mazes* is a guide to types of labyrinths and their locations around the world.

Pierre Brunel's *Companion to Literary Myths, Heroes and Archetypes* includes chapters by André Peyronie that examine in detail the symbolism of the labyrinth and the Minotaur. The section on the labyrinth draws on examples from ancient times to the twentieth century, exploring the origin, development, and variations on the theme and its associated characters in literature. Arnold Van Gennep's classic *The Rites of Passage*, with its description of the three stages of initiation, suggests, to me, a parallel to the labyrinthine journey and a way to understand the labyrinth as transformative.

Penelope Doob's *The Idea of the Labyrinth: From Classical Antiquity Through the Middle Ages* brings two streams of labyrinth scholarship together: the work of those such as Pliny the Elder, who was most interested in the physical structure of the labyrinth, and those who, like Ovid, were most interested in the mythical theme of the labyrinth as story or metaphor.

Doob addresses the perplexing tendency of classical and medieval writers to confuse the distinctly different unicursal and multicursal forms and explains how Pliny, Ovid, and Virgil were most responsible for the way the labyrinth was perceived in the Middle Ages. She examines the function of the labyrinth in stories from Homer to Chaucer.

In tandem with Doob, Craig Wright examines the origins of the labyrinth, both Greek and Egyptian, and delineates the ways in which medieval Christianity adapted the classical myth and remade it with Christ as the heroic figure. Wright's *The Maze and the Warrior: Symbols in Architecture, Theology, and Music* relates the labyrinthine musical structures of the Medieval, Baroque, and Neoclassical periods to the theology and philosophy of the Church, revealing how they converge and interpenetrate one another, and how the labyrinth finally emerges in non-religious music.

J. Hillis Miller's *Ariadne's Thread: Story Lines* examines story through the metaphor of Ariadne's thread in an exploration of the nature of narrative as an epistemological compass. Miller relates the concepts of line, character, anastomosis (or interpersonal relations), and figure to literary theory, showing how each unravels if followed far enough. His examination of nineteenth- and twentieth-century literary works complements Penelope Doob's literary approach while bringing it forward in time.

Mark C. Taylor believes religion and personal experience mirror the complex, interlocking systems of culture, society, nature, and technology, mutually dependent and "co-emergent," that must be taken into account to understand contemporary existence. Each of us is in a maze that connects with the mazes of others to form a network of mutual influence in a postmodern world. Taylor elucidates the constant "oscillation" he sees between structure and the breaking of that structure, a necessary and unavoidable dialectic similar to the tension between a unicursal labyrinth and a multicursal maze. Taylor's *Erring: A Postmodern A/theology* is an exposition of his thesis on structure and deconstruction in the context of religious studies, with wider implications for literature, culture, and society.

Joseph Campbell is not usually ranked among postmodernists, but in *The Masks of God: Occidental Mythology* he emphasizes that modernity makes individual experience the final arbiter of meaning. Campbell is usually classified as Romantic and Modernist, but his thinking here opens the door to the multivocality and plurality of postmodernity. Campbell invokes the theme of the Grail quest as maze and names the redemption of the Wasteland as the task of each individual in an age when the old certainties of faith no longer hold, when "there is no more any fixed center, any Mecca, Rome, or Jerusalem" (522).

Wendy Doniger examines the possibilities of myth in a postmodern age in *The Implied Spider: Politics & Theology in Myth*. Myth creates tension, showing us what could be as well as what is, and in this sense is like a maze with multiple paths. If dogma represents a Ptolemaic universe, in which all revolves around an enshrined "truth," myth, Doniger says, represents an Einsteinian universe of relativity with no fixed point. I contend that myth can in fact become dogma and support a favored definition of truth, and that it tends to do this at the cultural level. From a microscopic viewpoint, there are competing (or complementary) truths, and Doniger's universe of multivocality becomes the maze of postmodernity.

Miller's, Taylor's, and Jacques Derrida's deconstructive handling of narrative unravels not only ultimate meaning but history, the sense of self, and Ariadne's thread as the line that holds all together. Deconstruction does away with the center, the possibility of shared meaning, and myth all in one fell swoop. While these writers reflect the predicament of postmodernity and describe the experience of the maze as a metaphor for both the human condition and epistemology, I place their dismantling of the Christian myth (and of much of the narrative of Western history that mirrors it) in the context of a critique of a myth that in some ways no longer serves our diverse and polyphonic Western culture.

In this vein, I include James Hillman's exploration of what he considers the natural polytheism of the soul in *Re-Visioning Psychology*, a work that dethrones and de-centers the ego. In de-literalizing the tenets of religion, Hillman shows how multiple realities are always present. The monotheistic god gives way in Hillman's thinking to a world of multiple stories, multiple gods, and multiple paths, a maze worthy of Borges's "The

Library of Babel," if somewhat less grim.

Lauren Artress explores the history and lore of the labyrinth in *Walking a Sacred Path: Rediscovering the Labyrinth as a Spiritual Practice,* but her primary focus is the labyrinth's role in contemporary spirituality and the meaning of the unicursal labyrinth as a contemplative aid. She compares the different mindsets involved in walking a labyrinth and a maze and shows how each leads to a different experience. From a thoroughly non-religious perspective Jacques Attali, in *The Labyrinth in Culture and Society: Pathways to Wisdom,* puts forth his thesis that the labyrinth (in its multicursal form) is the operative metaphor for the complex systems of modern life, from social networks, to communications, to the economy, to the World Wide Web.

The work of philosophers from Plato and Aristotle to René Descartes, Friedrich Nietzsche, the phenomenologists, and Jacques Derrida tells the story of the changing tides of Western thought that correspond to transformations in the labyrinth as symbol. In the fourth century BCE, Plato invoked the labyrinth and was likely the first to use it purely as a metaphor, separating it entirely from its role in the myth of Theseus. In *Euthydemus,* his labyrinth is an image for the mental confusion that challenges a thinker's capacity for clear reasoning and sustained argument. More than two millennia later, Nietzsche, in *The Birth of Tragedy,* criticized Plato for his focus on unchanging certainty, believing that the mystery of eternal dissolution and formlessness (the Dionysian principle) is, as many myths acknowledge, what really underlies the temporary Apollonian play of forms. The Platonic splitting of spirit and matter and the separation of the labyrinth from the myth are not unrelated: both herald the birth of rationalism and the Western mind and an accompanying distrust of myth and ritual.

Descartes dealt a final blow to the body when he declared that nothing, not even sensory information, could be trusted; the only truth to be found was in rational thinking, a statement indicative of anxiety about uncertainty that reflects the mazelike process of reasoning endemic to the seventeenth century. Susan Bordo examines the legacy of Descartes in both its positive and negative consequences (*The Flight to Objectivity: Essays on Cartesianism and Culture*), tracing the further development of the mind/body split in Cartesian anxiety over philosophical uncertainty and the accompanying attempt to deny the reliability of sensuous experience. Of particular relevance to this study of the labyrinth is Bordo's examination of the anti-female bias that accompanied the mind/body split during the Enlightenment period (an echo of a much earlier denigration of the feminine that accompanied the rise of patriarchy).

Ernest Becker's *The Denial of Death* examines the attempt to distance oneself from the body, nature, and the female as a way to deny or stave off death. Based on the insights of Sigmund Freud, Otto Rank, and Soren Kierkegaard, the book details the struggle to accept the facts of bodily existence in the face of individual and cultural repression of awareness of mortality. Becker's insights give weight to the conception of birth as the first labyrinth humans ever experience.

In his later writings, Sigmund Freud focuses increasingly on Eros and Thanatos as two of the primary drives in human nature and culture. In *Beyond the Pleasure Principle*, Freud argues that death is the ultimate goal of life, and the return of organic matter to a state of equilibrium is built into the very nature of cells. Paradoxically, mankind's greatest fear is the fear of annihilation, Freud argues, and most human beings cope with this fear by turning it into aggression. A related response to the fear of death is the attempt to conquer it, and this unspoken agenda is, as John T. Irwin points out in *The Mystery to a Solution: Poe, Borges, and the Analytic Detective Story*, at the core of Theseus's story (314). (It is also at the heart of much of modern science and technology.) Thus our modern scientists and technologists can be seen in one sense as the heirs of Theseus, attempting to defeat death and casting the same shadow as their sword-wielding ancestor.

A number of writers are helpful in considering the labyrinth as form, a necessary step in unraveling its meaning. György Doczi studies recurring patterns in nature that suggest an underlying order and harmony and inquires into the possible significance of such an order. In *The Power of Limits: Proportional Harmonies in Nature, Art, and Architecture*, he examines certain recurring proportions, growth and structural regularities (including

29

the spiral), and the joint presence of unity and diversity, the macroscopic

and the microscopic, that are present throughout the natural world.

In *The Mystic Spiral*, Jill Purce looks at the spiral in nature, in

philosophy, in religion, and in great works of art. She examines the spiral as

an archetypal form connecting the transcendent and the immanent, spirit

and matter, divine and human; her discussion has great relevance to my

analysis of the labyrinth as a "connecting" metaphor. In *Melville's* Moby-

Dick: *A Jungian Commentary*, Edward Edinger not only analyzes *Moby-Dick*

from a Jungian perspective but also gives attention to recurring motifs in

the novel, including that of the spiral, which Edinger parses as a metaphor

for an encounter with the unconscious. In *The Poetics of Space*, Gaston

Bachelard examines the phenomenology and significance of ordinary space,

with chapters on "Shells" and "Corners" that are particularly relevant to the

labyrinth.

At the heart of my study are the writers who tell the stories about

the labyrinth, "dreaming the myth forward" in shifting conceptions of

reality, truth, and the place of humanity in the cosmos.

Plutarch's *Lives* draws on material from many earlier sources to

create a detailed, coherent narrative of the myth of Theseus, treated here as

a semi-historical figure. Allen Mandelbaum's authoritative translations of

The Aeneid of Virgil and *The Metamorphoses of Ovid* and E. V. Rieu's classic

translation of Homer's *Iliad* are my other sources for important classical accounts of the myth of the Cretan labyrinth.

In Dante's *The Divine Comedy*, the depiction of the poet as lost in a bewildering forest—a type of maze—is contrasted to the journey through Inferno, Purgatorio, and Paradiso, presented by the poet as a series of long spirals, first descending (in Inferno) and then ascending (in Purgatorio and Paradiso). In Dante's spatial metaphors, the forest maze is the equivalent of losing one's moral compass and falling into sin, while the unicursal spiraling journey leads to redemption and—ultimately—union with God.

P. M. Matarasso's *The Quest of the Holy Grail* is a translation of the *Queste del Saint Graal*, which I use to expand on Campbell's and Doob's interpretation of the quest as a mazelike journey, in which each knight enters the woods, "striking out into the forest one here, one there, wherever they saw it thickest and wherever path or track was absent" (Matarasso 52-53). In this thoroughly Christian version of a labyrinthine journey, it is nonetheless clear that the individual path is unavoidable if one is to temper his character and grow toward a more perfect knowledge of God. Doob's observation that the interchangeability of the two forms of the labyrinth in the Middle Ages seems to point to a reluctance to confront the contradiction between doctrine and individual works as the preferred means to salvation is relevant to the Grail story (Doob 62 n. 25). In Campbell's view, the importance of choice and the solitary path signals the rise of the individual in modernity.

William Shakespeare's *A Midsummer Night's Dream* presents a break with the long tradition of the spiritual labyrinth, using the maze as a motif of carnival and magic as the lovers experience confusion and disorientation in the woods at night. Significantly, Theseus is a character in the play, the King of Athens who rules the city with strictness but has no power over the mazy night world of the forest, where most of the action takes place.

In John Bunyan's *The Pilgrims Progress*, we return once more to the path as a unicursal (and universal) labyrinthine journey undertaken by all Christians, with a known destination and predictable encounters along the way. Once again, detours from the path are possible but involve moral error and danger.

Herman Melville's *Moby-Dick*, replete with images of coils, spirals, and whirlpools, depicts a mazelike journey upon the open ocean, in which the voyage leads inexorably to an encounter with the white whale. While the journey itself meanders and changes course, the encounter with the whale at the end of the novel is characterized as a downward (unicursal) spiral toward destiny and death, so that the novel juxtaposes the labyrinth in both its forms.

Robert Browning's "Childe Roland to the Dark Tower Came" is a Victorian version of the knight's quest, in which the motive, the meaning, and the outcome are all murky, and the center, if it is a center, appears to hold nothing but death. The poem is an example of an attempt to understand the labyrinthine journey at a time when traditional Christian faith has been challenged by the scientific discoveries of the day and the fabric of society itself is changing due to economic, political, and cultural shifts. I contrast "Childe Roland" with another knightly tale, the fourteenth-century *Sir Gawain and the Green Knight*, to reveal how the early modern Christian labyrinth of individual piety has devolved into a godless wasteland beyond redemption.

I will also examine the nineteenth century's favored versions of the literary labyrinth, the Gothic novel and the new detective novel. Wilkie Collins's *The Woman in White* bridges both genres with a labyrinthine plot that requires the weapons of intelligence and perseverance of its strong-willed protagonists. While these qualities win a victory for them, the essential darkness of the labyrinth in an evil world precludes a truly "happy" ending. The way through this Darwinian labyrinth does indeed depend upon the "survival of the fittest." The same is true of the Gothic-toned *Jane Eyre*, although Jane's labyrinth of deception, cruelty, and danger overlies a labyrinth of love. She must navigate them both, and in doing so she secures not only a solution to the puzzle but true love. In this sense, *Jane Eyre*, though dark in atmosphere and tone, is the more optimistic of the two novels.

Turning to the twentieth century, I will examine several works that emphasize the solitary experience of the labyrinth as maze, doubts about the ability of rationality to solve a maze, or the nature of the maze as consciousness or literary process. In Lawrence Durrell's *The Dark Labyrinth*, set after World War II, a disparate group of vacationers is on its way to visit the legendary labyrinth of Crete, which has been discovered and touted as a tourist attraction by enterprising locals. When the group enters the labyrinth and becomes lost, the experiences of each individual mirror the character and expectations he or she brings into the maze. This psychological study combines a postmodern attitude toward the flexibility of myth and its capacity to hold multiple meanings with an imaginative interpretation of what it means to penetrate to the heart of the labyrinth.

Jorge Luis Borges's collection of short stories, parables, and essays (*Labyrinths: Selected Stories & Other Writings*) draws on the symbolism of myth to critique culture and literature. The work has influenced many other writers, including Umberto Eco, who specifically cites Borges's short story, "The Library of Babel," as a direct and important inspiration for his novel *The Name of the Rose* ("Borges and My Anxiety of Influence" 124). In this short story, the library, a towering structure with spiraling stairs, is the universe itself. In another Borges story, "The House of Asterion," the narrator is the Minotaur, who explains how the labyrinth looks from his point of view. Another story, "The Garden of Forking Paths," reveals the ultimate secret of the labyrinth: it is a book that encompasses all imaginable pasts, presents, and futures.

John Barth's "Lost in the Funhouse" playfully deconstructs the narrative, as well as the funhouse maze, as the main character, a teenager on a family trip to an amusement park at Ocean City, tells alternate versions of his own story and considers the role of the storyteller as the builder of the maze.

In Umberto Eco's *The Name of the Rose*, the labyrinth is seen as a quest for knowledge. An older monk and his young protégé attempt to solve horrific murders in a medieval monastery in which the library is constructed as a labyrinth and the librarians hold the key to the mystery. Eco examines differing attitudes toward knowledge, both conservative and liberal, as the protagonists find themselves enmeshed in a maze that is literal as well as figurative. His conclusion that logic may be the undoing of those trying to solve a maze leaves open the question of what true wisdom consists of.

Finally, I will discuss contemporary appearances of the labyrinth in the film *Inception*, in Bruce Springsteen's *Tunnel of Love*, and in other phenomena such as the corn maze "craze" and the labyrinth revival, both of which have launched an industry of labyrinth-building, particularly in the United States, in both non-religious and religious settings.

Organization of the Study

In Chapter 2, I will examine the earliest Greek example of the labyrinth myth, that of Theseus. My examination of the myth will probe the

35

Greek attitude toward epistemology while also investigating Theseus's anti-heroic aspects and what they reveal about the shadow side of the classical period. Theseus's story mirrors the pattern of Eurocentric/Christian consciousness in its dominating and conquering style and its hostility to forms of wisdom other than rationality. This chapter demonstrates how the myth (when presented as a "heroic" account of the noble founder of Athens) contradicts its own surface story by detailing the subsequent failures of Theseus to behave heroically. I will suggest that these two apparently conflicting levels of the myth result from the gradual change in Greek culture from mythic to philosophical thinking; the myth retains residual evidence of its roots in ritual as well as an overt preference for the conquering behavior of its hero. The labyrinth here becomes a trap when approached in an overly aggressive manner unguided by intuition. Theseus is faced with many possible paths and must overcome the Minotaur before finding his way out. His "success" is partly his own and partly Ariadne's doing, since he is able to face down the monster but must rely on Ariadne's thread to extricate himself from the maze. The thread narrows down all the possible choices to a single correct path.

Plato viewed choice as the possibility of error, of losing one's way in reasoning. Plato sees the possibility of ending back where you started as the chance you take when you enter the labyrinth; you must reason well to avoid getting lost or getting nowhere (*Euthydemus* 447). He is the first thinker aside from Herodotus to separate the labyrinth from the myth and use it purely as metaphor, a move Peyronie identifies as marking the decisive shift from mythos to logos. Thus Plato's use of the labyrinth as identical with *aporia* ("puzzlement") identifies the very basis of the Western philosophical tradition (Peyronie, "The Labyrinth" 689).

In Chapter 3, I will examine the treatment of the labyrinth in the Middle Ages. Here, I am most interested in Dante's *The Divine Comedy* and the thirteenth-century *Queste del Saint Graal*. The theme of this chapter will be the very different symbolism of the well-worn path, with its named destinations and characters and predictable progress, and the individualistic experience of the multicursal maze. I contend that the unicursal movement is the inner journey guided by dogma and religious experience. One encounters shadow figures and demons along the unicursal path, but this trip "comes with instructions" and with the expectation that he who stays the course will find truth (and salvation) in the end. This offers a sharp contrast to the journey of the maze, whose main characteristic is a multitude of choices, uncertainty about the way to the center, and doubt about the journey's outcome. For a medieval Christian, the journey was always moral as well as epistemological.

In *Queste del Saint Graal*, various Knights of the Round Table pledge to undertake the quest and enter the woods, each at the place he judges to be best. There is no well-formed path, and many seekers of the Grail become hopelessly ensnared in temptations, delays, and wrong turns. Very few who undertake the quest ever find the Grail Castle, and many never return to Camelot. The Grail Quest reflects the experience of lone individuals venturing out with little more than the guidance of their own religious faith (and conscience) as individual compass. Here, instead of a beast, one seeks the rarest of spiritual treasures, which nonetheless has the power to destroy the unprepared and leaves even the worthiest knight utterly changed in the encounter. Striking out on one's own, though laudable, is hazardous indeed.

The labyrinth (in the strictest sense) does not appear in medieval literature, and certainly not in vernacular literature, except in those religious texts stemming from the classical, Latin tradition (Peyronie, "The Labyrinth" 691). However, clerics often wrote specific descriptions of the mythical labyrinth in their commentaries on classical texts. There are many references in the romances and in courtly literature to wandering, as in a forest or a dream, through difficult or narrow passages or paths. Where difficult or tortuous "maze"-like motifs appear in religious texts, they are generally associated with *this* world, the world of sin and error, and sometimes with heresy, specifically. Christ is often identified with Theseus in church labyrinths in France and Italy; he provides guidance on the one true path to God. This world is the labyrinth, and God's realm is the goal, and it can only be achieved by escaping the world of sin. This is certainly true for Dante's pilgrim, whose mazelike wanderings in the forest constitute the state of being truly lost. Chapter 3 will analyze the prominence of the unicursal labyrinth in *The Divine Comedy* and relate it to the phenomenon of the church labyrinths of the Middle Ages. I will suggest that Dante was likely influenced by (and certainly shared the vision of) the architects of these great churches. He was also familiar with their use of sacred symbols, including the labyrinth, and incorporated that symbolism into the architecture of his own work.

In Chapter 4, I examine the changing image of the labyrinth during the Renaissance and Enlightenment periods. The appearance of the maze for the first time as a physical structure in the landscape (and not merely as metaphor or literary motif) in the fifteenth century marks a corresponding turn to humanism and a blossoming interest in all branches of artistic, cultural, and scientific knowledge. A new openness to multiple paths of discovery and enterprise in the human world is expressed, I believe, in the new function of the maze as an amusement and a game and no longer merely as a somber religious road to salvation or damnation. The West at this time was entering into what Charles Taylor calls "the mind-centered" view as opposed to the earlier "God-centered" or "enchanted" view, another revolutionary shift in terms of Western thought and belief (31).

I interpret the playfulness associated with the new garden mazes, found in non-religious settings, in terms of what Mark C. Taylor calls the "aberrance of carnival," in which social stratifications break down and comedy supplants tragedy (*Erring* 15). I will take up an example of this non-religious, comedic treatment of the labyrinth when I discuss Shakespeare's *A Midsummer Night's Dream* (1594-95). In this play, Theseus appears as the heroic king of Athens but has no jurisdiction over the intrigues of the lovers, who are overtaken by the spirit of dreams and magic in the woods. All is set to rights by the morning's light, however, and order prevails at the play's end, signifying a shakeup of established values that, while revivifying and transforming, is to some degree temporary. Order emerges out of chaos at the end of the play, in the same way that the seemingly haphazard and inexplicable paths of a multicursal maze may reveal an inherent order once the labyrinth has been traversed.

The uses of the labyrinth during the Enlightenment are varied and contradictory. First, I will examine the maze as a metaphor for the deceptive appearance of the world. The labyrinth may appear as an initiatory experience in which the individual learns to distinguish reality from appearance, as in *Don Quixote* (1605-15). The labyrinth here stands for the transitory and deceptive aspects of the world. The labyrinth may, alternatively, be treated as the path to enlightenment; the unicursal labyrinth is not dead in the seventeenth century, by any means. Bunyan's *The Pilgrims Progress* (1678) is a work in this vein; the protagonist learns to avoid the

40

pitfalls and snares of the world by making his way through it, and the labyrinth is a single road.

I will show that the labyrinth may have either negative or positive connotations during the Enlightenment; it may be depicted as the path to deception or the road to knowledge, a divided view that coincides with the anxiety over certainty expressed by Descartes. In Vivant Denon's "Point de lendemain" (1777), for example, the labyrinth represents an initiation into love and sensory experience, but after the adventure is over, the hero is unsure how much was real and how much imagined; he doubts what he has learned (Peyronie, "The Labyrinth" 700). Thus, during the Enlightenment, both non-religious and religious uses of labyrinth imagery are common. The Baroque and Enlightenment periods also saw a flurry of musical interpretations of the labyrinth, building on a tradition begun in the Middle Ages. I will argue that these musical labyrinths, occurring as they did in the Age of Reason, are an example of an increasingly abstract interpretation of the labyrinth, moving away from the bodily enactments that flourished in Renaissance dance and seventeenth- and eighteenth-century landscape architecture.

In Chapter 5, I will explore the labyrinthine journey in a few examples of nineteenth-century literature. This period produced possibly the most important development in labyrinth literature apart from the Renaissance. Whereas the Renaissance labyrinth broke with the spiritual,

41

mythical, unicursal labyrinth of the Middle Ages, the nineteenth century broke even more radically from the very idea of the center being the goal (Peyronie, "The Labyrinth" 702). That break is still significant in modern and postmodern treatments of the labyrinth, which often replace the quest for the center with the search for the way out. In the nineteenth and twentieth centuries, it is sometimes possible to find a way out, and sometimes the attempt is futile.

The labyrinth in the light of pre-Darwinian discoveries in the sciences, particularly geology and anatomy, and an early modern encounter with loss of religious certainty (Parker and Hayford ix) is the subject of *Moby-Dick*. Ishmael learns to approach mystery with humility and a reverence for nature, while Ahab, with a maniacal insistence on overcoming the white whale, the face of nature itself, inevitably falls into a spiral of death. In *Moby-Dick*, the whale is the Minotaur, an ambiguous but terrifying apparition—for one character, it means salvation, and for the other, death.

Robert Browning's "Childe Roland to the Dark Tower Came" depicts a world in which meaning and religious certainties have been lost. I will contrast this tale of a dark errand with the lively medieval romance of *Sir Gawain and the Green Knight*, revealing the former as a maze that leads not to spiritual enlightenment (like *Sir Gawain*) but to death. This modern version of a knight's tale has many parallels to the *Queste del Saint Graal* and the myth of Theseus, but its passage to the heart of the labyrinth leaves us

42

in doubt about not only the outcome but also the meaning of the journey. I will argue that the poem leaves the door open to alternate interpretations, and that its ambiguity is characteristic of the skepticism of a scientific age that has lost its gods but not all of its longing for them and for a world imbued with meaning.

In Chapter 6, I will examine some variations of the labyrinthine journey in postmodern fiction, including Umberto Eco's *The Name of the Rose*, Lawrence Durrell's *The Dark Labyrinth,* and Borges's *Labyrinths*. I argue that the tenets of Jung's theory of individuation dovetail somewhat with the themes of postmodernism, which stress that the truth changes depending on the point of view of the individual and that in effect there are multiple roads to truth. Literary labyrinths also play with the nature of narrative itself, revealing that the illusion of a single story hides the possibility of multiple stories and multiple outcomes starting from a single point, as in Borges's "The Garden of Forking Paths" (1941) and John Barth's "Lost in the Funhouse" (1967).

Umberto Eco's *The Name of the Rose* (1980) is a curiosity, a novel about a labyrinth in medieval times, centuries before the first multicursal labyrinth (as maze) was ever constructed. Eco may be teasing us about a modern tendency to see labyrinths everywhere, but his metaphor of the labyrinth as a guardian of secret knowledge sums up the dilemma of modernity in which the center no longer holds and reason is suspect as an infallible guide.

Our contemporary fascination with the labyrinth and its accompanying proliferation in gardens, churches, and public places signifies that the return to the center is still a desirable goal; I will examine the ways in which this attitude manifests itself in the arts as well as in the labyrinth revival movement. The journey of an individual life still has an archetypal similarity to other individual lives in the universal trajectory from birth to death; the human condition still has a common landscape. Yet the maze, popular as an amusement and similar in form to a computer network, best represents, for many postmodern thinkers, the contemporary quest for truth. As Mark C. Taylor puts it, postmodernity mirrors complexity on complexity. Modern life consists of interlocking systems of culture, society, nature, and technology, mutually dependent and "co-emergent," which must be taken into account if we are to make sense of contemporary existence ("Refiguring" 112-14). Taylor refers to the "enigma" of living forms, which Norman O. Brown sees as "an invitation to the dance" of life (qtd. in *Erring* 177). Each of us is in a maze that connects with the mazes of others to form a network of mutual influence in which the Minotaur *is* the maze, and we are all partners in a vast cosmological dance.

But are unicursal and multicursal paths mutually exclusive? Has the maze forever overtaken the unicursal labyrinth as the fitting emblem of multivalent truth in which tradition is no longer relevant? In Chapter 7, I will argue that it is more appropriate to see the two images as superimposed, fitting the maze inside the unicursal labyrinth. One can then see them as opposite ends of the telescope, recognizing, along with Wendy Doniger, that we see the universal in the particular and vice versa. It is possible to see, with this kind of double vision, the two forms of the labyrinth as co-equals, existing one inside the other, once we separate the unicursal path from the dogma of a particular myth—in this case, Christianity. When we replace dogma with imagination, the quest for knowledge—both macroscopic and microscopic—opens anew, and the labyrinth represents the possibility of unity. The coexistence of the two forms of the labyrinth mirrors the ongoing quest for truths both personal and universal that each of us experiences over the course of a lifetime.

For Campbell, as for Jung, myths refer to the past, present, and future and are reactionary as well as revolutionary, just as Wendy Doniger describes them in *The Implied Spider* (107). A once living myth may become fossilized and in need of reviving; thus, the unicursal labyrinth can (and did) become stifling, and the multicursal maze then became not a prison but a symbol of freedom and individual destiny. However, as is true of any symbol, it, too, holds a dark side in need of balance.

Even in a postmodern world, there are common threads that define human experience and weave us all together as a species. In a postcolonial environment, with many individual stories clamoring to be told, it is just as vital to remember what holds us all together as to acknowledge what makes each of us unique. Postmodernists describe the experience of today's individual, searching for ultimate ground in a culture that no longer offers it except in the form of science (which is itself subject to questioning and revision). And yet the fact that most of us continue to experience continuity in our own lives is apparent—all of us share the human condition and have at least the basic facts of biology in common. Nor can we deny the fact that even when we are told that life in the contemporary age has no meaning because God is dead, most people continue to find that life is full of meaning from their own point of view.

Probably no postmodernist would argue against the universal biological necessities common to all humans: the facts of birth and death, the need to eat, drink, breathe, and receive adequate shelter. Human life has a recognizable pattern. Joseph Campbell, who believed that the individual was the ultimate authority in discovering his or her own truth, had faith that each quest for truth connected with the past and also prospected new territory never before seen. In subsequent chapters, we will see how, through the centuries, the labyrinth holds the paradox of both positions within its manifold twists and turns.

Chapter 2
A Riddle From Ritual and Myth

> The head is the inner sanctuary of the temple of man's
> body, both created and protected by the windings of the
> labyrinth. With each turn man completes a stage in his
> evolution. In the centre of the spiral he meets himself. . . .
> At the centre of the spiral labyrinth, man meets,
> overcomes, and thus unites with, Humbaba or the
> Minotaur, the 'monster' of his own hidden nature, and is
> reborn into a new state of wholeness. The centre is thus a
> symbol for the state of balance, of no-time or infinity.
>
> — Jill Purce, *The Mystic Spiral: Journey of the Soul*

The Greek Myth and Its Antecedents

This chapter examines the Greek myth of Theseus and what it

reveals about the Greek epistemological orientation, showing how

Theseus's story prefigures Eurocentric/Christian consciousness in the

dominating, conquering style of its hero. I will demonstrate how on one

level the myth contradicts its own overt assumptions by detailing Theseus's

failures to behave heroically after his adventure in the labyrinth. I am

suggesting that the two conflicting levels of the myth reflect a gradual

change in Greek culture from a nature-based society to one that celebrates

the values of civic life and culture; nonetheless, the myth retains strong

evidence of its roots in ritual along with its manifest preference for the

heroic behavior of a patriarchal city founder and ruler. The labyrinth, an

erstwhile sacred place, has become a trap; Theseus escapes it, but only with

Ariadne's help. The labyrinth is still an initiatory path, but its original

47

purpose of ritual renewal has been transformed by an unspoken desire to overcome the negative aspects of nature, and it is now a test of the hero's ability to defeat a monster. Nature, death, the body, the "lower" instincts—any and all of these are symbolized by the half-man, half-bull Minotaur, the "sacred monster" (Peyronie, "The Minotaur" 821). In *Language and Desire in Seneca's* Phaedra, Charles Segal delineates the ways in which the labyrinth, for Theseus's son Hippolytus, has become synonymous with the womb of Pasiphaë, mother of both Phaedra and her half-brother, the Minotaur. The labyrinth here represents an illicit and dangerous sexuality, which means female sexuality in general, "and especially maternal sexuality" (112). No longer the shining path in a ritual celebration of fertility, the womb of Mother Earth, and the life-giving sun, the labyrinth has become the "sinister labyrinth" and, paired with the Minotaur, "is the recurrent symbol of lust" (35) and, especially, "emblem of female lust" (44) in Seneca's first-century CE play.

We will begin with the myth itself. Although different tellers of the tale emphasize different parts of the story, and some incidents may be left out of a particular version entirely, a general outline of the story, derived largely from Ovid and Plutarch, begins with King Minos and his wife, Pasiphaë, and ends with the death of Theseus in a foreign land many years later. The tale begins with a sacred bull sent to Minos by Poseidon. The bull is intended as a sacrifice, but Minos covets the magnificent white animal and attempts to substitute an inferior bull so that he can keep the sacrificial beast for himself. In the meantime, Pasiphaë develops an intense passion for the animal and persuades the great architect and builder, Daedalus, to construct a wooden cow that she can enter in order to mate with the bull. The result of this union is the flesh-eating half-man, half-bull Minotaur, an object of shame for both Minos and Pasiphaë; Minos orders Daedalus to construct a labyrinth to hide the Minotaur and demands a terrible tribute from Athens in reparation for the killing of his son Androgeos: the Athenians are required to send youths and maidens to Crete every nine years as prey for the voracious Minotaur.

Eventually, Theseus, the son of Aegeus (king of Athens), and already a hero of many exploits, volunteers to go as one of the contingent of sacrificial youths. In Crete, he wins the love of Ariadne, King Minos's daughter, and she gives him a thread with which to find his way out of the labyrinth if he succeeds in killing the Minotaur. In some versions, she gives him other gifts as well, including a lighted wreath, a sword, and a ball of pitch to throw into the Minotaur's mouth. Theseus goes into the labyrinth, encounters the Minotaur, and kills him. Finding his way out of the labyrinth with the thread, he escapes Crete with Ariadne, her sister Phaedra, and the now-freed Athenian youths and maidens. He then abandons Ariadne on Naxos, although the reasons for his doing so vary according to who is doing the telling. In some versions of the tale, he has decided to marry

Phaedra, so his leaving Ariadne on Naxos is a cruel and capricious abandonment. Ariadne, however, is soon comforted by the god Dionysus, who marries her and sets her wreath as a crown in heaven. In some versions of the story, Ariadne is already married to Dionysus when she assists Theseus. This and certain other clues strongly suggest that Ariadne may originally have been much more than the hapless girl she appears to be in later stories.

Theseus and the other youths stop in Delos on their way to Athens and perform a celebratory dance called the Crane Dance, which imitates the twists and turns of the labyrinth as well as their escape from it. Theseus sails for home but forgets to change the color of his sail from black to white so that his anxious father will know he is returning alive and well. Aegeus sees the black sail and jumps into the sea, killing himself in despair over what he believes to be the death of his son.

King Minos, angered by Daedalus's role in constructing the cow for Pasiphaë and in helping Ariadne assist Theseus, orders Daedalus and his son Icarus to be imprisoned in the labyrinth. Even Daedalus cannot find his way out of the labyrinth unaided, so he constructs wings for himself and Icarus. They escape the labyrinth and Crete, but the youthful Icarus ignores his father's warnings and flies too close to the sun, causing the wax on his wings to melt so that he plunges into the sea and drowns. In some versions of the myth, such as Ovid's, Minos offers a prize to anyone clever enough to thread a spiral shell, thus luring Daedalus out of hiding. Minos knows that Daedalus alone will be able to solve the riddle, which indeed he does: by tying the thread to an ant and placing a drop of honey at one end of the shell, he induces the ant to travel all the way through it. Minos tries to have Daedalus killed, but well-wishers help him escape, and Minos is killed by Daedalus's allies.

Theseus succeeds his father as king and rules for many years. He continues to have exploits, battles, and adventures with women, but a domestic problem eventually destroys his family. Phaedra, his queen, falls in love with her stepson, Hippolytus (the son of Theseus by an Amazon queen). Spurned by the boy, she makes false accusations against him to Theseus. The boy is eventually killed by an enormous bull that rises from the sea, at Theseus's request, to take vengeance. The story ends with Theseus in exile, dying alone in a foreign land.

Some of the details in the story appear to be relatively late additions to the literary myth, such as the episode of Daedalus and the wings. Although the wings appear much earlier in vase paintings, early stories do not mention them, so later poets may have produced episodes to explain their presence. Two of the most complete and well-known versions of the myth, Ovid's and Plutarch's, are very late (first century CE); some of their sources are known, and some are not. What is known is that from Homer's first mention of Ariadne's dancing floor to Plutarch's quasi-historical treatment of the story and its characters, the myth is transformed repeatedly in the hands of its tellers to reflect the changing preoccupations and beliefs of Greek society.

Along with a look at Plato's transcendental labyrinth, this chapter will examine the labyrinth in the myth of Theseus as presented in the writings of Virgil, Ovid, and Plutarch. Prior to an analysis of the myth, a summary of the history of the labyrinth will establish the context of these late literary accounts, all of which were written well after Plato's non-mythic reference to the labyrinth. The sources for these accounts are in some cases sketchy. Plutarch preserves a number of now missing sources (Doob 20 n. 4), but a well-established tradition is evidenced not only by the familiarity Plutarch, Ovid, Seneca, Virgil, and other writers assume of their readers in connection with the myth (Doob 34) but also by abundant pictorial evidence of the myth's characters and motifs on vessels, mosaics, and other objects. Some of the known sources are included here to establish the antecedents of the classical writers whose work was so influential on later artists, poets, philosophers, and scholars as well as on the popular imagination.

Plato and the Philosophical Labyrinth

Ovid's treatment of the labyrinth in his *Metamorphoses* (c. 8 CE), and indeed, his treatment of most of Greek mythology, was slyly satirical; in describing the labyrinth, rather than dwelling on its terrors, he uses the

52

metaphor of a river doubling back on itself:

> As in the Phrygian fields, the clear Meander
> delights in flowing back and forth, a course
> that is ambiguous; it doubles back
> and so beholds its waves before they go
> and come; and now it faces its own source,
> and now the open sea; and so its waves
> are never sure that they've not gone astray.
> (Mandelbaum, *The Metamorphoses of Ovid* 8.162-66)

Plutarch, using a very different approach in his *Lives* (75 CE), chooses to

render his Theseus as a historical personage, explaining his rationale this

way:

> after publishing my account of Lycurgus the lawgiver and
> Numa the king, I thought I might not unreasonably go
> back still farther to Romulus, now that my history had
> brought me near his times. . . . it seemed to me that I must
> make the founder of lovely and famous Athens the
> counterpart and parallel to the father of invincible and
> glorious Rome. May I therefore succeed in purifying Fable,
> making her submit to reason and take on the semblance of
> History. (Plutarch 3, 5)

In both Ovid and Plutarch, we see a movement away from religious

reverence for the myth toward something else—either comedy or

historical/political commentary.

Long before either Ovid or Plutarch, in fourth-century Athens,

Plato, writing in a philosophical and not a mythical context, portrays the

labyrinth as a trap and a problem of choices—but without any

accompanying story. In his *Euthydemus* (380 BCE), the maze symbolizes the

possibility of error in reasoning; rather than the danger of death, it represents the danger of reasoning badly. Theseus and the Minotaur have vanished completely in Plato's bloodless labyrinth, and Ariadne is nowhere in sight. In the dialogue, Socrates tells Crito, speaking of a disputation with two visiting philosophers:

> we were in a most ridiculous state; like children who run after crested larks, we kept on believing each moment we were just going to catch this or that one of the knowledges, while they as often slipped from our grasp. . . . at this point we were involved in a labyrinth: when we supposed we had arrived at the end, we twisted about again and found ourselves practically at the beginning. (*Euthydemus* 447)

Plato sees the possibility of ending back where you started as the chance you take when you enter the labyrinth; you must reason correctly to avoid getting nowhere. While this intellectual labyrinth appears to be very different from the terrifying psychological and physical trap that is the Cretan "maze," both versions reveal negative attitudes toward the labyrinth and a distancing from its ritual origins. Furthermore, ending up back where you started is not a desired outcome but rather a sign of failure for Plato. Reasoning is not meant to be circular!

Plato's move goes further than the myth in severing any ties to the labyrinth as a bodily experience. Plato is the first (aside from the historian Herodotus) to separate the labyrinth from the myth; he is the first to use it purely as metaphor, a move Peyronie identifies as marking decisively the shift from mythos to logos in Western thought (Peyronie, "The Labyrinth"

688-89). His argument reveals the movement away from a mythic orientation to the world—in the sense Hatab ascribes to the word "mythic," as indicating an immersion in immediate, sensuous, communal experience (4)—toward one based on rationality and the mind, a legacy our civilization has inherited, for good or for ill. Plato's conceptual use of the labyrinth represents the very foundation of the Western philosophical tradition (Peyronie, "The Labyrinth" 689). In *Euthydemus*, the labyrinth is no longer a physical structure through which one moves but rather a mental structure one navigates with the aid of reason alone; furthermore, the labyrinth is a trick that may lead one back to the starting point, thus symbolizing the hazards of a faulty argument. To an even greater degree than the Greek myth, Plato's metaphor distances itself from any religious, ritualistic, or bodily experience of the labyrinth as a structure or dance. Neither Theseus nor Socrates sees the labyrinth as anything but a trap from which it is desirable to escape as expeditiously as possible, but in Socrates's case the trap is not even a physical one. Plato's labyrinth is completely disembodied and exists only in the airy regions of the mind.

Timeline of a Symbol

Historically, as we have seen, the term "labyrinth" has had three separate meanings: it can be a dance, an elaborate building, or a maze. Kern, Kerényi, and others believe the labyrinth was originally a dance, a ritual that may have been related to the movements of the sun or the stars, though, unfortunately, there is no clear evidence to support this beyond some tantalizing clues (Kern 31-33). The labyrinth dance may have been part of a ritual intended to help move the sun through its cycle, facilitate the growth of crops, and secure the fecundity of the land. There is pictorial evidence to support its relationship to fertility rituals (for example, the Tragliatella pitcher), although it is not conclusive. A certain Bronze Age petroglyph in Pontevedra, Spain (c. 900-500 BCE) depicts a crude phallic figure penetrating a womb-like labyrinth (Kern 36). It is possible that natural formations such as caves and the organs of the body (i.e., the birth canal) suggested the connection to the birth process. Kerényi discusses a ritual dance from the Indonesian island of Seram that celebrates the death of the mythical maiden Hainuwele, an event that made human life possible, since her body under the earth yielded the fruits on which people subsisted. Although other scholars now suggest that this story is of much more recent origin than Kerényi supposed, he interpreted Hainuwele as a parallel to Persephone, whose abduction by Hades took her to the Underworld, and whose return to the upper world in the spring coincides with new growth and first flowerings. The post-labyrinth dance at Delos, Kerényi states, was a dance to honor Aphrodite, "by which was meant Ariadne, whose nature coincides both with Aphrodite's and Persephone's" ("Kore" 134). The labyrinth has been associated with initiation as a process of birth, death, and rebirth (Kern 30-31; Chevalier and Gheerbrant 643); certainly in the

Indonesian myth, as interpreted by Kerényi, the way to life is through death, as humans must ritually recapitulate the death of the maiden, who made their life possible, in order to escape a second and final death. This is accomplished through the labyrinthine Maro dance, with its nine-circled spiral, which Kerényi connects to not only the Crane Dance at Delos but also to the mysteries at Eleusis; he theorizes that the mysteries there involved, among other things, a dance of the initiates ("Kore" 135). The chief event of the Greater Mysteries at Eleusis, Kerényi says, was the recovery of the Kore ("Maiden"), who was Persephone, as well as the initiates' identification with the mother goddess, Demeter. Demeter's recovery of her daughter means a recovery of herself (both goddesses are aspects of a single goddess), and the rebirth of the goddess signals the rebirth of the participants in the ritual (137-39). Whatever the details of the Eleusinian mysteries, they were powerful enough to make the initiates lose their fear of death forever once they had undergone the ritual.

The basic pattern of the labyrinth-as-ritual is this: the initiate enters the labyrinth and negotiates it successfully without getting lost, returning from the darkness to the light to reveal his triumph over death. A story of this kind appears in many mythical traditions, including the cult (and associated rituals) of Persephone. The tale of Theseus certainly fits this pattern. Thus, the myth likely echoes a very ancient tradition, albeit greatly transformed.

The labyrinth as an ancient fertility ritual may have suggested the representations of the "Cretan" pattern that showed up on coins, rocks, mosaics, and other objects and surfaces throughout Europe, especially in the Mediterranean area (not to mention other parts of the world). When the pattern appeared on a dancing surface it was probably meant to guide intricate, choreographed movements whose ritualistic origin was obscured as time went on; eventually, the labyrinth as dance was transformed or combined with the mythic tradition of the labyrinth as maze (Kern 26).

In Kern's view, a labyrinth is not the same as a spiral, so any attempts to connect them are unfounded (33). He points to the fact that even if it is unicursal a labyrinth employs a great deal of indirection, taking the longest possible route to reach the center; a spiral, on the other hand, proceeds smoothly and in one direction. Kerényi is more convinced that the two symbols are related, and he treats them as comparable in his analysis of the Hainuwele and Ariadne/Persephone myths ("Kore" 133-35). Furthermore, Kerényi argues in *The Gods of the Greeks* that, "Originally the Labyrinth was not a maze, but a spiral through which one could return after reaching its centre" (270). Whether or not this is true, the labyrinth and the spiral have significant features in common, and Kerényi makes a strong case that the similarities overshadow the differences. Both have a central goal and an inexorable movement toward the center and then away from it; if the labyrinth is unicursal, the way in is almost certainly the way out, as it is in a spiral.

The labyrinth in its simplest and most ancient form was usually depicted as a series of loops forming concentric circles. Perhaps the windings of natural formations such as caves or the intestines or brain of the human body suggested this shape to early humans; associations with the womb and ovaries have also been noted (see above). Since late Neolithic times, as we have seen, the spiral has been connected with the idea of birth, death, and rebirth (Freitas 5276-77). The double spiral, in particular, represents an inward or underworld journey of symbolic death and a return to life. If the unicursal labyrinth is not related to the spiral (as Kern believes it is not), we can at least talk about the characteristics they share. Both lead to a center, but the labyrinth emphasizes the appearance of indirection and circuitousness, whereas the spiral is circular but proceeds in a single direction. The more highly developed labyrinth form, unlike the spiral, represents the unexpected twists and turns of life—but it still reveals an overall sense of order, narrative, and a definite destination.

Labyrinth patterns appeared perhaps as early as the Late Neolithic Age (2500 BCE), when human society was typically organized in small groups. These patterns, very similar to what were later called "Troy towns" (derived from the supposed connection—exploited by Virgil in the *Aeneid*'s Book 5—between the labyrinth design and the "Trojan ride" equestrian exercise), were found as petroglyphs in Galicia in the northwest region of Spain (Saward 20-21). During the rise of civilization and trade in the Bronze Age period, "Troy town" patterns continued to appear, and labyrinths were found across the Mediterranean region on stone, pottery, and other surfaces (Kern 28; Saward 19-21).

An especially intriguing (and early) written reference to the labyrinth occurs around 1400 BCE, on a Linear B clay tablet found at Knossos. The inscription on the tablet reads "One jar of honey to all the gods, one jar of honey to the Mistress of the ? *Labyrinth*." Kern speculates that this reference is related to the labyrinth pattern (possibly a dance pattern) depicted on a clay tablet found at Pylos at roughly the same time (25). In addition, fragments of clay pottery found in Syria at Tell Rifa'at depict labyrinths surrounded by human and animal figures. This vessel possibly dates from around 1200 BCE, though Saward notes that the disturbed condition of the remains casts doubt on their age (42). Both pictographs on the fragments depict the labyrinth as the basic "Cretan-style" design.

There is more evidence of the labyrinth's connection to dance from the eighth century BCE in the form of a Salian priest dance; there are also petroglyphs dating from this time, in addition to written references to a "Game of Troy." Kern speculates that "truia" in this context may mean "arena" and have no connection with the city of Troy (79). Of special note is the seventh-century *Oenochoe* ("pitcher") from Tragliatella, in the Cerveteri region of Italy, with its depiction of a seven-circuit labyrinth and an accompanying "Trojan ride" with human figures. The pitcher also includes depictions of copulating couples, which suggests a connection between the labyrinth, the ritual (in this case involving horses and riders), and fertility rites.

In Homer we find an early mention of the labyrinth as well as a "lady of the labyrinth" with a specific name: *Ariadne*. In the seventh century BCE, Homer's *Iliad* contains his celebrated description of the shield of Achilles with its depiction of a dancing floor, which Homer likens to the one Daedalus created in Knossos for "lovely-haired" Ariadne (18.590-606). In Hesiod's *Theogony* (c. 700 BCE), Ariadne is mentioned: she is a mortal, whom Zeus makes immortal after her marriage to Dionysus (947-49). Kern believes that if the labyrinth was a structure important enough to be named and associated with the goddess it must have had a vital religious significance. If the labyrinth were intimately connected with fertility rites, or with birth, death, and rebirth ceremonies, as Kerényi has suggested, it would certainly have held a central role in the religious life of the people (Kern 25). Ariadne, as the lady of the labyrinth, was likely a much more powerful figure at this early stage than she was to be later.

In some ancient societies, labyrinths were in fact set up in front of cities, residences, or important buildings as part of a defensive strategy, symbolizing the desire to guard something valuable or precious; in southern India, for example, where evil spirits were believed to travel only in straight lines, a labyrinth was a most effective foil (Kern 31, 81). These labyrinths had a civic and/or religious significance as the protectors of a temple, tomb, sacred space, or fortified city with the implication that only worthy initiates would succeed in navigating their twists and turns. The reward for choosing wisely among the labyrinth's confusing courses was initiation into the secret at its heart, or the gaining of its treasure (Chevalier and Gheerbrant 643). Thus, the adventure of the labyrinth could represent the necessarily difficult path to inside knowledge, hard-won spiritual wisdom, or even the material rewards of civilized life, depending on the context.

To continue with our timeline, we turn next to the architect Theodorus, who, roughly contemporary with Homer, was writing modestly about a "labyrinth" of his own design, the Heraeum, likely on the basis of its size and impressiveness and not because of any mazelike qualities (Kern 25). Beginning around 500 BCE, coins from Knossos appeared that depicted the Minotaur and meander-style designs, later evolving to portray elliptical Cretan-style labyrinths. Despite this, and even though the myth of Theseus and the Minotaur points to the existence of a labyrinth at Crete, which has variously been assumed to be an actual structure, a cave, or an underground level in a palace, evidence for any of these actually being the labyrinth of legend is flimsy or nonexistent, according to Kern (42-44).

Saward suggests that a labyrinth did exist at Crete and consisted of a large and elaborate palace and temple, later identified by Homer as the palace of King Minos. Egyptian frescoes from 1550 BCE (found in Avaris, in the Nile Delta) display meanders along with youths leaping over the heads of bulls and are, Saward believes, clearly the work of Cretan artisans. This evidence suggests that the association between Crete, the labyrinth, and the bull was well established and widely known by that time (Saward 20-21).

The idea of the labyrinth as a welter of interconnecting rooms was known in Egypt as well as Europe, and the ancient palace/tomb of Amenemhet III, a XIIth Dynasty pharaoh (1842-1797 BCE), was described by the historian Herodotus, who toured the upper part of the structure and gave the first written account of it (c. 484–430 BCE). Herodotus's *Histories* describes the Egyptian labyrinth, near "the city of Crocodiles," as a vast and impressive structure; he makes no connection between this labyrinth and the one on Crete, though later writers, such as Diodorus and Pliny the Elder, do (Kern 57).

Matthews names the sixth-century BCE Cretan poet Epimenides as an early writer who describes Theseus's escape from the labyrinth with the help of Ariadne's shining crown, a gift to her from Dionysus (20). Fragments of the work of fifth-century BCE mythographer Pherecydes of Athens (not to be confused with Pherecydes of Syros) contain what, according to Peyronie, is the first documented reference to the labyrinth in the myth (c. 450 BCE); Cleidemus (c. 375 BCE) is another early Greek source (Peyronie, "The Labyrinth" 687). Pherecydes may have been the source of the story of Theseus killing the Minotaur with his sword, which was then copied by later writers, although this is not certain.

In the fourth century, Dicaearchus (later cited by Plutarch) writes of the Crane Dance performed by the companions of Theseus on Delos; Palaiphatos's *Mythographi Graeci* has a reference to the labyrinth as a cave, and Plato's *Euthydemus* contains the crucial reference to the labyrinth as metaphor for a philosophical "quandary" that we have already discussed. Also dating from this time is graffito in the Acropolis depicting a square labyrinth (Kern 28, 73).

Around 300 BCE, we find Callimachus, in his *Hymn to Delos*, describing the labyrinth both as a dance and as a confusing edifice with winding paths. There is a record of expenses from a Delian temple from this time period apparently connected with a ritual dance, as well as construction receipts from Didyma referring to a momentous building project as a "labyrinth." At Callipolis (modern-day Gallipoli), an impression of a Knossos-style labyrinth seal has been found on a clay fragment dating from the late Classical period.

Starting in the second century BCE, Roman floor mosaics begin to feature labyrinths (some of which were square). Then, in the first century BCE, two important literary references occur in Virgil's *Aeneid*: one is a description of the Game of Troy enacted by Aeneas's son and other boys as part of Anchises's funeral games (in Book 5) and the other is a description of the labyrinth on "Daedalus's door" (in Book 6). The latter is a reference to the labyrinth depicted on Daedalus's marvelous door at Cumae—a memorial of the original labyrinth in Crete—that Aeneas stops to admire before venturing into the Sibyl's cave. In addition, other authors such as Varro (cited in Pliny the Elder's *Natural History*), Diodorus (in his *Library*), and Strabo (in his *Geography*) all refer to a labyrinth as a structure with confusing paths, proof of the widespread currency of the idea at this time.

In the first century CE, Pliny the Elder's *Natural History* mentions both the Game of Troy and the labyrinth as a structure (including a reference to the labyrinth at Crete), and there is graffito from a Pompeii residence depicting a square labyrinth with the notation *Labyrinthus Hic Habitat Minotaurus* ("Labyrinth. The Minotaur lives here."). Kern speculates that the graffito was the work of a prankster done just before the eruption of Vesuvius in 79 CE (Kern 74). Doob points out that so many references to the labyrinth were to be found in classical literature by around 60 CE that it had almost become a cliché (17). Ovid's *Metamorphoses*, Pomponius Mela's *Chorographia*, Apollodorus's *Library* and *Epitome*, and Dio Chrysostom's *Orationes* all refer to the tortuous paths of the labyrinth.

References to the labyrinth may only imply or simply ignore the myth, but on the other hand, a number of writers mention it specifically. In the myth, Theseus is a conquering hero who overcomes the monstrous Minotaur and emerges from the imprisoning labyrinth in triumph. In his *Lives*, Plutarch gives a detailed account of the life of Theseus, whom he treats as a semi-historical figure. Ovid tells the story of Theseus and the labyrinth in *The Metamorphoses*, but his interest is purely in the myth and not in historical or semi-historical structures or people. Seneca tells the story of Theseus, his wife Phaedra, and his son Hippolytus in *Phaedra*, on several occasions mentioning the labyrinth, which appears as a tragic foreshadowing symbol of the events in the play.

Visual and Literary Testaments

Doob points out the striking fact that although the multicursal labyrinth is firmly entrenched in the literary tradition, and many pavement labyrinths include illustrations of episodes from the myth, virtually all visual depictions (with two exceptions, at Knossos and Poitiers) show a unicursal design (40). An "early" depiction of the multicursal labyrinth (a true maze) comes very late in the scheme of things: it dates from the fifteenth century (Kern 30). As we know, depictions of the unicursal model go back to prehistoric times and include cave carvings, Egyptian seals, frescos, Greek coins, vases or pitchers, mosaics, and pavements. Most have distinct centers, and although most are circular (the so-called "Cretan" type), some are square or rectangular. Doob notes that Pliny (first century) and Boccaccio (fourteenth century) both commented on the discrepancy between the unicursal visual depictions and the mazelike literary labyrinths, although the difference seems to have gone unremarked by virtually everyone else (41).

Doob contends that this was not an oversight: she believes that classical and medieval artists were simply more concerned with what was the same about the two labyrinth types than with what was different. The concept of "bivia" (forked paths necessitating choice) was common to both the biblical and the philosophical tradition, and the multicursal maze, which offers a whole series of bivia, is a natural expression of moral or philosophical difficulty (46). Doob states that a person in the labyrinth has no way of knowing whether it is unicursal or multicursal, whether there is a center, or whether she will be able to find her way out again—the distinctions we see when looking at the labyrinth "from the outside" as a design or a symbol are not at all clear to the one who experiences the labyrinth "from the inside" as process (55-56). (However, we may assume that if a person encounters no choice of paths, she will realize she is in a unicursal labyrinth.) The maze presents itself as inextricable, confusing, frightening, and even dangerous if one enters it without guidance. In such a case, most of the responsibility for getting through the maze rests with the individual and the choices he makes (57).

In contrast to the confusing and multifarious pathways of the maze, the basis of the unicursal labyrinth is the single path, however

67

winding and roundabout it may be. It is easy to follow a path that does not branch, but the person following it may still become disoriented and remain totally in the dark about where he is going. Unlike a maze, which may provide a fairly direct path to the center or goal if one makes the correct turns, the unicursal labyrinth requires not choice but perseverance. Its hallmark is not bewildering choices but the greatest amount of circuitousness possible; one must trust to the path itself to show the way (Wright 18; Doob 50).

Thus the form of the labyrinth suggests two different types of experience—the universal and the particular. As Doob puts it, the person in a unicursal labyrinth, "is Everyman, not an individual" (50). He is forced to follow the path laid out for him, if he chooses to follow it at all. A walker in a multicursal maze is also subject to the constraints of the design, but within those constraints he can choose how to proceed. Such an experience requires an active, thinking participant, one who is conscious of himself, the path he is on, and his choices. The unicursal labyrinth walker's choices are few (though they include whether to enter the labyrinth in the first place and whether to continue). Such a labyrinth parallels the universal human experience of being born, living, and dying. Intelligence plays no role in deciding to enter this labyrinth; one merely continues, goes back, or stops.

Furthermore, classical (and medieval) commentators almost never stress the superiority of one type of labyrinth over the other, although many of them mention the convertibility of either type from perceived chaos to order and back again, depending on the maze walker's perspective (Doob 52-53). There is after all (usually) a way through a maze, and there is often only one way. In reality, the way through is a one-way path, and the branching paths are only false starts. However, one may go all the way through a maze and out again (as Theseus did) and be just as unable to make sense of the path as he was in the beginning.

The Roundabout Quality of the Maze

Doob believes the circuitousness—the roundabout quality of both types of labyrinths—is the most important quality, not the choice or lack of choice of paths. In her view, the fact that the way is not straightforward but involves delays, diversions, and difficulty is the primary characteristic of a labyrinth. Whether it is unicursal or multicursal, she believes, has no bearing on the subjective experience, good or bad, of being in it. It is possible for a multicursal labyrinth to take one fairly quickly to the center (assuming there is one) if the walker is able to discern the way (53-54).

Of course, a unicursal labyrinth may represent "difficulty" in the sense of offering only a frustratingly circuitous path, but this is not the same type of difficulty experienced in a maze, where the problem lies in choosing among the options one confronts. In light of our interest in the labyrinth as a metaphor for epistemology, Doob's discussion of the labyrinth as a model for learning, either by precept (the unicursal model) or by active participation (the multicursal model) is significant. Doob believes the unicursal design served to represent both labyrinth types in visual renderings for so long because the difference between the two types of labyrinths was not thought to be "important" during classical and medieval times. It was not until the sixteenth and seventeenth centuries that the multicursal maze began to replace the unicursal design in artistic renderings, and since then, the multicursal maze has come to represent the general meaning of "labyrinth" in Western art and imagination. But there is something else. On closer inspection, Doob suggests, the opposition of the two types of labyrinths in visual representation versus literary tradition reflected a dynamic interplay between authority and the individual, or determinism and free will, that medieval thinkers may have been reluctant to fully confront (62 n. 25). While Doob suggests this possibility in a footnote as "deconstructive fancy," it seems likely that the crux of the matter lies in just such a medieval unwillingness to emphasize free will as we will later see in Dante.

Tellers of the Tale

Doob identifies three writers who were especially influential in shaping the way early Christians (and later, people in the Middle Ages) viewed the labyrinth: Virgil (70-19 BCE), Ovid (43 BCE-17 CE), and Pliny the Elder (23-79 CE) (17).

Pliny was interested in the historical/geographical facts of labyrinths as great or notable structures, an approach that goes back at least to Herodotus. Pliny focused on the Egyptian labyrinth, the Cretan labyrinth, the one at Lemnos, and the one at Etruria, in Italy (Kern 58). He wrote of the labyrinths as both impressive architectural achievements that were monuments to their makers and/or patrons and confusing, inextricable structures. As we have seen, he was especially detailed in his description of the Egyptian labyrinth, which he described as magnificent as well as complicated; he thought it was a temple to Egyptian sun gods. On the other hand, he knew the Cretan "labyrinth" (or palace) only by reputation since it had disappeared by 1400 BCE. Its ruins were only discovered in the twentieth century by Sir Arthur Evans, who found ample evidence of a cult of bull worship practiced at Knossos as well as a decorative meander pattern (on plaster) resembling a multicursal maze (Matthews 29). Doob identifies this meander pattern as the earliest depiction (and a rare one) of a multicursal maze (25 n. 12).

Ovid, as we have seen, was mostly interested in the story and its characters, and he emphasized the negative aspect of the labyrinth as a trap in both *The Metamorphoses* and *Heroides*. In *The Metamorphoses*, Theseus enters the bewildering maze boldly and slays the Minotaur, finding his way out again with Ariadne's help (Mandelbaum, *The Metamorphoses of Ovid* 8.169-76).

The hero then sails off with Ariadne, only to abandon her abruptly on Naxos.

Virgil combined the approaches of Pliny and Ovid, joining an interest in labyrinths as structures with a literary exploration of the labyrinth as myth and metaphor. He and other classical writers tended to stress the labyrinth as process, and the negative connotations of the labyrinth as a trap were prominent in their work. The *Aeneid* and *Metamorphoses* assume of their readers some familiarity with the myth, but the sources for this knowledge, other than a few commentators here and there, are unknown (Doob 25-26).

Virgil's contribution in the *Aeneid* is significant: he describes the Game of Troy in detail in the scene involving Anchises's funeral games, in which the young boys perform elaborate maneuvers on horseback, weaving in and out in alternating stages of mock battle and peace (Mandelbaum, *The Aeneid of Virgil* 5.727-94). The game was well known in Roman times and may go back to the seventh century BCE or beyond (the Etruscan Tragliatella pitcher depicts a scene from this game labeled with the word *truia*). Part of the mystery surrounding the Game of Troy centers on the meaning of *truia*. It may mean "Troy" (in the Etruscan tongue) or "dancing floor" (in Latin). Virgil may have been the first to associate the two-dimensional static design (such as might be left by horses' hooves on a surface) with the three-dimensional structure: he compares the *lusus Troiae* with the Cretan labyrinth in Book 5 (lines 772-79) of the *Aeneid*. Doob believes Virgil's association of the two may have contributed to the later confusion, persisting through the Middle Ages, of a unicursal labyrinth design with the multicursal structure of classical literature. The identification was common by Pliny's day, and it may have been inspired by Virgil's description (29-30). Virgil describes the *lusus Troiae* as multicursal, but in other writers' accounts (Pliny's, for instance) it is not clear if the path is multicursal or unicursal (Doob 30 n. 18).

Virgil's famous description of the Daedalus door at Cumae includes a retelling of the legend of Crete, and his emphasis is on the labyrinth as a trap and a prison, with the artistry of the design taking a decided back seat to its associations with shame, error, sin, lust, suffering, and death. Virgil's descriptions here are later echoed by most other writers, including Ovid and Pliny. Virgil played with the meanings of "labor" and "labyrinthus" (the labyrinth as "travail"), and others imitated him; to a large extent, the metaphorical meaning of "labyrinth" current in the Middle Ages was based on Virgil's treatment (Doob 31-32). In medieval times the story was known as a legend, not as fact, despite Plutarch's well-known "biography" of Theseus.

Theseus as the Founder of Athens

Plutarch (45-120 CE) presents the story of Theseus, the legendary founder of Athens, as a semi-historical tale in his *Lives*; for Plutarch, Theseus's history is a parallel to the story of Romulus, founder of Rome.

73

Plutarch's sources for the life of Theseus include Pherecydes, Demon, Philochorus, and Cleidemus. Some of his other sources have been lost and are now known to us only through his work.

Plutarch summarizes many tales told of Theseus from diverse sources and includes both favorable and unfavorable views of his actions. Kern summarizes his telling of the story at some length because of its wealth of detail and inclusion of so many earlier sources (which, disagree, however, as to the identities and relationships among Theseus, Minos, the Minotaur, and Ariadne) (41-42). What emerges in Plutarch is the story of a hero dedicated to the establishment of Athens as a democracy formed from a group of towns and communities in Attica and joined under his leadership to pursue unified interests. Theseus was an admirer of Heracles (Plutarch 15), and his story somewhat parallels that of the famous hero, both in his many battles with local tyrants and monsters and in his exploits with women, which cast a shadow on the positive aspects of his character. Plutarch links Theseus with numerous women, from Ariadne and her sister Phaedra to Antiope (or Hippolyta), the Amazonian queen, to Helen of Troy, whom he is said to have abducted. In one version of the story, which Plutarch attributes to the Greek historian Philochorus, the Minotaur is a formidable but entirely human general under Minos, with whom Theseus does battle during funeral games held for Minos's son Androgeos (Kern 41-42). The labyrinth is here presented as an actual prison, and Ariadne is the girl, present at the games, who falls head over heels for the valiant and sinewy Theseus. Plutarch concedes that most sources credit Ariadne with giving him the thread that lets him find his way into and out of the Labyrinth, killing the Minotaur and freeing his fellow Athenians (37). After he leads them to freedom, they all sail away from Crete, taking Ariadne with them. Theseus either abandons or forgets Ariadne on the isle of Naxos (in one version, he intends to return but does not), and later he and the Athenian youths perform the celebratory Crane Dance on the island of Delos, supposedly in imitation of the intricate twists and turns of the labyrinth from which they so recently escaped.

Theseus and the Archaic Past

A generalized portrait of Theseus emerges from the various literary accounts of the classical period: he embodies strength, courage, and fighting ability, heroic qualities that allow cities to be established and civilizations to flourish. Yet he finds himself entering a labyrinth, a structure of very ancient lineage, symbolic of nature, the goddess, and the Mysteries, whose origins appear to be much older than civilization, if the evidence of the Neolithic artifacts cited by Kern and others is to be believed. Theseus uses his strength and courage to battle the Minotaur, but he relies heavily on Ariadne's gifts (which may include weapons as well as the guiding thread) to win the battle and find his way back. His labyrinth is a multicursal labyrinth, designed by the architect as a prison. Theseus—warrior, future king, and founder of a city—faces and overthrows the archaic forces represented by the labyrinth, the Minotaur—and Ariadne.

It is the older, matricentric, goddess-centered culture that Theseus, representative of the patriarchy, symbolically opposes. Until the coming of the Indo-Europeans around 2000 BCE, the earlier inhabitants of Greece lived in a matricentric society, worshipping powerful goddesses who ruled over the agricultural cycles of life and death. The portraits of the Greek goddesses that have come down to us from classical Greece are, according to Christine Downing, watered-down versions filtered through a patriarchal lens. In *The Goddess: Mythological Images of the Feminine* she writes, "The classical literature is explicitly patriarchal, though it is imbued with a profound sense of continued threat from the older order" (20). Since Theseus is emblematic of the new warrior-hero, the forces he defeats must be suitably reprehensible; not only the Minotaur but also the labyrinth itself (now a structure designed and built by a man) are associated with doom and death. Therefore, what was formerly approached reverentially (as the heart of a mystery) is now approached with enmity and the goal of destruction. Ariadne, the former goddess, has been relegated to the role of a lovesick girl left behind by the ungrateful (or is it the merely absent-minded?) Theseus. The awkwardness of this abandonment stems from the fact that Ariadne's original stature as goddess and mistress of the labyrinth does not translate easily into such a reduced form. Her original primacy is implied by

76

Theseus's dependence on her to find his way through the labyrinth. Once he has defeated the Minotaur and escaped Crete, however, the hero and representative of the warrior culture "forgets" her as soon as possible and moves on to other conquests.

Evidence of changing values and beliefs in Greek society exist in the uneasy layering of archaic symbolism and heroic struggle that we see in the myth. Theseus begins his adventure courageously, but things start to go awry soon after he emerges from the labyrinth. Far from having achieved spiritual victory, he has instead established a pattern of destruction that is repeated, either intentionally or unintentionally, in his subsequent actions. From a Jungian perspective, we might say that Theseus's approach is too one-sided. It relies too much on physical prowess and the use of force and amounts to a violent attack. The formerly sacred precinct of the labyrinth has become a battleground, and its mysteries have been transformed into a death-giving enemy. Awe and reverence have been replaced with a determination to defeat the enemy by a force of arms. As Downing puts it:

> Theseus is the male hero who continually finds himself in conflict with the matrilineal world, the "king must die" world. As the hero most deeply aware of the danger and the appeal of the feminine, he spends his life battling against being overtaken by it. Not only Theseus but the heroes of many of the Greek myths that we know best . . . seem to represent precisely the moment of transition in Greek cultural history from the matrilineal to the patrilineal. In the earlier period the sacred was experienced most powerfully as feminine; political power, if not directly in the hands of women, was defined by one's relation to

them . . . the Greek myths as we get them from Homer and Hesiod, from Aeschylus and Sophocles, are written from the perspective of the patriarchal period, a perspective that issues in the reduction of ancient goddesses into figures with whom men can safely deal. (57)

Theseus enters the labyrinth as a conqueror and not as an initiate. Because he does not go seeking knowledge, he does not find any. He wins a soldier's victory but not an increase in consciousness or the humility that might result from a true encounter with what lies in the collective psychic past. He repudiates the distant origins of his own story. For him, the labyrinth is no longer a return to "Mother Earth" but a descent into the underworld of death and subsequently another victory to add to his belt.

The shadow cast by Theseus's heroic stance is huge, though unspoken. Although he goes on to become the king of Athens, his career is marked by missteps from the time he leaves the labyrinth, as if his one-sided approach (and abandonment of Ariadne) has left him off-balance. His thoughtlessness upon approaching Athens results in his father's suicide when he forgets to change the color of his sail. His attack on the Amazons seems further proof of his warlike spirit and determination to overcome powerful feminine figures. There are further transgressions against women: he kidnaps Helen of Troy when she is still a child, and he tries to help his friend Pirithous abduct Persephone (a goddess and queen!) (Morford and Lenardon 611).

Having married Ariadne's sister Phaedra, Theseus is eventually undone when Phaedra falls in love with her stepson, Hippolytus, the son of Theseus and the Amazon queen Antiope. In a mirror image of the passion that began the adventure of the labyrinth, Phaedra falls in love illicitly and is ashamed when her secret is discovered. The result is not only her death but also Hippolytus's. Although Theseus realizes his error in time to reconcile with his son, Hippolytus still dies.

Theseus goes on to become a protector of the helpless and oppressed and is considered a wise and just king, but he has lost much along the way. Despite such noble actions as defending the mothers of the seven heroes against Thebes and sheltering Oedipus at Colonus, Theseus's life ends in failure when he is driven into exile and killed on an island (Morford and Lenardon 612-13).

As hero, Theseus snatches a warrior's victory from the jaws of death, defeating the monster utterly, and he could not have accomplished even this questionable victory without the help of Ariadne. Her presence and crucial role in the myth is, as we have seen, a holdover from an earlier time in which goddess worship was prominent, and Ariadne was a mother-goddess connected with not only birth and death but with the soul, "the archetypal reality of the bestowal of soul, of what makes a living creature an individual," according to Kerényi, writing in *Dionysos, Archetypal Image of Indestructible Life* (124). Kerényi goes on to say that, "Soul is an essential element of *zoë*, which needs it to transcend the seminal stage" (124). Ariadne's pairing with Dionysus represents the soul-giving principle that animates each life and is present within that life from its inception in the unconscious. As Downing puts it, this unconscious is "a source of continual renewal rather than a depository for what has been banished from the world of the living" (64). Thus it appears that the mystery of what the center of the labyrinth held in archaic times was no less than Ariadne herself, the giver of soul. As the myth changed to reflect the changing values of the culture, Ariadne's role was diminished, but her continuing presence was a reminder that the original labyrinth may have represented a woman's body, or the body of Mother Earth, from which each individual was born. Although Theseus makes his way into and out of the labyrinth, which has now become a prison, he abandons Ariadne soon thereafter, as if to say she was not so very important after all. In the patriarchal scheme of things, she no longer is.

As Sophie Mills suggests, the Theseus of the early myths is different from the Theseus presented in later accounts, particularly those of fifth-century Athenian tragedians. Theseus appears in the plays of Sophocles and Euripides (as he does in Plutarch) as an Athenian hero; in these plays, some of the episodes connected with his life, and particularly his abandonment of Ariadne, do not suit the portrait of a beloved hero and king. It is clear that the story has been shaped over time to reflect changing concerns and circumstances (Mills 2). The noble Theseus of later legend (as seen in *Oedipus at Colonus*, for example) has had his character burnished so as to shed a good light on the city of Athens, which he represents. Bits and pieces of conflicting information from various sources account for the complicated portrait of Theseus (misogynist? fair-minded king? brave warrior?) that emerges as a composite.

Who Is the Minotaur?

As we have seen, Theseus is plagued by a succession of bulls throughout his career, not the least of which is the strange hybrid he encounters in Crete. The Minotaur is a complex symbol, half-man and half-beast, often thought of as a joining of humanity's "higher" and "lower" natures, rational consciousness and instinctual animal. In place of a man's head (the seat of rationality and wisdom) is the bull's head; the instincts are driving the beast without the restraining influence of thought and higher consciousness. Thus we may think of the Minotaur as Theseus's own shadow. From this perspective, Theseus's victory over the Minotaur is a pseudo-victory over brute nature and instinctual passions that should be acknowledged and owned if humanity is to move out of a primitive existence. Peyronie characterizes the Minotaur in this light, when "at the very moment of the confrontation, Theseus suddenly saw his own inverted image rise before him, represented by the Other" ("The Minotaur" 821). Peyronie recognizes that it is not possible to destroy the Minotaur. "At the very most we can sacrifice it, in other words transform it, or else it 'completes' us" ("The Minotaur" 821).

Traditionally, scholars give the Minotaur's name as Asterion, or "star" (Artress, *Walking a Sacred Path* 57; Kerényi, *Gods of the Greeks* 110-11). This indicates that the Minotaur may truly be a somewhat unrecognizable sun god, a source of light, life, and growth, in a disguised and debased condition. The Minotaur *is* a monster, more animal than man, but as such he represents a powerful source of primitive, unconscious wisdom. Kerényi writes, "The Minotaur of the older myth was bull and star at the same time. If he lived in the labyrinth, he lived with the 'mistress of the labyrinth,' his mother [Ariadne]. . . . The mistress was at the center of the true labyrinth, the underworld; she bore a mysterious son and conferred the hope of a return to the light" (*Dionysos* 117-18).

The Minotaur's ferocity is not to be underestimated or trifled with. He represents power, strength, and vitality, especially sexual vitality, but also violence, untamed animal ferocity, and tyranny. The bull is associated with fire and water, sun and moon, the celestial and the underworld realms (Chevalier and Gheerbrant 135). Though connected with the forces of creation (as in the Hebraic El, the sacred bull), it also has associations with death and rebirth (132-33)—which brings us back to the labyrinth's connection with the Mysteries.

In many cultures, it is the hero's job to tame or sublimate the fury of the bull, transforming it into spiritual or moral strength. In the story of the Golden Fleece, for example, Jason does not kill the fire-breathing bulls, but instead yokes them, symbolically gaining control of his own passions in the process (Chevalier and Gheerbrant 136). The Greek conception of the bull recognized both its ferocious, violent aspect and its associations with fertility. Perhaps these are not as different as they seem; birth is not a gentle process but an incredibly bloody one, steeped in agony and sometimes danger, or even death. Dionysus, the male god of fertility who is associated with both Demeter and Persephone (as well as Ariadne), presides over rites that are incredibly violent; his Maenads were capable of tearing a grown man (such as the hapless Pentheus) limb from limb while under the influence of Dionysian ecstasy.

From a psychoanalytic point of view, gaining control of the bull represents integration of the passions and animal energies in the maturing personality. Though an individual may fear the power of his animal nature and wish to murder the beast, he will never succeed in doing so—nor would it be desirable to succeed, even if it were possible. To deny one's animal nature and primitive (even violent) instincts is to deny the biological aspect of consciousness and to split oneself off from the natural world. Going to the center of the labyrinth means recognizing one's animal nature while acknowledging the ultimate mystery of life's origins—its "givenness," to use Hatab's term (26).

Hatab makes much of the messiness and disorder—the imperfection—that mythic consciousness experiences in the world as opposed to the distancing from immediate experience that philosophical abstraction creates. As he sees it:

> there *is* a moral and structural sense in early Greek religion, but not moral perfection or universal regularity. The flux and contest of forces in the world are not eliminated but rather apportioned and celebrated as such, thereby implying an affirmation of the whole of life.
> . . . . Perhaps we can understand this contrasted with Christian transcendence and the Greek philosophical development of rational abstraction from the lived world . . . . both developments represent a *reform* of the lived world, the contentious plurality of sensuous experience and existential concerns. For this reason both traditions will maintain that there is something flawed in the way we first encounter the world, which is in need of correction by either spiritual transcendence or rational abstraction. (50)

In terms of the labyrinth, the correction supplied by philosophy transforms it from a bodily experience into a metaphor for knowledge or experience gained by rational thought or moral struggle. The transformation was never complete, but the movement from ritual dance to mental or moral quandary is present as a definite metamorphosis corresponding to the epistemological change from mythic givenness to rational abstraction.

The journey through the labyrinth, practiced in a religious spirit, approaches knowledge wreathed in the unknown. This knowledge may be thought of as mythic consciousness or the collective unconscious, but either way, it corresponds to a very ancient form of knowledge and way of being in the world. It is no easy task to access this knowledge when human history is viewed as progressive and the ancient past as wholly savage and without merit. Like any form of wisdom that truly matters, it must be approached by circuitous means, with a receptive attitude, rather than by direct assault.

The Labyrinth and the Bull

The symbolic combination of labyrinth and Minotaur expresses several interrelated meanings: an earlier goddess-oriented religious perspective, a reverence for the mystery of life and death, an acknowledgement of the mythic consciousness that precedes (and informs) philosophical consciousness, and a representation of the collective unconscious that contains the memories, instincts, and drives, including the violent, murderous urges, which the human race has inherited from its forebears. The labyrinth's origins in dance and bodily movement are understandable in terms of a non-rational, mythic understanding of nature that springs from a direct immersion in the sensuous world. This experience is expressed in the movement in and out of the labyrinth, a pattern understood intuitively and through the body—not by the head alone, or even primarily by the head. This is the movement from life to death to rebirth that we have been discussing, which existed in ritual as the labyrinth dance.

It is important to note, however, that the entire movement includes an approach to the center *as well as a return*. It is not possible or desirable to return to the mythic past, the Golden Age, or the Garden and stay there. The gifts of civilization—culture, ethics, and the rule of law—are vital and necessary advances for humanity. This does not negate the fact that the mythic consciousness they spring from continues to function in our individual and collective lives and institutions. The past and the present live side by side in our inner and outer worlds.

An important aspect of the labyrinth's symbolism is its association with man's inner journey toward consciousness and wholeness (Purce 13). The labyrinth may also represent the feminine, intuitive side of human nature, the side that perceives patterns and does not rely on logic alone to understand problems (Artress, *Walking a Sacred Path* 52, 67). Here again, we see an association of the labyrinth with the feminine in some form. This aspect of the mythical Cretan labyrinth eludes even its builder, Daedalus, who is not able to find his way out unaided—and it certainly eludes Theseus. It is no wonder, since the labyrinth is much older and more mysterious than either its builder or its "conqueror." A prominent characteristic of the labyrinth maze, as we have seen, is its difficulty, which keeps the unworthy or unprepared from penetrating to its heart. Likewise, one who has found his way to the center must be able to find his way back, or else the journey was in vain. By the time the myth featuring Theseus as the hero (and Ariadne as a subordinate character who provides the "cheat sheet") had gained currency, the labyrinth was no longer welcoming to its would-be "initiates" and had taken on the character of a terrifying prison.

In one of his adventures before coming to Crete, Theseus had captured and sacrificed Poseidon's bull (Plutarch 27). Sacrifice denotes an appropriate humility, a healthy characteristic in a hero; Theseus had performed the appropriate action but perhaps honored the wrong god, or at least failed to honor other important gods. He had sacrificed to Apollo, the god of light and reason. Perhaps Theseus believes when he sails for Crete that his heroic triumphs in previous exploits have prepared him to take on the labyrinth and the Minotaur with brute strength and bravery alone. According to most accounts, he volunteers to accompany the Athenian contingent and seems confident that heroic will, courage, and deeds of arms will see him through the ordeal. In the event, however, these alone are no match for the disorienting experience of the labyrinth. Theseus is out of his league when faced with this great task, which requires a different approach, or at least a complementary approach, to the one inspired by a warrior's values.

Before entering the labyrinth, Theseus receives Ariadne's gifts and is thus able to meet the Minotaur with additional defenses; he is also assured of a way out. Ariadne provides the thread, and in some variations of the story, a crown or wreath that lights the way, as well as a ball of pitch that Theseus can throw into the Minotaur's mouth. Ariadne's Cretan name, Aridela—"the utterly clear"—(Kerényi, *Dionysos* 104) and archetypal associations of the guiding thread with inner awareness (Artress, *Walking a Sacred Path* 14) suggest that Ariadne does not give Theseus weapons of destruction alone but also weapons representing intuition and perception. Theseus will not be able to force his way in or think his way through, so Ariadne gives him the gifts of a more ancient wisdom—which he must follow blindly, as it were. The warrior is utterly dependent on Ariadne's thread, which is truly his lifeline.

Ariadne's role in the tradition is depicted differently from the time of Homer onwards than it was in the earlier "unwritten texts—pictorial representations and dances" (Kerényi, *Dionysos* 90), in which she was an important goddess, the consort of Dionysus from the beginning, rather than an abandoned girl picked up by the god on Naxos. Kerényi believes the mistress of the labyrinth referred to on the clay tablet from Knossos (1400 BCE) was Ariadne herself, and that the offering of honey dedicated to her (equal to that offered to the rest of the gods together) confirms her high status (Kerényi, *Dionysos* 90). Christine Downing, Sophie Mills, and others point to Ariadne's connection with Dionysus as the proof that Ariadne was originally a goddess, reduced to a mortal only in later versions of the myth. There are indications that she may have been an early version of Aphrodite (Kerényi, *Gods of the Greeks* 270, 272); Plutarch mentions the worship of Ariadne-Aphrodite on Cyprus (43). This joining of the goddess of love and the goddess of the labyrinth makes sense in the context of the labyrinth as a birth passage; Ariadne knew its secrets of birth and rebirth. Again, this suggests that the basic meaning of the labyrinth involves a ritual approach to the origin of life, to the womb, or to Mother Earth.

Kern points out that the Hopis of North America have a labyrinth in their mythology that symbolizes birth and the movement between two worlds. The identical symbol appears as far away as India, and Kern believes it possible that it was spread by cultural transmission, citing the Hopi creation story, with its account of tribal founders making an extended water journey in search of the Fourth World, as suggestive of "transpacific transmission" (298). Whether by cultural diffusion or spontaneous emergence of a universal idea, labyrinths (or labyrinth-like structures) have been found in many societies in both the East and the West.

Ariadne was a powerful figure in the matrilineal era. Along with Kerényi and others, Downing identifies her as the Lady of the Labyrinth, who was always associated with death, but a death that includes rebirth.

Downing cites other authors who describe her cult on Crete, which was deeply concerned with water and islands. In that culture, there was less of a clear delineation between life and death (unlike classical Greek culture, in which the border between life and death was definite, at least until the advent of the mystery cults). Life and death were intimately bound together in Minoan Crete, so Ariadne may be seen as a source of life *and* a source of death (Downing 63-64).

Originally, it was Ariadne who occupied the center of the labyrinth, though she was gradually reduced in stature as the Greek culture demoted the all-powerful goddesses into split-off, less potent figures. It is no accident that the "heroic" stance eventually coincides with the rise of ego consciousness in clear distinction to the earlier mythic consciousness. One can see the progression, even in a culture still as imbued with myth as ancient Greece was, toward a style of thinking that placed consciousness above and apart from nature and in opposition to it. The forces of nature, and the gods that represent them, are often hostile to the Greek heroes.

Bruce Lincoln and Vera Bushe are among the commentators who read the Greek myths (in particular, the Demeter and Persephone myth, which both authors analyze in detail) in terms of patriarchal consciousness as opposed to an earlier matricentric sensibility. Lincoln refers to the coming of the Indo-Europeans (the dates are disputed, but he tentatively suggests 1800 BCE), with their patriarchal traditions, as an event that profoundly changed the matricentric orientation of the existing tribal culture in Greece, resulting in the displacement, demotion, or alteration of many of the goddess-centered rituals (Lincoln 167). According to Bushe, who references Charlene Spretnak on the subject, "Jane Ellen Harrison found the pre-Olympian body of mythology to be different in many ways from the patriarchal Olympian system" (Bushe 173). Bushe recognizes that we have inherited the attitudes and style of consciousness associated with patriarchy, so we must take that into account when trying to understand the myths that evolved with it, which includes, of course, the myth of Theseus. "What we have is patriarchal mythology and patriarchal archetypes," Bushe observes (173). Although this is true, we still see glimpses of the archaic view.

Myth reflects the "being-in-the-world" view of a people as well as the universal being-in-the-world experience of being human. It is a direct existential engagement that acknowledges the mystery from which life springs. While philosophy attempts to explain the world, categorize knowledge, and seek predictability and certainty about what can be known, myth celebrates the *experience* of living. The ancient ritual labyrinth expresses receptivity toward the mysterious source of things; it is only later that the maze begins to express a problem-solving drive toward solutions.

The labyrinth, in its ritualistic and mythic origins, presents an approach to this source as a sacred journey. In the myth of Theseus, we see the ritual meaning of the labyrinth already altered to reflect changing values. The labyrinth is now an initiatory experience for a hero, the founder of Athens and the slayer of monsters, not a religious experience open to all. In an earlier culture, the center of the labyrinth contained the source of things. In the myth of Theseus, that source has been transformed into an enemy to be overcome.

Herodotus and Plato (in the fifth and fourth centuries BCE, respectively) were the first to discuss the notion of "labyrinth" in a non-mythical context, as we have seen; Plato's contribution is especially significant because he was likely the first to use the labyrinth as a metaphor, separating it from its role in the myth (Peyronie, "The Labyrinth" 688). In *Euthydemus*, as we have seen, Plato used the labyrinth as an image for the mental confusion that challenges a thinker's capacity for clear reasoning and sustained argument. A journey in the labyrinth, he said, is a quest for knowledge in which the unwary or incapable may find himself lost. This metaphor of Plato's is not merely an elegant literary conceit: untethering the image from the myth signals no less than the shift from mythos to logos— from mythic thinking to philosophizing—that Peyronie describes as the foundation of the Western philosophical tradition ("The Labyrinth" 689). The shift, though decisive, was not complete, and something was lost as well as gained in the transition. Furthermore, it is not necessary to come down on the side of mythos or logos for once and for all; the two types of labyrinths reveal the hazards and benefits of thinking mythically and of thinking philosophically and actually suggest a way out of their opposition.

In the Beginning

What was lost and what was gained in the move out of mythic and into philosophical consciousness? As David Abram describes it in *The Spell of the Sensuous*, a direct immersion in the phenomenal world of nature was the ordinary daily experience of early humans. Continuing in the tradition of such twentieth-century pioneers of phenomenology as Edmund Husserl and Maurice Merleau-Ponty, Abram insists on the primacy of sensory, bodily experience in our knowledge of the world. Humans have evolved, with the rest of the natural world, as part of a matrix of mutually influencing and perceiving entities; from the human point of view, the nonhuman entities and forces in nature comprise what Abram terms "the Others" (7).

In primitive societies, far removed from our scientific age of abstraction and objectification of matter, tribes relied on their shamans to contact, placate, forestall, or encourage, as the case might be, the mysterious and powerful forces of nature they sensed as active all around them. They experienced the world in a fundamentally different way than our "civilized" understanding encompasses (an understanding based on "distance" from our direct experience and a preference for analyzing and conceptualizing what we see). For them, nature was alive (Hatab 20-21). Spirits were present in the phenomena of the natural world and in the continuing presence of the ancestors. People enacted their experience of participation in the natural world through such rituals as the labyrinth dance. Rituals expressed their belief in their ability to influence the world of spirit and matter of which they were an active part. The rise of philosophy, with its emphasis on reasoning and abstraction, began to replace mythic immersion in sensory experience with the habit of thinking about and reflecting on experience. One of the results of this shift was the ability of the subject to separate himself from events and observe both himself and the world around him "objectively" (26-27).

In defense of pre-philosophical "being-in-the-world" Merleau-Ponty points out that scientific objectivity (and I would add, philosophical abstraction) has its origin and basis in the older stratum of direct, lived experience. In *Phenomenology of Perception*, he describes the state of affairs thus:

> The whole universe of science is built upon the world as directly experienced, and if we want to subject science itself to rigorous scrutiny and arrive at a precise assessment of its meaning and scope, we must begin by reawakening the basic experience of the world of which science is the second-order expression. . . . To return to things themselves is to return to that world which precedes knowledge, of which knowledge always *speaks*, and in relation to which every scientific schematization is an abstract and derivative sign-language, as is geography in relation to the country-side in which we have learnt beforehand what a forest, a prairie or a river is. (ix-x)

Philosophers and physicists, along with everyone else, live in the phenomenal world, which has never entirely disappeared, though it has been obscured by the abstract style of thought pioneered by Plato and his philosophical labyrinth. This ever-increasing tendency to conceptualize what had formerly been a bodily experience gained impetus from Aristotle's emphasis on "empirical" reason as a means of understanding the natural world (Hatab 260).

The twin streams of Platonic Idealism and Aristotelian empiricism were both influential in the Middle Ages, although Aristotle's brand of rational, scientific enquiry eventually became the predominant mode of understanding the world. Plato's influence eventually revealed itself mostly in the spiritual etherealism of Christianity's otherworldliness, which coexisted, albeit somewhat uneasily at times, with Aristotle's scientific pragmatism, up through the scientific revolution ushered in by Nicolaus Copernicus (1473-1543) and Galileo Galilei (1564-1642). As we will see in the next chapter, the labyrinth was adopted by the Church as a symbol of an outlook that places God as the central authority and source of all that is. Although the labyrinth represented the way to God, it was often portrayed as a thorny "moral" path through the snares of the world (Doob 145; Wright 76). The labyrinth led to transcendence but only if successfully negotiated; it could also lead the unwary to the devil.

Abram intuits the original purpose of the labyrinth set forth in this chapter. He refers to the interplay of the living body and the natural world in which it is enmeshed as a dance: "this improvised duet between my animal body and the fluid, breathing landscape that it inhabits" (53) and "this ceaseless dance between the carnal subject and its world," adding, "at one moment the body leads, at another the things [in the world]" (54). It is possible, then, to embrace the philosophical labyrinth while at the same time celebrating the dance of which it is an outgrowth. Philosophy and science are embedded in the mythic/sensuous ground from which they spring. Instead of an either/or situation, or a historical progression in which philosophy and science take their "rightful" place as the enlightened successors to the uninformed thinking of an earlier time, mythic receptivity and philosophical conceptualizing can and do co-exist. All of the labyrinth's meanings—as dance, as puzzle, as initiation, as a moral difficulty or descent into the underworld—continue to inform one another.

A problem arises, however, with the twin developments of Christian thought and rationalism as they developed in the Middle Ages. Both assume, as Hatab points out, an essential flaw in our uncensored and sensuous experience of the world that each, its own way, seeks to correct. Hatab says:

> The pluralism of Greek myths expresses the acute sense of worldliness reflected in early Greek culture. . . . The historical link between [Christian transcendence and the

Greek philosophical development of rational abstraction]
(e.g., in Medieval philosophy) becomes easier to
understand when we notice their common dissatisfaction
with sensuous immediacy and the disorder of the lived
world. . . . And since the Greek myths are nothing more
than a presentation of the lived world, both traditions did
battle with these myths. The subsequent demythification
of the world resulted in a secularization (or profaning) of
the world, which had two significant consequences:
Christian dualism and scientific naturalism. (50)

It is not necessary to deny the value of science in order to find a way out of

the conundrum posed by strict objectivity. What is required is the recovery

of sensuous appreciation and a recognition that mythos and logos are not

mutually exclusive. During the Middle Ages, however, the road to

knowledge was split: one path consisted of the scientific, rational approach

and the other of idealization of a transcendent God. We will turn now to an

examination of what the labyrinth meant in the Middle Ages and how the

Church transformed this very pagan symbol into a very Christian one.

Chapter 3
Knights Errant and Climbing Poets

'And what do you go about seeking, thus accoutred?'
'Along with the rest of my companions, Sir, I am
seeking the adventures of the Holy Grail.'
'Seek them you may,' replied the priest, 'but find them
you will not. For were the Holy Grail to appear before
you, I do not think you would be able to see it any more
than a blind man would a sword before his eyes.'

— P. M. Matarasso, *The Quest of the Holy Grail*

Early Christian and Medieval Commentators on the Labyrinth

As Christianity took hold and spread and the Church began to
adopt and incorporate certain images and beliefs of the ancient world to
suit its teachings, commentators continued to mention the labyrinth, first in
works related to its ancient origins, and eventually in connection with
Christian beliefs. The labyrinth appears in various guises in the work of
writers from the second through the sixth centuries. Pausanias's *Description
of Greece* (second century CE) describes the labyrinth in terms of a marble
pavement then intact at Knossos; his *Description*, along with Philostratus's
Life of Apollonius and Hyginus's *Fabulae*, contains references to a labyrinth of
confusing paths. In the third century, the use of the labyrinth as a metaphor
for heresy or philosophical quandary surfaces in Hippolytus's *Labyrinth of
Heresies* and in Lactantius's *On the Wrath of God*; in both cases, the authors
are Christian writers.

99

In the fourth century, Marius Victorinus writes of the labyrinth as dance, Claudian makes a textual reference to the labyrinth as a cave, and St. Jerome's commentary on Ezekiel and St. Augustine's *City of God* continue a Christian predilection for equating the labyrinth with quandary. In what may be the earliest example of a church labyrinth, a mosaic in the Basilica of Reparata (founded in 324 CE) in Orleansville, Algeria, depicts a square Roman labyrinth with a thread leading from its entrance to the second turn. At the center of the labyrinth is a "letter poem" spelling out "Sancta Eclesia" ("Holy Church") in various directions (Kern 88). This labyrinth clearly references both the classical myth and a Christian context. Kern notes that its placement near the west entrance of the church (an arrangement later copied by other churches) meant that it was the first sight encountered by worshippers entering the building. Reparata's labyrinth was apparently intended to represent the Christian way to truth through a tangle of heresies, which Kern speculates may refer in this case to the Donatists, a North African group that argued against the authority of church officials it considered unfit.

In the fifth century, John Malalas's *Chronographia* lists the labyrinth as a cave, and Christian writers Prudentius (*Apotheosis*) and Sedulius (*Carmen Paschale*) reference, once again, the labyrinth as "heresy." Boethius's well-known *Consolation of Philosophy*, from the sixth century, contains a reference to a labyrinth as a philosophical quandary posed by Lady Philosophy.

From the sixth through the eleventh centuries, scattered references to labyrinths occur, notably in the seventh-century writings of Isidore of Seville (which were inspired by Pliny the Elder) and the ninth-century work of Rabanus Maurus (which was in turn based on Isidore). The only other labyrinths noted by Kern in the ninth through the eleventh centuries appear as illustrations in manuscripts and are of various styles and shapes (29). Many of these are the elliptical "Cretan-style" labyrinth and consist of seven or so circuits. In the twelfth-century *Etymologicum Magnum*, a well-known lexicon, a labyrinth is defined as a cave. Meanwhile, the Greek scholar, Eustathius of Thessalonika (c. 1110-98), in his commentary on Homer, connected the Crane dance on Delos to the scene depicted on Achilles's shield in the *Iliad*, a significant linkage since it helped situate Homer's scene in the tradition of labyrinthine dances that includes the horseback scene on the Tragliatella pitcher, the Crane dance described by Plutarch, and the Trojan Ride in Book 5 of the *Aeneid* (Greene 1413-14).

The first church labyrinths (after the much earlier one at Reparata) appeared in Italy in the twelfth century. The heyday of church labyrinths in the medieval period was the thirteenth century, when cathedrals in northern France began incorporating labyrinths into their pavement designs. Chartres Cathedral was completed 1194-1221 and dedicated in 1260 (Wright 39), with a labyrinth as wide as the nave. Unlike other commentators, Kern doubts that Chartres's labyrinth ever contained an illustration of Theseus,

101

Ariadne, and the Minotaur on a now missing metal plate in the center, stating that "northern French pavement labyrinths did not serve to perpetuate ancient traditions" (153). Wright, however, alludes to a document written by a church historian in the seventeenth century describing just such a plate at Chartres (41). With the possible exception of churches in Germany (St. Severin, eleventh century) and Italy (Pavia and Piacenza, both twelfth century), Kern believes the battle between Theseus and the Minotaur to be absent from pavement labyrinths altogether (153). Wright, however, believes the battle portrayed on the central plate at Chartres continued the traditional depiction of Theseus and the Minotaur in the labyrinth's center that was found in the old Roman mosaics as well as in the Italian churches (41).

Mapping the Labyrinth

According to Penelope Doob, the very concept of the labyrinth contains contraries—pattern and process, time and eternity, static and dynamic, single and multiple (189). Furthermore, she emphasizes the importance of taking account of the medieval understanding of the term to include single and multiple paths simultaneously rather than imposing our modern view of the labyrinth onto an earlier age. She also points out the distinct tension that exists between literary and artistic presentations of the labyrinth in classical, early Christian, and medieval times. Artistic renderings are often elaborate and beautiful, presented as works of skill and ingenuity

102

to be admired; the builder of the labyrinth, whether human or divine, is admired as an author of great craftsmanship. Literary labyrinths, on the other hand, generally suggest confusion, heresy, and sin and represent a sinful world or the snares of the devil (144).

In addition, the labyrinth may be a metaphor for either inextricability or impenetrability, two related but distinct possibilities (Doob 1). A labyrinth may be difficult to penetrate, keeping the unworthy from discovering its secrets, or it may be difficult to escape, serving as a trap. Inextricability can apply to either reasoning or morality (or sometimes both); a labyrinth might be self-made, due to the missteps or waywardness of the individual. Moreover, inextricability and impenetrability can be positive or negative. Impenetrability can be a protective metaphor, as used by the Romans in their heraldic devices vis-à-vis the Minotaur, pictured in at least one sixteenth-century illustration—hearkening back to an earlier tradition—with a finger to his lips to signify secrecy. Here the symbol represents the importance of keeping close counsel (Kern 201). Later, the quest for the Holy Grail will involve this type of impenetrability, which hides knowledge of the ineffable from those unworthy of achieving it. Inextricability, too, can be a desired outcome if the labyrinth leads to God and a triumph over sin and death.

In the hands of some medieval writers, a labyrinth has an obvious pedagogical purpose, symbolizing hard-earned knowledge that sticks with the learner because it is obtained with such terrible (and painful) effort. As we have seen, impenetrability may refer to something desirable but difficult to obtain that is hidden in the center; the goal may be to find something, not merely to find the way through. The medieval labyrinth is a spiritual journey as well as (sometimes) an intellectual one. The knowledge one seeks is the knowledge of God. For many early Christian writers, however, a choice of paths is something to be feared. Just as they emphasize the one true God, they emphasize the one true path. (Though nothing is simple when it comes to a labyrinth: a single path can also lead to the devil, as Gregory Thaumaturgus points out.) Moreover, the form of the labyrinth—unicursal or multicursal, impenetrable or inextricable—may not be as crucial as the fact of guidance being available, as Gregory of Nyssa suggests (Wright 75).

A maze is sometimes a metaphor for heresy in early Christian writings, or for paganism and the worship of multiple gods. Prudentius writes of the "cross paths" as being synonymous with heresy, while the one true path is provided by Christ. In contrast, Symmachus likes multiple approaches to God (Doob 77). Gregory Thaumaturgus approved of the study of various philosophies and approaches advocated by Origen, which he thought led inevitably to God (78-79). Despite these few advocates for the multiple way, however, inextricability is most often linked to evil in medieval use of the labyrinth metaphor.

Thus, Augustine equated labyrinthine design to paganism; in his formulation, Christ provides the true path, free of error, an idea later seen in Dante's *The Divine Comedy*. Meanwhile, sixth-century philosopher Simplicius of Cilicia (a pagan commentator on the writings of Aristotle) was writing about the labyrinth as a metaphor for infinity (Doob 82)—which reveals just how complicated the concept of the labyrinth actually was in the Middle Ages.

In addition to its use as an image of faith (or doubt), the labyrinth had astrological associations as well (even in Christian works), which tied it to ancient rites involving the seasons, the planets, and the movement of the spheres. Illustrated manuscripts often included labyrinths with pictures of calendars and zodiac charts (Wright 134). Wright links this cosmological meaning to the Christian *choreia*, a ring-dance performed to celebrate Christ's victory over Satan and the initiation of new Christians. Just as the characters of the ancient myths gave way to Christ, his followers, and Satan, so the ancient *choreia* (the Greek name for the ancient maze dance performed at Knossos and other places) was transformed into a dance of triumph over the powers of Satan. The ring-dance was connected with the ideal, eternal form of the circle in Greek philosophy, an association that was adopted by the early Christians (Wright 133). The dance of the Virtues Dante joins in Purgatorio is a ring-dance (29.121, 31.103-04), and the spirits who greet Dante in Paradiso also dance in circles (7.4-7, 8.19-26, 8.34-36), as do the planets in their spheres.

The ring-dance survived as a Christian rite performed at Easter and was danced on labyrinths in several churches. The most detailed account of this dance, which was probably performed at Chartres, Reims, and other places, comes from records of the cathedral at Auxerre, also the source of the round "classical" labyrinth design adopted from the earlier "Cretan" type by Christians. Records describe the dancing of church officials to the tune of a hymn and the throwing back and forth of a leather ball. While this dance was officially sanctioned, Wright also mentions similar ring-dances performed by church members that were not officially approved (138-39). Early in the history of the Church, performances of this dance at Easter took on a risky character as they often had the air of a pagan rite of spring, as a description by St. Basil in the fourth century shows:

> Casting aside the yoke of service under Christ and the veil of virtue from their heads [at the end of Lent] . . . they [the women] shamelessly attract the attention of every man. . . . hopping about, they dance with lustful eyes and loud laughter; as if seized by a kind of frenzy they excite the lust of the youths. They execute ring-dances . . . transforming the Holy places into the scene of the lewdness. (qtd. in Wright 138)

This description of what we today might call "spring fever" brings to mind the ancient Tragliatella pitcher and its sexually explicit scenes. Information about these dances in the church records is understandably thin since the pagan nature of the proceedings must have been obvious to all. Eventually, the ring-dances were likely confined to those performed on the labyrinth itself, and these, too, sometimes included dancers of both sexes (Wright 138-39, 145-47). Wright believes that the many depictions of church labyrinths as places of symbolic pilgrimages to Jerusalem during the Middle Ages were anachronisms fabricated during the nineteenth-century Gothic revival (210). So, dancing, yes—pilgrimage, no.

Difficulty of Process

When Christian writers emphasize the teleological aspect of the labyrinth, the difficult process of navigation is purposeful and beneficial, leading to a desirable result. The complex task may even be likened to the structure and workings of the brain, as remarked by Galen and other commentators (Purce 98; Doob 84). Traversing a labyrinth becomes a metaphor for mental processes and learning via the dialectical method—a crucial pedagogical device in both classical and medieval Christian education (Doob 87). Seen from this point of view, tracking and backtracking along various mental paths in a series of trials and errors serves to sharpen the reason.

Alternatively, labyrinthine reasoning may be seen as a waste of time or, worse, a snare, as Plato describes it in *Euthydemus*. Thus, Aristotle's labyrinth, taken by Doob to mean the main body of Aristotle's thought on dialectic, logic, categories, syllogisms, etc. (199-201) was often disparaged by commentators in the Middle Ages. Even Augustine, though, admits the usefulness of the labyrinthine method as a learning tool in the hands of a good teacher, with the repetition and delayed approach of "trial and error" leading to deeper understanding and retention of knowledge once successfully completed. Indeed, "this knowledge could not be reached so effectively by a direct route, a short-cut, for the process itself determines whether the product will be understood" (Doob 89). However, the teacher must match the student with the right level of difficulty; for the average Christian, anything resembling a multicursal labyrinth may, depending on which writer one consults, be overly demanding—and therefore a moral and spiritual danger. Thus, most commentators emphasize reliance on doctrine and the teachings of church authorities over personal experience or independent reasoning.

Origins of Medieval Thought on the Labyrinth

Christian and medieval writers developed their idea of the labyrinth from the seminal writings and commentaries of Virgil, Ovid, Pliny, and Plutarch. The mismatch between the concept of the labyrinth as beautiful art (seen from the outside or above) and the labyrinth as suffering and evil (when experienced from within) began with the treatments these classical authors gave the subject. As Doob points out, the labyrinth as a structure (in Pliny's descriptions, for instance, or Virgil's account of the labyrinth on Daedalus's door in the *Aeneid*) was usually seen as a noteworthy architectural feat and admired as such. When the reference was to the classical myth and Theseus's entry into the labyrinth, the association was with fear, error, confusion, and death (38).

Furthermore, although a unicursal labyrinth may (and often does) represent a path to God or to good, it can also represent a one-way path to hell or the devil if it is the *wrong* labyrinth—the one the Christian should not have entered. Thus not only the choices one makes inside the labyrinth but also the particular labyrinth in question (and whether one chooses to enter it) may carry moral implications.

The labyrinth as such does not appear in vernacular medieval literature; it only appears in religious texts stemming from the classical tradition, until the thirteenth century (Peyronie, "The Labyrinth" 689). Clerics wrote very specific descriptions of the labyrinth in their commentaries on classical texts. On the other hand, there are many nonspecific references in the romances and in courtly literature to wandering, as in a forest or in a dream, through difficult or narrow passages or paths that sound very much like labyrinths. Theseus sometimes appears alone in these descriptions, without a labyrinth per se (Peyronie, "The Labyrinth" 691). Where difficult or tortuous "maze"-like motifs appear in Christian texts, they are associated with *this* world—the world of sin and error, and sometimes heresy—they represent traps for the unwary. Dante goes further in depicting hell itself as a kind of downward spiral in *Inferno*.

In *The Quest of the Holy Grail*, the Desired Knight destined to obtain the Grail is Galahad; early on, he signifies his desire to follow the left-hand path (Matarasso 66), which eventually leads him to his goal. The standard advice for solving a simple maze is to keep one's left hand on the wall at all times (Fisher 12; Saward 32). Even Dante, who follows the path Virgil chooses in *Inferno*, is led by this logic: "his steps turned to the left" (10.133); "the poet / held to the left, and I walked at his back" (18.20-21); "We turned again, as always, to the left" (23.68). The left or "sinister" path is generally considered the wrong path in Christian dogma, the one that leads away from God. Prudentius tells us that Saint Hippolytus of Rome dabbled in heretical ideas before coming into the Church's fold and encouraging others "away from the path on the left," urging them instead to "follow where the way on the right calls" (Doob 80-81). The mystical, or left-hand, path is the road less taken in many spiritual traditions, including Christianity, but it is exactly the route one takes in solving a maze (or for that matter, a classical Chartres-style labyrinth). The requirement to move to the left may be one of the reasons the labyrinth stood for sin and error in medieval times. The necessity to go in the "wrong" direction was built into its very structure. Yet in *The Quest of the Holy Grail*, and *The Divine Comedy*, too, it is impossible to avoid this maze on the way to knowledge of God. The difference between the two is that the Grail Quest truly involves separate paths; Virgil's guidance effectively reduces the maze of *Inferno* to a single, narrow path.

From Cretan Labyrinth to Christian Icon

Wright describes the process by which ninth-century Christian clerics near St. Gall and Reichenau in Switzerland adopted and transformed the elliptical, unicursal Cretan labyrinth, rounding it into a perfect circle. The number of circuits in the new Christianized design gradually changed from seven to eleven, with eleven symbolizing error, sin, and incompleteness in Christian iconography. Finally, a French cleric was inspired to superimpose a cross pattern on top of the concentric circles, creating the pattern that we now know as the classical "Chartres" design, even though it appeared in manuscripts three centuries before the cathedral labyrinth was built in Chartres (Wright 21, 23).

Once this design had been created, it remained largely unchanged. Its meaning, according to Wright, was perfectly contained in the circular form (indicating divine perfection), the cruciform pattern, and the eleven circuits. "The moral imperative of these Christian labyrinths is always the same," says Wright. "Do not deviate from the path of rectitude if you hope to arrive at celestial Jerusalem" (27). It is as if in the adoption of the symbol by Christian clerics and writers, the ancient idea of multiplicity, whether of paths or of divinities, was so unpalatable that the labyrinth was transformed into its opposite. From an image of complexity the labyrinth was

111

transformed into a symbol of the single path, provided by clinging to the one true faith. Theseus, parsing out the precious thread as he penetrated ever deeper into the dangerous recesses of the labyrinth, had to choose his steps according to his own wits; the thread showed him the way out once he had reached the center but not the way in. Ariadne's thread, interpreted as the rough equivalent of "truth" by these Christians, now becomes the path itself, unmistakable and certain.

Christ often takes the place of Theseus in the church labyrinths created in Italy in the twelfth century and in northern France in the thirteenth century; he provides guidance on the one true path to God. This world—the horizontal realm—*is* the labyrinth. God's realm—the heavens, and therefore on a vertical plane—is the goal, and it can only be achieved by escaping this world, as Daedalus escaped the labyrinth. The truth for which man strives is not here, but *there*, and the idea is to get out of the labyrinth altogether. This is certainly true for Dante's pilgrim in *The Divine Comedy*; his mazelike wanderings in the forest of *Inferno* constitute the state of being hopelessly lost in the world of sin. It is only by moving first down, into the Inferno, and then up, through Purgatory, on his guided journey to Paradise, that Dante regains his footing and his hope of salvation. The saving knowledge he seeks is knowledge of God and is not achieved by reason or will alone but through greater attunement to the love and grace of God.

The stars (once again, the symbolism of life-giving celestial bodies) are guiding lights for Dante's pilgrim, whose quest is to find both God and his own moral center. But as magnetic as the stars are, drawing the eye irresistibly to heaven, they are also remote, existing far beyond the realm of human experience. Furthermore, the way to them is not a direct path but a very roundabout one; the way down is the way up. The overall movement of *The Divine Comedy* is dizzyingly vertical. The movement of the soul is not horizontal, nor is it a straight line; when Dante is on level ground, in the dark woods, he is lost and going nowhere. He is caught in a labyrinth in which three beasts, not one, prevent him from taking the direct route on Mount Purgatory, three beasts representing the sins of lust, pride, and avarice. The way out of this quandary takes the physical form of a slow spiral, the movement of a first narrowing and then expanding gyre, as Dante navigates first the Inferno, then Mount Purgatory, and finally the spheres of Heaven (Purce 48).

Dante's path is deceptive in classic labyrinthine fashion—in the beginning, he is much farther than he appears to be from his goal; his initial attempt to climb the mountain and leave the woods by the shortest route is premature, as if he attempted to climb over the wall of a maze instead of proceeding through it. Yet he draws ever closer to the stars even as he clambers down to the coldest part of hell, the icy pit that is the final destination in *Inferno*. In Dante's geography, hell is at the center of the earth, and Dante and Virgil climb out of the pit by reversing direction. Their terrifying downward spiral ends unexpectedly when they climb headfirst into a cave with a view of the night sky:

> we climbed—
> he first, I following—until I saw,
> through a round opening, some of those things
> of beauty Heaven bears. It was from there
> that we emerged, to see—once more—the stars. (*Inf.*
> 34.135-39)

The stars, of course, have been there all along. They serve as beacons during an immeasurably long journey and are a part of what Dennis Slattery, writing in *Renascence*, calls *kairos* ("sacred time"), shining out across the great divide of eternity to touch Dante, a creature of mutable, historical time ("Dante's Image" 25). In this Christian treatment of a labyrinth, characters from classical myth appear as denizens of *Inferno*: Virgil and Dante encounter both Minos, who is a judge there, and the Minotaur, who rages at the edge of the Seventh Circle, where the violent dwell (5.4-24, 12.11-27). Virgil names both Theseus and Ariadne when addressing the Minotaur (12.16-20). Virgil's address to the Minotaur supports the idea that Dante, by virtue of his safe passage and guide, is not following a maze, appearances to the contrary: " 'Be off, you beast; this man who comes has not / been tutored by your sister; all he wants / in coming here is to observe your torments' " (12.19-21). There is no suggestion that the

Minotaur is a star that lies misshapen and disguised in the darkness. However, Satan himself was once a bright light in heaven, although the frozen lake in which he dwells has long since extinguished his flames. No redemption for the fallen is possible in *Inferno*.

For Dante, vertical geography represents a display not of unity but of opposites—high and low, heaven and hell, light and shadow, human and divine. In the symbolism of medieval Christianity, heaven and hell rest above and below the earth, respectively, and the realm of human existence is relatively flat (Peyronie, "The Labyrinth" 689). For salvation to occur, the soul must move, and leaving its sinful state means leaving the plane of normal existence. As a Christian (heavily influenced by Aristotle's belief in the Prime Mover, perfect beyond all things), Dante's vision is directed upward toward the eternal realm, beyond the world of daily life. His God dwells in the outermost heavens, and his cosmos is consistent with an Aristotelian/Ptolemaic view of the universe with the Empyrean beyond.

Sources of Dante's Geography

Aarati Kanekar hypothesizes that Dante, writing in the early fourteenth century, may have taken the structure of Gothic/Byzantine churches, redolent with cosmic symbolism from the rose windows to the labyrinths inscribed in the floors, as the structural model of his poem. Kanekar writes, "These considerations raise the interesting possibility . . . that the poem might thus express spatial motifs that were familiar to its readers" (136). The three-part structure of the poem, in this view, echoes the structure of the churches, from the labyrinthine underworld of the crypt (or the labyrinth itself), to the middle world of congregation and ritual activity, to the vault of the heavens.

Moreover, Dante's spiritual geography is consistent with other mythologies throughout the world that have employed the spiral or the labyrinth as a metaphor for creation and the subsequent unfolding of the universe. Annemarie Schimmel and Allahbakhsh Brohi both comment on Islam's mystical view of the vertical and horizontal as geographical metaphors for the world of matter and the divine realm (Schimmel 105; Brohi 12). For the Dogon of West Africa and the Hopi of North America, the narrowing and widening gyre reflects a transition from one world or state of being to the next, as it does for Dante. Dante's spiraling path reflects the pilgrimage each soul makes in drawing closer to the divine creator, a process that occurs through a series of inversions revealing the true but paradoxical nature of things. As Alison Cornish notes:

> The entire last third of [Dante's] narrative is plotted across the template of the physical heavens, and the basic form of the universe with its concentric revolutions is a model for the arrangement of sinners orbiting Satan at the rotten nadir of Hell, and of penitents in Purgatory spiraling up the mountain at whose summit lies the garden of first innocence. (1-2)

The "negative vortex" (downward gyre) in Dante's Inferno is not unlike a vast whirlpool or a mountain turned on its head. In literary works from *The*

Odyssey to *Moby-Dick* to Edgar Allen Poe's "A Descent into the Maelstrom," the downward spiral leads to death and destruction *unless* the hero knows how to look into the depths without being pulled in. For the wise, the experience, though terrifying, is ultimately healing. In Jungian terms this encounter with the whirlpool or downward gyre is an encounter with the potentially destructive (but ultimately creative) aspect of the Self (Edinger, *Melville's* Moby-Dick 138-39). In terms of the labyrinth dance, the pull to the center results in death as well as rebirth.

For Dante the pilgrim, who has the opportunity to see both Satan's frozen lake and the divine light at the center of the celestial rose, there is a clear distinction between two *different* centers. To understand either, however, he must know its opposite; there is no joining of the two but rather a movement away from one and toward the other. This is why Dante's first attempt on the mountain fails; he is not ready for the climb. As Helen Luke points out, the dark woods and the descent are necessary preconditions to the ultimate bliss Dante seeks. As Luke puts it, "to know meaning is to glimpse the joy of the end" (x-xi). Dante is given a passport through hell, though his "safe-passage" seems to dangle by a thread at times. As he struggles to understand what he sees in *Inferno*, he circles and descends successive levels. Each level represents a particular state of consciousness, or constriction of that consciousness, that results in an arrested state of development, illustrating, in turn, incontinence, violence, and finally, fraud. Inferno, at its lowest point, is icy cold, a frozen lake. It is an inhuman and ungodly place "frozen into immobility—that is the final state of sin" (Dorothy Sayers, qtd. in Luke 41). Dante is forced to face the potential for evil that, according to Christian belief, exists in every human heart in a variety of forms. The Inferno is the beginning of Dante's path to salvation, which enters the redemptive phase when he and Virgil climb into the cave with the stars in view, arriving in the region of Mount Purgatory. At this point, he has entered a *new* labyrinth. Exactly at the moment of deepest despair, Dante finds that he and Virgil have changed direction and are now moving up instead of down. Like many labyrinth walkers, he finds himself closer to his goal just when it seemed impossibly distant; the curves in the path prevent him from seeing what is ahead.

Climbing the Mountain of Purgatory

While the earthly woods at the start of the poem and Inferno itself (to some extent) are mazelike, Purgatorio has the clean lines of a unicursal labyrinth. Consequently, the journey here is a bit anticlimactic. It is more a test of endurance, a labyrinth with countless circuits that leads one inexorably on. The didactic function of the labyrinth and of Dante's guides is very emphatic. Dante's role is to listen and learn. His outcome is a reward in heaven; he is only required to stay on a path he can clearly see and learn from the example of others. The exchanges with his guides and with the souls he encounters in Inferno, Purgatorio, and Paradiso are dialectical, mirroring the labyrinthine and instructive route he takes. His labyrinths are somewhat "Augustinian."

The Catholic Church viewed Purgatory as the place where sinners suffered to expiate their sins before moving on to heaven. The inhabitants of Purgatorio move, but unlike the souls in hell, they *advance* from one circuit to another, as in a unicursal labyrinth. Instead of purposeless and passive movement, they follow a distinct path. Each circuit of the mountain brings them closer to their ultimate goal; they know where they are going, and they will eventually arrive.

The highest point of Purgatorio is the mythical beginning of human life, the Earthly Paradise or Garden of Eden. Dante and the sinners he encounters in Purgatory are spiraling inward toward the primal state of innocence. Here, for the first time since the start of the poem, there is a union of opposites, as Dante meets his soul guide, Beatrice. Dante's Ariadne is Beatrice—at once soul mate, beloved, teacher, and voice of wisdom. They meet in the Earthly Paradise, which in some ways resembles the return to the primal beginning that we witnessed in Neolithic ritual labyrinths. But Dante, being Christian, moves beyond this primal state of earthly origins into another realm envisioned to be superior.

Aarati Kanekar has pointed out that Dante seems more specific and concrete in describing Inferno than in depicting his other realms, especially Paradiso (142); Winifred Hunt notes that Inferno is physically closer to the world of everyday "reality" in which the story originates, the dark wood of the story's opening (18). Purgatorio, too, is close by; indeed, the base of its mountain adjoins the dark woods. Is it an accident that Inferno is so vividly portrayed and Paradiso so ephemeral? Is Dante's vision of bliss at the end of Paradiso the true emotional center of the poem as he intends, or is it his reunion with Beatrice in the Earthly Paradise? As a medieval Christian, Dante would answer these questions in one way only, although his use of labyrinthine imagery and focus on his earthly love for Beatrice sometimes undermine his purpose.

The Paradoxical Vision

The Divine Comedy is full of paradox. Dante's final vision of the image of humanity enclosed within the three circles of eternity represents the ultimate union of flesh and spirit, transcendent divinity and immanent humanity, symbolized by Christ. But it is so mystical that Dante is baffled:

> so I searched that strange sight: I wished to see
> the way in which our human effigy
> suited the circle and found place in it—
> and my own wings were far too weak for that. (*Par.* 33.136-39)

This vision is only offered when Dante goes beyond the nine spheres, beyond the Primum Mobile, penetrating into the heart of the circles of the Empyrean—a movement toward an ineffable center.

The overall movement of *The Divine Comedy*, in labyrinthine motion, mirrors the repetitive rhyme scheme of the poem, the A – B – A, or terza rima, that Slattery suggests is the movement of psyche reaching for wisdom. Dante moves forward, takes a mental step backward to reflect, then moves forward with a deeper understanding "that rests on imitation and remembrance" ("Dante's Terza Rima" 7). Though one seems to regress, "one step forward, two steps back," as the saying goes, it is the falling back that creates deeper awareness, making the next step, taken now in greater wisdom, possible. This slow, backtracking movement is the structure of a labyrinth, and the truth toward which it leads here is knowledge of God. Even if that knowledge is ultimately beyond human understanding, one continues to move closer.

Larry Allums describes the geography of *The Divine Comedy* as a full circle, "not away from but toward home" (173). In this interpretation, Dante's journey teaches him his own true nature: the light he seeks not only shines from the distant stars but also radiates from within. In this Christian universe, the journey to God leads toward a "peace that passeth all understanding." If this is home, it is not an earthly home, not even one in the original Paradise, but rather a spiritual realm only reached after a dizzyingly vertiginous climb. There is an earthly labyrinth, an infernal labyrinth, and a heavenly labyrinth, and while one may offer a glimpse of the other (as Beatrice does for Dante), they are ultimately different labyrinths—either horizontal (earthly life) or vertical (the infernal regions and their mirror, the heavenly spheres).

Many writers have noted the textual quality of Gothic cathedrals. Matthew Reeve observes, "The famous statement of Gregory the Great (d. 604) that 'images were the books of the illiterate' stood at the centre of the medieval justification of images in medieval buildings" (3). Kanekar notes that "Dante might have drawn at least partial inspiration from the real architectural masterpieces that he saw around him" (136), mentioning in particular the Gothic/Byzantine cathedral of San Marco in Venice as a church with which Dante was familiar (156 n. 4).

The cathedrals were a visual representation of the world view spelled out in Dante's elaborate geography, a map of the spiritual universe for the illiterate or those without the leisure, ability, or inclination to read poetry. John Leyerle states:

> Cathedrals and important urban churches can give very illuminating indications of medieval habits of mind because such buildings were a major influence on artistic expression in the high middle ages and, in turn, reflect the aesthetic attitudes they helped to create and focus. As Mario Praz has observed, 'Architecture and costume, being the arts which are closest to everyday life, offer the clearest indications of the temper of an age.' A manuscript illumination was out of sight in a closed book most of the time and only seen by relatively few; by contrast, a rose-wheel window [or a labyrinth] in an urban church was seen by hundreds or thousands of people on a daily basis, year after year. (291-92)

Intriguingly, Charles Radding and William Clark point out in *Medieval Architecture, Medieval Learning* that the logical problem-solving habits of medieval philosophers such as Abelard, in which alternatives between conclusions are tried, tested, and either discarded or adopted, was a philosophical approach that influenced some medieval builders and the choices they made.

In the case of the learned master Abelard, who was not a builder but who influenced many of the thinkers of his day, his habit of mind was formed by his study of logic, and specifically his study of the issue of universals. Plato's theory of forms addresses this issue by promulgating the existence of universal ideas or forms that are "distinct from tangible objects" (Radding and Clark 58). Aristotle, in reaction against his famous teacher, argued against the existence of universals beyond concrete experience, coming down on the side of immanent reality. His brand of rational, empirical philosophy eventually formed the mainstream of Western thought, a philosophy that is evident in the work of twelfth-century thinkers like Abelard. He believed that "universals" are simply words: what is real is the particular, concrete individual.

According to Radding and Clark, one of the most important aspects of Abelard's work on logic was his method of interrelating various philosophical problems (60). He adjusted his earlier analyses as further reflection caused him to alter previously held positions in a process of trial and error—the same problem-solving method used to solve a maze. His method of alternately testing and adjusting his theories made him the great logician of his time and put him on a more "scientific" basis than many earlier and contemporary twelfth-century philosophers. Here we see the stirrings of individual initiative and decision-making that were soon to appear in the *Queste del Saint Graal*, written some time between 1215 and 1230.

The famous labyrinth in Chartres's cathedral was completed between 1215 and 1221 (Wright 41). The cathedral familiar to us was built after a major fire that destroyed most of an earlier Romanesque church; Kern places the dedication of the newly built Gothic structure in October of 1260 (153). The famous West Rose Window, symbolizing the celestial (Wright says "stellar") character of God, is noteworthy for being nearly the same distance from the floor as the labyrinth is from the west entrance. Furthermore, the labyrinth and the window are nearly the same size, so that if the west wall fell inwards, the Rose Window would be superimposed on the labyrinth, which contains a rosette pattern at its center (Wright 43). Here, in the form of symbols, are the two opposed labyrinths of earthly and spiritual life so distant from one another in *The Divine Comedy*.

As it happens, Chartres is also an important center of Marian devotion because of a relic housed there, said to be Mary's cloak (Kern 153). It is interesting to speculate on the presence in one church of symbols of the sacred feminine in two forms: Mary's veil and the labyrinth (although the latter was now Christianized, its ancient roots remained). Although other churches not dedicated to Mary also had labyrinths, the labyrinth at Chartres is the largest ever built in a church—12.85 meters in diameter (Wright 38, 41). Mary, a Christian Ariadne who helps the faithful achieve grace as an intercessor with God, resides in the Celestial Rose in *The Divine Comedy* and is key to navigating the labyrinth of worldly life on the way to God.

Thus the symbolism of the divine circle is carried out in Chartres both above and below. The rose and the labyrinth are echoed in *The Divine Comedy*, which ends with Dante's vision of the Celestial Rose of Heaven and the famous vision of the reflecting circles enclosing a human form (*Par.* 33.115-38). Dante's vision superimposes the circles of creator and creation in a symbolic depiction of the Incarnation of Christ (*Par.* 33 n. 127) but presents this revelation as mystical and ineffable, as if Dante cannot quite make sense of it.

The Incarnation and the Worldly Labyrinth

During the Middle Ages, the Church struggled with the relationship of body and spirit, and human and divine, a struggle that led to many divisions and ruptures whose reverberations continue down to the present day. The gnostic offshoots of Christianity, according to Edward Edinger, were guilty of a more complete separation of matter and spirit than the mainstream Church ever promulgated (*The Psyche in Antiquity: Gnosticism* 42-43). Wisely, in his view, the Church attempted to maintain a more concrete theology emphasizing the Incarnation and humanness of Christ and thus his relation to the rest of humanity. The centrality of the doctrine of Incarnation was one factor ensuring the connection of spirit to the material world of the body. Thus for the Church, the separation of the world of spiritualized forms first delineated by Plato is tempered by a somewhat inconsistent sense of the sacredness of the created world, which God himself deigned to participate in.

The difficulty of the Church's position lay in both the Idealism of its Platonic heritage, which effectively split matter and spirit, and the emphasis on the perfection of the Prime Mover—promoted by Aristotle—as Hubert Dreyfus and Sean Dorrance Kelly explain in *All Things Shining* (133). Both of these tendencies led away from the embodied Christianity the Church was attempting to advance. Hatab writes:

> Platonic spirituality and rationalism were intimately related in Christian thought; monotheistic religions share at least one disposition with rationalism and empiricism, namely, a rejection of "primitive" mythology. Furthermore, spiritual, rational, and scientific developments in a way share a moral element, namely, a devaluation of the passions (which impede both purity and an objective methodology)
> . . . .
> The underlying element . . . is the ascendancy of the conscious mind. (215)

From Plato to Aristotle

The influence of Aristotelian philosophy fell on fertile ground once his works were rediscovered, translated, and interpreted by such Christian thinkers as Saint Bonaventure, Thomas Aquinas, and Albert the Great. Erwin Panofsky believes that the period of High Scholasticism (beginning with the turn of the twelfth century) coincides with and reflects the age of High Gothic. Both movements reached their apogee with the reign of Saint Louis (1226-70) and both were based within one hundred miles of Paris (4-5). Scholasticism reflects a movement away from Plato to Aristotle's more scientific objectivism and forms of logic (though Aristotle's metaphysics, of supreme interest to the Church, features a transcendental move of its own). Nonetheless, Scholasticism coincided with the new emphasis on the individual and individual authority then beginning to take root.

Dante, writing *The Divine Comedy* from 1306 to 1321, was influenced by Aristotle's philosophy through the work of two of his favored thinkers, Albert the Great and Thomas Aquinas; like other medieval writers and philosophers, he explored the relationship of reason to faith in the wake of both High Scholasticism and High Gothic. In the end, for Dante, faith is more important; rationality and will are subordinate to the love of God and are only instruments of that love. Nevertheless, like the mighty cathedrals of his day, the rigidity of Dante's highly structured hell, purgatory, and heaven owes as much to Scholasticism as it does to Neoplatonism. For Dante and for other religious thinkers, logic was a road that led inevitably to God and was in that sense a one-way street—just like the unicursal labyrinths located in many of the great cathedrals.

God is often portrayed as the ultimate designer in early Christian writings, and his grand labyrinthine designs seen in nature (i.e., ants' dwellings and bee hives) far outstrip the labyrinths of humankind, which are a pale imitation (Doob 67). This Platonic view of the ideal labyrinth of God is at the heart of *The Divine Comedy*. Dante's use of the labyrinth in this sense of divine pattern is also related to another of Doob's observations about the paradoxical nature of the symbol: a labyrinth looks very different depending on where you are standing. From within, it can seem endless and terrifying (even if it is unicursal). When seen from above, it may reveal a design unimaginable to those trying to navigate its windings (Doob 38). Thus what seems inexplicable at the immediate level may be understandable (and even admirable) when viewed from a macroscopic perspective. When the labyrinth is a model for epistemology, learning is what allows one to rise above the maze and see it whole instead of in parts. Dante is given the ability to soar above the earthly labyrinth, and looking down from the Sphere of the Fixed Stars, is able to see "Ulysses' / mad course and, to the east, could almost see / that shoreline where Europa was sweet burden" (*Par.* 27.82-84). From his standpoint high above Dante sees the entire picture of even pagan Odysseus's labyrinthine, wandering travels (now revealed to be "mad")—and far beyond.

In contrast to Dante's unicursal path to knowledge of God is the Christian epistemology presented in the thirteenth-century *Queste del Saint Graal.* In this most spiritual of the many versions of the Grail romance, the Knights of the Round Table are the pilgrims. The quest is their labyrinth, and the Holy Grail is at the center. A key difference between their quest and Dante's journey is that each knight takes a distinctly different path. The emphasis is on the choices each individual makes, and although every knight encounters a series of guides (and enemies), the path taken and the deeds enacted along that path are the individual's own.

In the *Queste*, it is Galahad who achieves the Grail, at the cost of his life (Matarasso 283); his holiness is practically without stain, making him almost superhuman in his saintliness. Snares and deceivers along his path fail to trip him up, and his mystical union with the Grail coincides with his disappearance from the earthly realm. As Lancelot's son, he represents the perfection Lancelot himself is unable to attain, largely because of his illicit passion for Guinevere, which the author of *Queste* presents as a decisive moral stumbling block. However, Lancelot persists in the face of many setbacks, seeks spiritual advice, and attempts to master his shortcomings. He comes close to achieving the goal, and although he does not attain the Grail, he is in some ways the most human of all the characters because (and not in spite of) his struggles. Other knights have their own failures; Gawain,

129

for instance, seems to lack seriousness; anger, lack of piety, and pride are other faults exhibited by the knights. With only one of them fully succeeding in the Quest (and seeming himself more angel than human), *Queste* ultimately seems to reflect human life as many people live it—a struggle full of missed opportunities, failures, and disappointments that also reflects achievements in the face of great odds, moments of glory, and hard-earned wisdom. While it is the impetus for a long journey, the Grail itself is an achievement that most properly belongs to the next world.

Queste takes free will seriously, and the end result is a strangely modern approach to the spiritual labyrinth. Unlike many of the early Christian commentators, who viewed the multicursal "maze" as a snare to be feared, the author of the *Queste* embraces the notion of multiple paths to a single truth. The symbol we have described as a fitting metaphor for the postmodern condition emerges in the hands of a thirteenth-century cleric/author as the necessary route to a mystical union with God. We are still in the grip of a single truth, no matter how varied the means for achieving it, because all of the roads potentially lead to God. In the end, moreover, only a few knights out of many actually see the Grail—unspoken, but implied, is the notion that this individual path to God is arduous and may not be for everyone.

Those who embark on the quest are special; they are the crème de la crème of Arthur's court, morally, spiritually, and physically. It is only the

Knights of the Round Table who undertake the difficult trip; the King and other members of the court stay behind. The Grail journey represents a religious experience that is individual and private and thus the opposite of a shared, communal undertaking. This raises the question: do the knights represent only an elect group whose "superiority" allows (or requires) them to take on the difficult task of searching for the Grail, or do they represent Everyman? Perhaps the fact that only a chosen few go on the Grail Quest is a representation of the difficulty of the task from the point of view of a medieval churchman. Perhaps it is, in truth, the mission of each human soul to enter those woods "wherever they see it thickest," but the dangers of the path keep most of the faithful on the "well-beaten track" of established faith and doctrine.

While Dante prefers the "beaten path" and the author of the *Queste* "the road not taken," the distinction between them is not always clear. Dante's pilgrim stays on the true path only because he is guided; Dante believes in this path but also believes the pilgrim has a choice in the matter; choosing wrongly can easily lead to disaster. On the Seventh Terrace of Purgatory, for example, Dante's guide warns him: " 'On this terrace, it is best / to curb your eyes; the least distraction—left / or right—can mean a step you will regret' " (*Purg.* 25.118-20). Dante views the unicursal route as good and the multicursal paths as divergences from the good that lead to evil. The *Queste* author also believes divergences can lead to trouble but suggests that these diversions have their purpose if a knight learns from the experience and is guided always by the desire to seek God; purity of intention and the ability to accept spiritual guidance will always lead an erring knight back in the right direction. In fact, there is no other way to find the Grail.

The Psychology of the Maze

The allure of the maze is real. While the unicursal labyrinth, with its single path to righteousness, obviously holds an appeal for the Christian looking for the sure way to God, the uncertain path, which the individual must discover for himself, leaves much to the imagination, fate, and even chance. In that sense, it is the more romantic alternative, allowing for the unfolding of a very individual journey, determined by the actions of the person caught up in it. The unicursal labyrinth has many twists but offers no choices; the individual may or may not know what lies ahead, but he will eventually achieve the goal if he continues. Patience, faith, and persistence are great virtues in the unicursal labyrinth. With the maze there is no such assurance. Unless one has exceptionally good instincts and a keen sense of direction, he is bound to make numerous mistakes and pursue many paths that lead him in circles or to dead ends. The knights in *Queste del Saint Graal* experience this kind of labyrinthine disorder in the various roads they pursue, crisscrossing one another's paths and trying first one, then another direction. In true labyrinthine fashion, a knight may come close to the Grail

132

without being able to grasp it; he may seem to be almost upon it but be completely unable to bridge the final distance. In *Queste*, Lancelot experiences what he mistakes as merely a dream of the Grail early in his journeying. Failing to grasp the significance of what he sees (the sick knight, the silver candlestick carried by unseen hands, and the Grail itself), he loses his chance to "pierce the secret" (Matarasso 82-83, 85).

The Paradoxical Labyrinth

Both Dante and the author of *Queste* depict the labyrinth as the means to access not earthly knowledge but transcendent truth; that is, the labyrinth leads to a place beyond this world. The appearance of an end-point in the center is merely an illusion, since the center is infinitely large, just as a magician's house seems small from the outside but holds an enormous number of rooms. Dante portrays the journey as one of great physical distance to signify the profundity of the experience. The *Queste* has its knights tracing complex and infinitely varied paths toward a goal that is not merely physically distant but psychologically and spiritually impossible for even the best knights to attain. Even when it seems almost within his grasp, Lancelot fails to do more than glimpse it from an adjoining room, "a great light flooding through the opening, as if the sun had its abode within" (Matarasso 262). His attempt to approach it more closely results in physical and psychic trauma so profound that he is rendered senseless for days (261-65).

It is one thing to read about the adventures of the knights on their mazelike quest and another to actually experience such a journey. It seems likely that the medieval writers who favored the unicursal labyrinth did so for this very reason. At a distance, the spectacle of valorous knights wandering to and fro in the forest, encountering damsels, mysterious castles, and riddling clerics, offers a dazzling adventure to the mind of the reader. To find oneself actually embarked on such a journey is a different matter. If one sets off on such a quest, he is certain to experience frustration, physical discomfort, anxiety, fear, tedium, and discouragement. To enter a maze is to take the risk of becoming irretrievably lost; one does not know what to expect when choosing one path over another and has no idea what may lie around the next corner, be it good or ill. In the medieval period, with its diseases, wars, roaming bandits, and other calamities, safe passage was highly desirable; life offered enough uncertainty as it was. The unicursal labyrinth offered an instructive view of a life path with many twists that nonetheless had a pattern and led one steadily in the desired direction (assuming one had entered the "right" church-sanctioned labyrinth and not one that led to evil ends). A multicursal labyrinth, under these circumstances, must understandably have seemed like a hazard only too likely to lead to disaster.

In comparing Dante's certain path to that of the Grail knights, a modern reader is struck by the somewhat constricted experience of the pilgrim. Dante goes where he is told to go, and despite the many wondrous events and personages he meets along the way, his role is somewhat passive. If, however, one imagines standing on the edge of a dark wood, alone and without guidance, with the prospect of great difficulty, danger, and discomfort ahead, the maze begins to seem much less attractive. Who would not, under these conditions, be grateful for the sudden appearance of a trustworthy guide such as Virgil? In the first canto of *Inferno*, Dante recapitulates such an experience and is psychologically astute in showing the terrors such "lostness" creates in the wanderer who has missed the path and experienced a darkness too terrifying to describe even long after the events have taken place:

> Ah, it is hard to speak of what it was,
> that savage forest, dense and difficult,
> which even in recall renews my fear:
> so bitter—death is hardly more severe! (*Inf.* 1.4-7)

The knights, on the other hand, are the epitome of action. There is an interesting tension in the mazy quest that does not exist in the structured, predetermined path of the unicursal labyrinth. For these reasons, *Queste del Saint Graal* is, from a plot standpoint, in some ways more satisfying than *The Divine Comedy*. The reader is pleasantly unaware of the twists of fate in store for each of the knights, not to mention the fact that the tale follows the adventures of several characters separately while weaving them all together. One experiences one of the pleasures inherent in the maze experience, that of continually turning corners to discover what is hidden from sight (Fisher 21). In comparison, the geography of Dante's universe, while dizzying to contemplate, begins to resemble, to the modern eye, a gigantic hamster cage. *Inferno* is arguably the most interesting of the three cantos because it contains dangers that are only held at bay by Virgil's protection. The descent is replete with horrifying if somewhat fantastical sights leading to the climactic encounter with Satan in the lowest circle. *Inferno* has the drama of a descent into a whirlpool. However, as soon as Dante begins the long climb up Mount Purgatory, there is no longer much doubt about the outcome for him or anyone he meets.

The climb to Paradiso is not only a one-way street, it is also an unsuspenseful and interminable spiral; there is little of the delay or unexpected turning characteristic of even the simplest unicursal labyrinth. One's ticket to paradise is assured when one reaches the shore of Mount Purgatory, though the way is still long. While the beauty of Dante's descriptions, especially those of the heavenly spheres, is often enchanting, one feels in some ways that *Paradiso* constitutes a long denouement after the wild descent into the pit of *Inferno* and the long-awaited reunion with Beatrice in the Earthly Paradise. The "labyrinth" in Dante's *Paradiso*, especially, lacks any element of challenge but proceeds smoothly toward Dante's final vision and salvation.

Joseph Campbell singled out the *Queste del Saint Graal* as a literary example of the changing emphasis in Western thought from reliance on authority (particularly the authority of the Church) to reliance on individual effort and initiative as the path to wisdom. Nonetheless, as distinct as each individual's own story may be, for Campbell the individual myth is always connected to collective archetypes. He believed that the individual was the ultimate authority in discovering his or her own truth but also thought that each quest for truth connected with the past (and the collective) while prospecting new territory never before seen. This is a definition (or at least an approximation of one) for individuation, Jung's term for the process by which an individual grows in self-knowledge while also growing into a conscious connection with that which is larger than himself (the Self or God). In "Conscious, Unconscious, and Individuation," Jung writes, "I use the term 'individuation' to denote the process by which a person becomes a psychological 'in-dividual,' that is, a separate, indivisible unity or 'whole' " (*CW* 9i: 490). Jung spoke in terms of a personal and spiritual quest for knowledge (in which the "Grail," or the center, is simultaneously within and without), and the double nature of the process has parallels in the epistemological journey of the Western mind. In discussing Perceval as the Grail knight, Emma Jung and Marie-Louise von Franz speak of the "widening of the continually changing horizon of awareness" that comes with maturation, or individuation (98). They write:

> Beyond this there is often *a numinous experience of this inner psychic wholeness*. This experience is usually accompanied by a profound emotion which the ego senses as an epiphany of the divine. For this reason it is practically impossible to differentiate between an experience of God and an experience of the Self. The manifestations of the Self, arising from the unconscious, coincide with the god-image of most religions and, when not personified, are distinguished by circular and square forms and very often (statistically considered) by quaternary formations. Jung, making use of an Eastern term, has called these structures *mandalas*. (98-99)

Here, they describe beautifully the design of the classical labyrinth as perfected by medieval monks in manuscripts and as it later appeared in the great Gothic cathedrals. They go on to describe the Grail castle as a type of this "mandala" formation, which represented, for many medieval Christians, a symbol of heavenly Jerusalem (in other words, the center of the labyrinth). As a "paradisal garden and a mysterious world centre," they write, it is a place where "the opposites are united, where the hidden treasure lies buried" (332). They go on to say that the center "is clearly a projection of the Self as an inner centre, extending far beyond the ego, which expresses wholeness and harmony and from which radiate healing, integrating influences" (333).

Campbell believed that both the guided path and the untracked waste lead, albeit in very different ways, to the same place: awe in the face of the ineffable. In his view, mythologies mostly protect against realizations too overpowering for day-to-day living. Nevertheless, those who follow established teachings (like Dante) can find the center just as surely as those who strike out on their own (like the Grail knights). In his view, the two paths are complementary.

On the other hand, the well-beaten path, for Campbell—while offering greater serenity (and less loneliness)—takes much of the adventure out of life. Campbell considers the individual unique and irreplaceable; he or she is responsible for finding his or her own place in the world. An individual life has great meaning because, by following his own path, each person takes part in the ongoing process of creation, participating in its shifting and weaving patterns as an artist who is both the painter and a living portion of what he paints. The predominant tendency in the West, at least since the late Middle Ages, has been to emphasize this individual authority. That is why the quest for the Holy Grail, in Campbell's view, is a tale that reveals a changing zeitgeist, a story of the individual charting his own course, finally independent of others, in search of what is true in the world and in himself (*Thou Art That* 30-31).

In the explosion of knowledge and renewed interest in discovery affecting all forms of human endeavor during the Renaissance, we see the spirit of individual enterprise blossoming. The quest of the lone individual on a singular, mazelike path in the *Queste* is emblematic of the scientists, explorers, artists, and inventors whose work opened up new vistas (literally) within a few hundred years of the time the work's cleric set pen to paper. The fever for prospecting new territory was inspired in part by the rediscovery of ancient works from the classical period. In the unmistakable and unabashed admiration for the human form, along with the celebration of reasoning, philosophy, sculpture, poetry, and other forms of art found among the works of the ancient Greeks, Europe found a source of new/old inspiration that brought the quest for knowledge down to earth. The Church was not so much abandoned as humanity was elevated; perhaps, in the telescopes of the new astronomers and the formulas of the new mathematicians, the heavens seemed a bit more within the reach of human grasp than they had in the past. Dante's ascent was no longer as high as it had been.

All of this came later, after the Grail romances and after Dante, who perhaps experienced the stirrings of change before they came fully to flower. Dante's geography, as we have seen, emphasizes the physical separation of the divine, the infernal, and the earthly, but his time in Paradiso affords him a glimpse of the circle identified by Nicholas Cusanus in the fifteenth century, "whose circumference is nowhere and whose center is everywhere; the circle of infinite radius" (Campbell, *Masks of God: Occidental Mythology* 522). It is certainly true that the end of Dante's *Comedy* affords a vision of the coming together of humanity and God as the final and climactic experience of Dante's sojourn in heaven (and one that is beyond Dante's understanding):

> That circle—which, begotten so, appeared
> in You as light reflected—when my eyes
> had watched it with attention for some time,
> within itself and colored like itself,
> to me seemed painted with our effigy,
> so that my sight was set on it completely.
> As the geometer intently seeks
> to square the circle, but he cannot reach,
> through thought on thought, the principle he needs,
> so I searched that strange sight. (*Par.* 33.127-36)

This final vision, the image that Dante chooses to leave us with, can be nothing less than a summation of the movement of the entire poem. God and man together in the circles of Dante's vision of eternity is perhaps a bit surprising after all of the trouble Dante has gone to in emphasizing the vast distances involved in traveling both within and between the three realms, but his image is at once Christian and humanistic.

It took the "secularization" of the labyrinth form and the transformation of the quest into a game and an amusement to usher in the next phase of the labyrinth's history. In Renaissance gardens, court dances, and the plays of Shakespeare, the labyrinth became a thing of wonder, dalliance, and joy unrelated to moral objectives and the quest for God and closer in some ways to its origins as ritual and dance. Chapter 4 will explore the ways in which the labyrinth was transformed from a place of trouble and difficulty to a place of pleasure and magic.

141

Chapter 4
Romance, Dance, the Pilgrim, and Music

By'r Lakin, I can go no further, sir:
My old bones ache: here's a maze trod indeed
Through forthrights and meanders. By your patience,
I needs must rest me.

— William Shakespeare, *The Tempest*

This is as strange a maze as e'er men trod,
And there is in this business more than nature
Was ever conduct of. Some oracle
Must rectify our knowledge.

— William Shakespeare, *The Tempest*

Labyrinths of Love and Play

André Peyronie points out that French, Spanish, Italian, and English literature all have instances of the new and revolutionary nonreligious labyrinth in the Renaissance period. The first appearance of the word "labyrinth" in English was in Chaucer's *The House of Fame* (1379-80), in which the poet compares the "House of Rumours" to a labyrinth. In Spain, Juan de Mena's *El Laberinto de Fortuna* (1444) marks the first use of the term in Spanish and the first explicit reference to the labyrinth as an orderly creation watched over by Providence. Francesco Colonna's *Hypnerotomachia Poliphili* (1499) likens a palace to the Egyptian labyrinth, mentions Daedalus's labyrinth in the context of a character's wandering and confusion, and includes a unicursal spiral water labyrinth with a dragon at its heart as a symbol of human life. The latter influenced Ariosto's *Orlando*

Furioso (1516-32), which connected the labyrinth to the forest, a popular

motif in medieval literature.

Peyronie believes Shakespeare's reading of the Italians may have

influenced *A Midsummer Night's Dream* ("The Labyrinth" 695), written in

1594 or 1595. Shakespeare's woods are the scene of an enchanted,

labyrinthine adventure; he specifically mentions the neglect of the custom

of "treading of the maze" in connection with the upheaval in the natural

order that occasions the plot. Shakespeare draws here on the venerable

English tradition of turf mazes and their associated ritual dances, which

brings us back to the ancient tradition of the labyrinth as dance (Peyronie,

"The Labyrinth" 696). Turf mazes were widespread in England and a few

other countries but not in France, which had church labyrinths instead.

England did not have church labyrinths but had numerous turf mazes,

usually similar in design to the "classical" French cathedral labyrinths (Kern

167-68). Kern observes that there is no way of telling which came first, the

turf labyrinths or the church labyrinths, but that in both cases what began

as a pagan symbol was adopted by the Church for its own use. In England,

many turf mazes were in fact located near churches. In any case, the

tradition of a turf maze was a familiar one to Shakespeare's audience,

though the use of the word "maze" leads one to believe that these

structures were multicursal when in fact they were not. The folkloric ritual

of treading labyrinths cut into the turf was said to move the seasons through their proper course, and within Shakespeare's play neglect of the dancing has turned the natural world topsy-turvy. Once the enchantment in the forest is broken and the dance is performed, the world is renewed—as it would have been by ancient solar rituals—and the seasons proceed in their proper course. Peyronie notes, "the expression 'to tread a maze' is used here in its original sense which is linked to dance and the religious function of the labyrinth" ("The Labyrinth" 696).

Mazes and Moonlight in A Midsummer Night's Dream

A new phenomenon, the hedge or floral maze, became popular during the Renaissance in England, France, the Netherlands, and elsewhere across Europe. Intended purely as amusements, these mazes were fashionable during Shakespeare's time. Is it a coincidence that they became popular just as Western Europe was experiencing an explosion of new ideas and a new focus on humanism, science, geographical expansion, and exploration? On the contrary—the maze, albeit in a playful manner, is an emblem of the open-ended spirit of inquiry that pervaded the age. The maze is a labyrinth that has been tied up in knots for the amusement of wealthy landowners and others with access to the gardens or parks containing them. It is notable that the maze was so popular in England, a country that already had turf labyrinths but no church labyrinths. It was probably a short step from a unicursal labyrinth in the turf to a multicursal maze with a variety of paths, especially for a landscape feature that had traditionally been used for games and rituals (Kern 168).

A Midsummer Night's Dream combines explicit references to turf mazes with a forest setting that also echoes the twisting paths of a maze. In using this motif, Shakespeare borrows from the conventions of medieval literature while changing the tone and circumstances from one of fear and dread to one of magic and romance. Instead of a forest populated with wandering knights battling for the sake of their souls, there are quarreling lovers and mischievous fairies. The maze has been transformed from a trek through a forest wasteland into an enchanted playground. The lovers seek not a spiritual object but each other, a task that proves to be almost as frustrating (if less prolonged) as the hunt for the mystical cup. To make matters even more amusing, Theseus, the hero of the labyrinth in classical times, appears in Shakespeare's play as a king and an authority figure on the eve of his own wedding. Despite his prowess, however, Theseus has no knowledge of and no authority over the kingdom of the night and the world of the fairies who, without his knowledge, have turned nature upside down in the course of their disagreements and made sport of the humans with whom they cross paths. Fleeing from a life or death ultimatum created by harsh Athenian laws, Hermia and Lysander collide with a wholly different set of rules controlled by the fairies. By the light of the moon and with the help of a fairy potion, tragedy is turned upside down in the forest labyrinth and transformed into comedy.

Mazes are mentioned by name in *A Midsummer Night's Dream* in Titania's speech to Oberon, when she lists examples of disorders in the natural world that have resulted from their quarrels. The labyrinth myth is invoked in the play by the presence of Theseus, whose impending marriage to Hippolyta is the springboard for the plot. Theseus is depicted as the authority figure, the ruler whose word means law. Hermia's father, Egeus, appeals to him for justice when Hermia refuses to marry Demetrius, the man he has picked out for her. Theseus is depicted as a firm enforcer of the law. He tells Hermia that she must either accept Demetrius, be consigned to a convent for life, or die. She has until "the next new moon" (four days hence) to decide.

Hermia and her true love, Lysander, then plot to run away together. Their plan is to steal away into the woods and make their way to the home of Lysander's widowed aunt, where "the sharp Athenian law / Cannot pursue us" (1.1.162-63), and there to be married. They take Helena, Hermia's girlhood friend, into their confidence. Helena is understandably resentful of Hermia, since she herself loves Demetrius; he has lately grown cold toward Helena and transferred his affections to Hermia, who wants nothing to do with him. Helena decides to tell Demetrius what Hermia and Lysander are planning, in the hope of regaining his favor. Thus, the foursome ends up in the woods near Athens on a summer night—the lovers in flight, Demetrius in pursuit, and Helena trailing Demetrius.

The four mortals are not the only ones wandering in the woods that night. The fairy king, Oberon, and his estranged queen, Titania, along with their followers are also afoot, and their quarrel over an orphaned child has fairyland and the natural world in an uproar. The seasons are occurring out of turn, and the flocks and crops are failing due to the inauspicious conditions. As Titania tells it:

> the green corn
> Hath rotted ere his youth attained a beard;
> The fold stands empty in the drownèd field,
> And crows are fatted with the murrion flock;
> The nine men's morris is filled up with mud;
> And the quaint mazes in the wanton green
> For lack of tread are undistinguishable.
> The human mortals want their winter here;
> No night is now with hymn or carol blest.
> Therefore the moon, the governess of floods,
> Pale in her anger, washes all the air,
> That rheumatic diseases do abound.
> And thorough this distemperature we see
> The seasons alter. (2.1.94-107)

Not only is fairyland on the move in the moonlit woods, so is a rustic group of craftsmen, or mechanicals, including Nick Bottom, a weaver. This homespun group is gathering to rehearse a play they plan to perform as part of Theseus's marriage celebration. Like the two couples, they are from Athens and therefore subjects of Theseus but find themselves in the woods at night, beyond the pale of the daytime world of law and order. Thus four separate groups are represented in the play: Theseus and his court, the four lovers, the King and Queen of faerie and their followers, and the craftsmen/thespians.

Theseus appears in the play as a respected ruler in his prime; the action of the play depicts him after his adventure with Ariadne, who is mentioned by Oberon as one of his past loves (and a rival to Titania, who dallied with Theseus). Even though Theseus now represents order and responsibility, he has a labyrinth in his past as well as a train of female conquests. As a conquering hero, he defeated the Minotaur and returned to Athens to take his place as king. Though this history is only alluded to and is already past during the action of *A Midsummer Night's Dream*, the inclusion of Ariadne and Titania in the list of Theseus's conquests brings these aspects of Theseus's history squarely into the plot. His majestic, somewhat stern persona in the play is undercut by these references to his past; he himself has been entangled in both a labyrinth and a long line of women. His heroic world has an underseam of darkness, erotic intrigue, and danger, and his kingly stature projects a long shadow represented by the woods, a place where logic, feelings, custom, and rules turn inside out. His character is essentially the same as it was in the Greek myth.

In the Renaissance, labyrinths of love were a popular precursor to the hedge mazes they resembled. These labyrinths were based on the pattern of the "church labyrinth" model—sometimes including connecting gates in the greenery "walls"—and were designed as a place for lovers to dally in (Kern 226). They are in that sense similar to a "Tunnel of Love" in a modern amusement park. That is exactly the purpose served by the woods in Shakespeare's play, as first Lysander, and then Demetrius, falls victim to a fairy potion that causes each man to switch his affections from Hermia to Helena. Thus Hermia and Lysander, who were certain of their feelings before being undone by Puck's magical herb, are set at odds, and Hermia takes Helena's place as the rejected lover. Although it is actually a kind intention of Oberon's (and Puck's mistake) that turns Lysander's affection for Hermia aside, the play implies that the lovers (or least the men) are somewhat to blame for being so gullible. Demetrius, after all, originally loved Helena and grew besotted with the indifferent Hermia before ever venturing into the woods. He, like Theseus, has toyed with more than one woman, so Theseus's insistence on enforcing the law on Hermia has an ironic, not to mention misogynistic, ring to it. Once again, the ancient association of the labyrinth with fertility rites surfaces in these erotic entanglements, and once more, Theseus misses the point.

Both of the women remain faithful while the men switch affections with comic ease. They are all under the eye of the moon, which is invoked several times in the play as a kind of silent presence overlooking (and perhaps influencing) the proceedings. Ariadne may have been, among other things, a moon goddess in ancient times, according to the evidence of coins from Knossos (Kerényi, *Dionysos* 104-06, 124). The maze of love and the maze of the nighttime world of dreams, parts of Ariadne's realm, interpenetrate one another. The women are less subject to confusion in this realm, just as Ariadne knew the way through the labyrinth because it belonged to her.

The only female character to undergo a change of heart is Titania, who falls in love with the ass-headed Bottom under the influence of Puck's flower, which Oberon characterizes as the fruit of a love shaft intended for one of the Goddess Diana's maidens—"a fair vestal" (2.1.158)—whose head was not turned. Although Puck famously declares mortals to be "fools," the fairy people are not immune to the effects of love potions, as Titania's sudden passion for Bottom makes plain. This forest labyrinth has its own bi-form creature, which might make us think of Pasiphaë and her offspring, although the ass's head makes this affair a farce instead of a tragedy.

Humans and fairies alike lose their way under the influence of moonlight and magic. References to their sudden reversals abound in the play, as in Lysander's remark that he has always heard, "The course of true love never did run smooth" (1.1.134). Bottom tells Titania that he is not wise, "but if I had wit enough to get out of this wood, I have enough to serve mine own turn" (3.1.135-36), to which Titania, happily lost in the labyrinth of love, replies, "Out of this wood do not desire to go" (3.1.137).

Oberon instructs Puck to lead the two mortal men astray to prevent them from fighting and give Puck a chance to use another herb that will renew Lysander's love for Hermia. Lysander and Demetrius hunt one another, but tricked by Puck's ventriloquism, get lost in a game of hide and seek. They are as mistaken in who they are following as they have been in who they love; what threatened to be a sad ending for Hermia and Lysander becomes a comedy of errors. This is no maze for deep philosophical pondering, no road map for a life's journey, but rather a light-hearted tumble through the vagaries of romantic love.

Oberon knows nothing of Hermia's and Lysander's plight when he first tells Puck to use the potion, but his sympathy for Helena's grief and vexation is an endorsement of true love and concern for a woman's grief. In the woods, at night, it is possible to challenge inflexible daytime laws and set things right. In this case, there is no Minotaur in the maze—the threat to the lovers stems from Theseus's brand of justice. Oberon assists the lovers in settling their predicament, so that "all to Athens back again repair, / And think no more of this night's accidents / But as the fierce vexation of a dream" (4.1.66-68). His influence provides a kind of Ariadne's thread, though it is prone to getting tangled. He also lifts the spell from Titania, and she and Oberon reconcile before performing the fairy dance that helps set the world right again. As Peyronie notes, they dance in the same place where the four lovers are sleeping ("The Labyrinth" 696).

Now that magic, moonlight, and dance all accord, the couples are reunited, and the mortals can be married. The fairies will grace the marriages by dancing "solemnly" at midnight in Theseus's palace, "and bless it to all fair prosperity" (4.1.87-89)—emphasizing the role of the ritual dance in bringing the couples together and blessing their future offspring.

When the night is over, and all the lovers have been restored to their proper states, they tell a confused tale of how they spent the night. Theseus is skeptical of their veracity. As he tells Hippolyta (who is less sure than he is of the insubstantiality of the lovers' claims):

> I never may believe
> These antic fables nor these fairy toys.
> Lovers and madmen have such seething brains,
> Such shaping fantasies, that apprehend
> More than cool reason ever comprehends.
> The lunatic, the lover, and the poet
> Are of imagination all compact. (5.1.2-8)

In view of his preference for rationality (and discomfort with the "lunatic" world of dream and fantasy), it is perhaps not surprising that Theseus, having made use of Ariadne's gifts of intuition, tossed her unsentimentally aside. His reliance on "cool reason" blinds him to the mysterious events in the woods, and he is closed off from the world of imagination. His limited vision is overruled because the fairies have already done their work. Peyronie notes that the triumphant ending of the play is "pregnant with the new life to come" ("The Labyrinth" 696).

Shakespeare's play, whether directly inspired by the labyrinths of love or not, weaves a plot infused with the same playful outlook. The use of the maze or "labyrinth" as an amusement or a game is a bridge between the serious theological and religious attitudes represented by the unicursal labyrinth and the increasingly non-religious attitudes toward knowledge summed up by the complexity of the maze and its transformation into ever more complicated designs. The certitude of Christian morality and dogma was giving way to the open-ended pursuit of knowledge symbolized by the maze—but not before this detour into the garden of play and romance, a rebirth of the labyrinth as "fertile ground."

French Court Ballet and the Labyrinth Tradition

Meanwhile, in France, the labyrinth evolved in a somewhat related direction in the art of dance. During a state visit from Polish diplomats to the French court in 1573, a command performance of a work by Savoyard choreographer Balthazar de Beaujoyeulx was inspired by the tradition of the labyrinth, according to several contemporary commentators. One striking feature of Beaujoyeulx's dance was a lightness and buoyancy in the movements that negated the darkness of the labyrinth *en malo*. Thomas Greene recounts a description by eyewitness Brantome that emphasized the "order in disorder" character of the dance, which repeatedly created movements in one direction followed by abrupt reversals, in addition to an intricate weaving of steps in a complicated pattern (1404-05). Another

154

contemporary description, this one by Jean Dorat, writing in Latin in a commemorative booklet honoring the occasion, refers to the dancers' movements as bee-like, meandering, resembling a flock of cranes, knot-like, "artfully entangled," dolphin-like, game-like, and sinuous (qtd. in Greene 1405-06). Even the description itself takes on the repetitiveness and rhythm of the dance (Greene 1406). Dorat makes direct references to the ludic dance performed at Anchises's funeral games by his grandson Ascanius, calling the French ballet a reprise of the performance described by Virgil in the *Aeneid*. This so-called "Troia" is usually translated into English as "the Trojan Ride" (though this may be a mistranslation of "Truia," meaning "arena" or "place to dance" (Kern 25). An important feature of this famous dance from classical times was, as we have seen, its connection with life, death, and resurrection and the need to trick evil spirits, which—in several traditions—were said to travel only in straight lines. Commonly performed at important funeral games (and, as Virgil notes in Book 5, lines 783-88, at the founding of the city of Alba Longa), the "Trojan Ride" thus had a protective function (Kern 77).

The history of the *Truia* is very ancient, though its exact origins are unknown. As we saw with the Tragliatella pitcher, the *Truia* is associated with an illustration of a labyrinth, riders on horseback, and copulating couples. The same word, "Truia," crops up in connection with medieval turf mazes and Scandinavian rock mazes, also known, respectively, as Troy or Troy-towns, and Troyaburgs, though the association with Troy may be an accident encouraged by Virgil's description of the *Troia*, as Greene notes (1410). Another example of the *Truia* appears in Plutarch's account of the life of Theseus, in which the hero and the other Athenian youths execute a complex dance in celebration of their freedom while visiting Delos. Greene believes this dance "may well act out the kind of acceptance of death as an inherent part of the life cycle that emerges from the Homeric 'Hymn to Demeter' " (1412); Virgil, too, would have known Plutarch's source and may have been informed by it.

Yet another reference, the illustration on the shield of Achilles described by Homer, may refer to a supposed tradition in which the dancers dance the solution of the maze for Theseus's benefit before he enters it. This Homeric dance may be the source on which Dicaearchus, Plutarch, and Virgil all base their descriptions (Greene 1413-14).

Greene's detailed account of the labyrinth dance as it appeared not only in French court dances but also in the masques of Ben Jonson (the earliest of which was performed in 1605) places these elaborate Renaissance productions within the long tradition of labyrinth as dance, myth, and structure. He comments on the apparently apotropaic function of labyrinth dances in ancient times as well as on the mysterious and seemingly ritual origins of the English turf mazes and Scandinavian stone labyrinths. Greene notes the muddied etymological tale that accompanies the story of the labyrinth through ancient, classical, medieval, and Renaissance times and the difficulty in grasping the original meaning of the symbol as it appeared in cave drawings. At the same time, he finds a common "thread" running throughout the descriptions of such disparate labyrinth dances as those performed at Auxerre by the church canons, the French court dances, the English masques, the "Troia" at Anchises's funeral games, and even the angelic dance in Book 5 of *Paradise Lost*. In addition to such characteristics as intricacy, complexity, and sudden reversals, the key characteristic Greene identifies in all of these dances is the joy invoked in the viewer (1415, 1460). Even God is said to take pleasure in the circling dance of the angels, as described by John Milton:

> mazes intricate,
> Eccentric, intervolved, yet regular
> Then most when most irregular they seem,
> And in their motions harmony divine
> So smooths her charming tones that God's own ear
> Listens delighted. (5.622-27)

Greene suggests that the dancers' ability to overcome the difficulty of the labyrinthine choreography and perform the steps to perfection is what creates pleasure and joy. "To tread flawlessly and religiously the windings of a maze would be to overcome all that it stood for," notes Greene (1458), going on to list confusion, lack of forward progress, danger, and the moral and experiential entanglements of human life as the most common experiences the maze represents. He goes on to say:

the balletic mastery of labyrinthine evolutions declares the possibility of human control. However bewildering, the balletic intricacy has been designed; everyone follows a plan, which is by definition a plan under control; the dance acts out a victory of the brilliant unicursal over the entrapments of the multicursal. Thus the irregularity is reassuring and healing. If the multicursal labyrinth had been misnamed during the Middle Ages as *labor intus*, inner travail, by the kind of false etymology that plagued this tradition, the performance of a complicated labyrinth design was calculated to free the performer from travail. The multicursal bewilderment could always be transformed into a unicursal progress. And if in the Renaissance a magical capability was attributed to dancing (or re-attributed), this addition could only heighten the intensity of the emotions. If the dance was understood to imitate the circling of celestial bodies, or to correct their irregularities, this imitation would only assist further the realization of a liberated human power. (Greene 1459-60)

The humanism Greene identifies transforms the labyrinth from a tool of medieval religious dogma into a jubilant declaration of human ingenuity and capability. As in ancient times, the labyrinthine dance form is ritual, and therefore transformative.

As Greene notes, the tradition of seeing dance as "imitative" (and possibly "corrective") of the heavenly dance was attested by Plato, Lucian, and others (1447). In the Renaissance dances, it is as if humanity, formerly in terror of hell and uncertain of the way to salvation without God's continual guidance, has thrown fear aside in favor of a new optimism and faith in its own abilities. Not only is the Christian less concerned with damnation, as the Church shifts its emphasis to Christ's humanity and message of redemption (celebrated in *The Divine Comedy* by an emphasis on the Incarnation), humanity is now in a position to "partner" with God in the unfolding story of Creation. Not only is man a "creature," he is also a "creator" in his own right—of new scientific theories, technological advances, art celebrating earthly life, and maps that re-draw the contours of not only the known world but even the skies overhead.

It is no wonder that the court dances and masques, as well as *A Midsummer Night's Dream*, are steeped in a sense of wonder and magic and exude a lightness miles away from Dante's dark wood or even the Grail forest. In Shakespeare's play, quarreling lovers, impudent fairies, and befuddled would-be actors replace devils and heretics. Instead of a man with the head of a bull, one encounters Bottom, a man with the head of an ass. Magical potions are responsible for many sudden reversals, which complicate matters for the lovers but create an enjoyable sense of mayhem and enchantment rather than a sense of danger. In addition, the diverted affections of the two men mirror and gently ridicule the inconstancy displayed by Demetrius and, above all, Theseus; men are easily led astray in the labyrinth of love.

The place of "magic" in Shakespeare's play is central to the action of the plot. Just as Greene notes a new (or newly rediscovered) magical quality in these labyrinth dances that reveals the power of humanity to act on and affect the material world, the fairies in *A Midsummer Night's Dream* are shown to be the keepers of potent magical knowledge. The world of

Athens, ruled by the kingly but inflexible Theseus, runs on a completely different set of wheels than the forest. In the woods, rules are made to be broken, and the clear distinctions between dream and reality, attraction and antipathy, and the human world and nature are blurred. Here is a region akin to the unconscious, with its upside-down logic and shifting shadows. As Robert Pogue Harrison suggests, the forest's place as "an outlying realm of opacity which has allowed [Western civilization] to estrange itself, enchant itself, terrify itself, ironize itself, in short to project into the forest's shadows its secret and innermost anxieties" (xi) goes all the way back to *Gilgamesh*, with its mazelike Cedar Forest (Harrison 14-18). In Shakespeare's forest, while affections and loyalties are tested and redirected, the agency behind the disruption is, even if mischievous, basically benign. The spirit of carnival reigns in the forest, and Oberon's interference actually makes things better than they were before. What Theseus could not control can be influenced by potions in this liminal place. Though himself a treader of labyrinths (by the grace of Ariadne's thread), Theseus has neither knowledge of nor sympathy for the realms of magic and nature, which are somewhat intertwined in the play. Shakespeare, while manifestly respectful of the power vested in Theseus as ruler, subverts this nod to authority by placing all of the real action, transformation, and change in the forest. The mood of enchantment that permeates "one of Shakespeare's happiest comedies" (Doran 146) derives from the fairies' ability to give the lovers a

160

happy ending in spite of Theseus, who does not believe fairies are real

(despite presumably believing the Minotaur was real). Theseus exhibits an

inability to comprehend greater powers at work in the world beyond kingly

authority, powers that burst exuberantly into view with a new humanism

that begins to test the bounds of old assumptions.

Mazes in the Garden

Concurrent with the appearance of the maze in Renaissance theatre

and dance was the advent of the garden maze. While English turf labyrinths

appeared at the same time the cathedral labyrinths were being built in

France, and garden labyrinths became popular in France in the fourteenth

century, garden *mazes* as we know them today, except for a few designs

from the fifteenth and sixteenth centuries (Kern 138, 198), were unknown

until the sixteenth, seventeenth, and eighteenth centuries. Kern states that

the garden "labyrinths of love" in France were very similar in design to the

church labyrinths that apparently inspired them. He speculates that their

placement in gardens may have been intended to connect them with the

idea of the garden of Paradise; gardens were often taken as symbols of

Eden (226). Labyrinths of love (the first known example of which appeared

in 1338 in France) were sometimes referred to as "Houses of Daedalus"

(*Maison Dédalus*), the same term applied to the cathedral labyrinth at Amiens

in a document from the same period (Kern 226). Based on this and other

evidence, Kern concludes that the French garden labyrinths may have had a religious significance, serving as a reminder of the loss of Paradise due to original sin. Couples who walked in these labyrinths of love may have been expected to recall Adam and Eve, especially since a Maypole representing a tree was often present at the center. In spite of the religious overtones of these French labyrinths of love, they, like their cousins the cathedral labyrinths, were also the center of festivities with ancient origins connected to fertility, such as dancing around the center pole, or "Tree of Life" (Kern 226). (Shakespeare alludes to May celebrations in *A Midsummer Night's Dream* performed by Theseus and members of his court: 1.1.167, 4.1.103, 4.1.132.)

These late medieval garden labyrinths (almost always unicursal) were sometimes constructed of hedges or flowers, but hedge *mazes*, popular across Europe, were a product of the Renaissance and Baroque periods. Many gardeners' plan books still extant include patterns for these sometimes highly elaborate and carefully sculpted mazes. Although many mazes were planted so that the walls would eventually be taller than the people walking in them, some were trimmed close to the ground so that the layout (and solution) could be easily seen. While some garden mazes were suitable for games and dalliance and getting lost (which in these settings was considered pleasurable and not lamentable), others were designed merely to delight the eye with their geometric exactitude and intricate designs (Kern 247). They presented a challenge to the eye and the mind without requiring an observer to enter to discover their secrets. These hedge mazes remained popular in England and other places until the advent of the English landscape garden and its more naturalistic conventions in the late eighteenth and early nineteenth centuries.

The Playfulness of the Maze

It is worthwhile to consider parallels between the garden mazes, created entirely for amusement, the forest maze in *A Midsummer Night's Dream*, and the exuberant labyrinth dances and masques created by Beaujoyeulx and Jonson. In each case, a sense of reversal, temporarily frustrating but ultimately enjoyable, playfulness, and a carnival-like overturning of everyday rules is the overarching theme. Certainly a playful eroticism permeates the mazes, with their garden settings, profusion of intertwined growth, and hidden spaces that create a tailor-made paradise for lovers. The forest in Shakespeare's play is a larger version of the same kind. While the more abstract sequences of the dances and masques may have been more formal and less overtly erotic, the physical exertion and amatory themes (particularly in the masques) suggest a stylized form of dalliance. There is a major difference between the court dances/masques and the mazes, whether of garden or of forest: in the former, delight is taken in the precision of the steps and the skill of the dancers in threading their way through a potentially chaotic sequence of shifting patterns. In the latter, the great delight is precisely in losing the way for a while and wandering with

163

no knowledge of what lies around the next corner. The court dances and masques, not surprisingly, still celebrate order and control triumphing over chaos. Considering their audience and purpose, this is to be expected and is closer in spirit to the religious labyrinths that preceded them. By the time of Shakespeare's play and the advent of the hedge mazes, abandonment of propriety and a very non-religious (if not pagan) enjoyment of the game for game's sake transforms the multicursal labyrinth into the Renaissance and Baroque version of a funhouse or "Tunnel of Love."

It is not too much to suggest a progression by way of an Ariadnean thread that links these related phenomena in a European world waking up to new possibilities after a long medieval dream steeped in Christianity. In the court dances and masques, disorder threatens but is overcome by the skill of the dancers. They are, if not co-creators, at least understanding participants who discern God's designs and dance to the music of the spheres (an image close in spirit to Dante's depiction of Paradise). In Shakespeare's play, a daylight world of strict and unyielding order is turned topsy-turvy in the forest so that lovers are matched with their true partners; when the night is over, the rule of Athens is imposed once more but because of the magical corrections that took place in the forest, it is rendered benign. And as for the hedge mazes, it may be assumed that even though there is always a solution to the maze that leads one back to the everyday world, what happens within is privileged and hidden from the outside. One might tread a different path each time she returns to it, so the maze offers a sense of multiple possibilities and experiences.

In the Gardens of the Sun

In France, the fashion for garden mazes in the late seventeenth century found its way into the gardens of the Sun King, Louis XIV. While the main gardens at Versailles consisted of long linear vistas precisely aligned with the palace, which symbolized the king himself, labyrinths provided for the more private amusements of courtiers. Leisurely walks through the forest labyrinth, installed some time between the 1660s and the 1670s, were a large part of the appeal, according to Sarah Cohen, who notes that the king's labyrinth was unusual for having no center. "The fragmented geometry of its pathways also wittily convoluted the linear order governing the central axis of the Versailles gardens," she writes in *Art, Dance, and the Body in the French Culture of the Ancien Régime* (105). Statues of Aesop and Cupid (with a ball of string) were stationed at the entrance, as if to signal a double meaning for the labyrinth: a labyrinth of love in which to get lost *as well as* a path to wisdom. "It was indeed not a goal but travel itself that visitors appreciated in the Labyrinth at Versailles," Cohen writes, adding that if the overall symmetry and order of the palace's gardens symbolized the king and his rule, the labyrinth offered "alluring pockets of disorder" meant to provide courtiers with "aristocratic pleasures and amorous engagement" (106-07). Again, the labyrinth is a playground that subverts the orderly world of a king's leadership, but in this case, it is completely sanctioned by the king. As secluded as it may have been, this labyrinth was still a reminder of the king's wealth and generosity in providing for the amusement of his courtiers. Whether there is a central goal or not, every trip through this elaborately conceived and ornamented labyrinth would have been a reminder of the source of this magnificence, the Sun King himself.

While the French monarchy made conscious use of solar symbolism to emphasize the absolute authority of the king, it is not clear whether anyone considered the ancient connection between the labyrinth and solar rituals in constructing the king's maze at Versailles. It is not likely that such a pagan connection would have been officially sanctioned; the French court was aware of the scientific heliocentric theories of Nicolaus Copernicus and René Descartes and incorporated them into every aspect of the buildings, decorations, and grounds at Versailles as an allegory of the king's power, but without the approval of the Church. While the association of the sun with political leadership and monotheism went back to biblical times, Louis XIV used it as a symbol of political might aligned with cosmic, material power (Cohen 85-87).

The Prince de Condé hired the king's garden designer to construct gardens, including a maze similar to the king's, at his Chantilly estate; there is record of an occasion in 1688 when guests were invited to dessert laid out in the labyrinth's center, a situation that created an enjoyable confusion for all the guests, who took different paths to reach it. This labyrinth featured statues of Ariadne and Theseus, and like the one at Versailles, was intended purely for pleasure. Cohen writes: "Roaming through these labyrinths must have felt something like performing a dance in a ball or ballet, for in addition to displaying oneself and observing others, movement enjoyed as *divertissement* was the object in a labyrinth, just as it was in dancing" (109). Once again, dancing, the labyrinth, and dalliance are joined in a single image.

Intellectual Labyrinths

The church labyrinths disappeared one by one from Reims, Auxerre, Amiens, and other cathedrals beginning in the late seventeenth century. Eventually, garden mazes also waned in popularity. Many of the garden mazes created for wealthy estate-owners and members of the royal families in France and England were either destroyed in favor of more naturalistic landscaping in the late eighteenth century or simply failed to weather the ravages of time. While the labyrinth underwent many transformations over the course of two or three centuries, it remained a recognizable concept despite the abstract appearance it sometimes took. Labyrinthine wanderings disappeared from the confines of ballrooms and noblemen's gardens but continued to appear in a more intellectual realm in the form of puzzles, verse labyrinths, illustrated spiritual labyrinths, and musical compositions.

Text labyrinths, illustrated labyrinths, and musical labyrinths were popular throughout the sixteenth, seventeenth, and eighteenth centuries. Script or verse labyrinths often contained secret messages pointing to spiritual knowledge in one form or another. Some verse labyrinths consisted of words situated on the page to create a labyrinth design, while others took the form of word puzzles in which the same word was spelled in various directions, or hidden words could be found upon close examination. A book of sixteenth century woodcuts by Italian architect Francesco Segala included many illustrated labyrinths in the form of elaborate figures. Many of these, in their detail and complexity, resemble the designs we see today in corn mazes. Segala included a jester, a man on horseback, a ship, and a crab among his designs (Kern 240).

While many of these labyrinths were designed for amusement and play, spiritual labyrinths, which appeared in pamphlets, books, broadsheets, and engravings, were still used for didactic purposes. Their meaning was similar that of the traditional church labyrinths: they often represented the snares and confusion of worldly life and the need to be vigilant against moral errors. Both the Catholic Church and the Protestant Church used the labyrinth to represent the "errors" of the opposing side. The center of the labyrinth sometimes symbolized Earthly Paradise, from which God guides the Christian to spiritual life and salvation (Kern 209, 211). Although labyrinths of love also appeared as illustrations, they sometimes served a didactic purpose as well, warning of the pitfalls and hazards of erotic entanglement.

In addition to Louis XIV, other monarchs also used the labyrinth for political purposes. Illustrated labyrinths produced during the Thirty Years War depicted allegorical references to the events and participants. The Pope, for example, was the target of Anglican and Calvinist illustrations depicting him as a devil or the new Minotaur (Kern 224).

Thus, while the Renaissance began with the lively dances and masques that celebrated the labyrinth in movement, it ended with the labyrinth beginning to de-materialize. Mazes went out of vogue, church labyrinths were no longer being built, and the influence of the Cartesian philosophical split between mind and matter turned the labyrinth into a plaything of the mind. With the spirit of inquiry, along with scientific rationalism, permeating European culture on the heels of Renaissance open-mindedness, the labyrinth followed suit by eventually shedding its playful and erotic associations to become a vehicle of mental manipulation and intellectual exercise.

By the eighteenth century, with the Protestant Reformation having swept aside the relics of medievalism, the church labyrinth had fallen into ill repute. Indeed, it was likely that the very popularity of the church labyrinths in France, on which parishioners—used to the new fashion in garden mazes—now enjoyed taking a stroll during services, led to their removal. According to church documents from the cathedral at Reims in 1778, church officials asked for the removal of the labyrinth, as its use by churchgoers was perceived to be distracting and unseemly (Wright 231-32).

The Enlightenment and the Labyrinth

As the Baroque gave way to the Enlightenment, the uses and interpretations of the labyrinth grew more complex and difficult to summarize. On the one hand, mazes, with their non-religious appeal and worldly settings, continued to be popular for a time. In the early seventeenth century, followers of La Pléiade (a group of sixteenth-century French poets who emulated ancient Greek and Roman models as they attempted to revitalize vernacular French) sometimes used the labyrinth as a symbol of worldly love, so non-religious uses of this imagery sometimes appear (Peyronie, "The Labyrinth" 700). In Miguel de Cervantes Saavedra's *Don Quixote* (1605, 1615) the labyrinth represents the illusions of worldly life that often masquerade as reality. In this novel, Peyronie sees early intimations of a questioning of religious belief itself ("The Labyrinth" 696-97). On the other hand, the spiritual labyrinth as the path to God took on a somber religious appearance in various literary works. In an age in which the central questions tended to involve what was real and what was deceptive (Peyronie, "The Labyrinth" 696), the labyrinth provided a ready-

170

made allegory for the errors and deceptions of worldly life.

The labyrinth of the world, featuring a path to truth amid deception, was a popular theme in seventeenth-century spiritual literature. All of the moral lessons of the medieval labyrinth are there, enmeshed in a more intellectual brand of religiosity favoring mind over matter. This conception of the labyrinth is depicted in such works as John Bunyan's *The Pilgrims Progress* (1678), which does not specifically mention the labyrinth but features a labyrinthine journey.

In *The Pilgrims Progress*, the advice of a trustworthy guide leads Christian in the proper direction, but there is plenty of room to veer off the path since false guides are also on the road, ready to send the well-meaning pilgrim "off course" at every turn. The true path is accompanied by deceptions and tricks, and it is up to Christian to see through these snares and stick to the unicursal path amid a tempting array of multicursal byways.

The Labyrinth as Pilgrimage

The emphasis on the lone individual's journey on the path to God anticipated centuries earlier by the *Queste del Saint Graal* comes to fruition in *The Pilgrims Progress* and other similar works, in a manner in keeping with Post-Reformation and Enlightenment spiritual earnestness. As Wright puts it:

> [The labyrinth] became, as it once was long ago with the patristic fathers, a simple metaphor for the route along which the solitary soul must pass. . . . This maze has no

demonic center. There is no implication of a round-trip journey by Christ. . . . The pilgrim may set forth toward Jerusalem at any time.

As he does so, he will find himself alone. In this early-modern maze, the emphasis has shifted from a collective symbol seen from without to an object for individual meditation experienced from within. We should recall that there are no records attesting to, or even suggesting, a personal journey on a church maze prior to the seventeenth century. . . .

Moreover, as the steps of the spiritual pilgrim literally began to efface the tracks of an older ritualistic symbol, the maze became divorced from the liturgical rites of the church. (213, 215)

Wright identifies a medieval work, Guillaume de Deguileville's highly popular *The Pilgrimage of Human Life* (c. 1331), as the inspiration for *The Pilgrims Progress*. In Bunyan's work, the solitary seeker presses forward amid perils, distractions, and false counsel to find the Celestial City. Although the emphasis on the personal journey is aligned with Protestant belief in the wake of the Reformation, the journey itself is almost Dantean at times in its depiction of treacherous pits, wrathful dragons, and other hazards.

Notwithstanding this similarity, this journey carries more suspense than Dante's since the emphasis is clearly on the pilgrim's personal choices: not only whether to begin the journey or not, but whether to continue, how to conduct himself en route, and how to tell good counsel from bad (good counsel almost always means the less attractive, more difficult alternative). The pilgrim can (and does) make mistakes, moves forward, strays from the path, and backtracks. Although there is a single "straight and narrow" path to his goal, there are many possibilities for error and turning aside; choices frequently present themselves. Thus, this very spiritual seventeenth-century labyrinth actually has more in common with the worldly hedge mazes and puzzle games then in vogue than it does with its predecessor in the Catholic Church, the unicursal pavement labyrinth. The journey toward truth here is no longer a collective one but rather one undertaken in solitude and loneliness.

Comparing Reality and Appearance

Peyronie identifies the motif frequently found in Enlightenment literature concerning the difference between "true" reality and mere appearances as the era's major religious/philosophical preoccupation ("The Labyrinth" 696). The labyrinth, on either a spiritual or a worldly plane, becomes an initiatory experience in which the individual learns to distinguish reality from false appearances. The protagonist of *Pilgrims Progress* learns to avoid the pitfalls and snares of a treacherous mazelike world with the help of good counsel and faith in God. His missteps are presented as a negative example to the reader, who, it is hoped, will learn to avoid the same mistakes. "The true path" leads to salvation, and deviating from it creates delays and danger, as seen in this exchange between Evangelist and Christian:

> *Chr.* Sir, what think you? Is there Hopes? [sic] may I now go back, and go up to the *Wicket Gate?* Shall I not be abandoned for this, and sent back from thence ashamed? I

am sorry I have hearkened to this man's counsel; but may my Sin be forgiven?

 Evan. Then said *Evangelist* to him, Thy Sin is very great, for by it thou hast committed two evils; thou hast forsaken the Way that is good, to tread in forbidden paths; yet will the man at the Gate receive thee, for he has *good will* for men; only, said he, take heed that thou turn not aside again, lest thou perish from the Way, when his wrath is kindled but a little. (Bunyan 20)

Distrust of Sensory Experience

 The labyrinth in *Pilgrims Progress* is very much an imagined one, a metaphor only. In a non-religious vein, Vivant Denon's "Point de lendemain" (1777) presents the labyrinth as an initiation into love and the sensory world, but after the adventure is over, the hero is unsure how much was real and how much was imagined (Peyronie, "The Labyrinth" 700). The maze has the form of a ritual initiation, but in true Cartesian spirit, the initiate doubts what he learned there.

 A distrust of bodily experience and a preference for mental investigation permeates the Enlightenment. In examining this mind/body split, Ernest Becker discusses Freud's theories about fear of the mother and the mother's body that is manifested by young children of both sexes as they come to associate the mother, her bodily processes—including menstruation—and her milk with the embodied experiences of mortality: sickness, suffering, and death (38-40). Not coincidentally, the labyrinth has been associated since ancient times with the female body, as we have seen—particularly the vagina, the ovaries, and the womb. As cultural critic

Jacques Attali points out, "[The labyrinth] is surely not unrelated to a sense of the first path a human being ever travels, at the end of which he or she becomes a person: the path that leads out of the maternal womb. *Every human being's first labyrinth is that of a woman*" (3).

The desire for separation from the mother's body and from nature, resulting from an anxiety to escape reminders of mortality and dependence, fueled the seventeenth-century flight to the rational world of the mind and the objectification of nature, as philosopher Susan Bordo argues in *The Flight to Objectivity: Essays on Cartesianism and Culture* (58, 107-08). To objectify nature is to sustain a hope of somehow controlling it. The separation of mind and body, or spirit and matter, received a decisive impetus from the rigorous rationalism expostulated by René Descartes (1596-1650). We have seen the beginnings of this duality as far back as Plato, whose philosophy modeled abstract thinking and the primary importance of Ideas as opposed to sensory experience. This "Idealism" was present throughout the medieval period and influenced the Christian tendency to look forward to the "next world" rather than dwell on the present, material, imperfect one. Despite this drawing apart of the material and the spiritual worlds, the separation was not complete. The Church's decision to emphasize Christ's Incarnation in the late Middle Ages is one indication of a belief in the Christian West that earthly life was sanctified by Divine presence. In addition, the popular cult of Mary in the Catholic Church indicated a

175

reverence for a maternal form of the divine presence.

Bordo discusses the problem of a new and growing alienation from nature and sensory experience that haunted Descartes and other Enlightenment thinkers more than two millennia after Plato. In her view, the Cartesian unwillingness to trust information from the outside world was a reaction to an inevitable shift in consciousness that occurred as people became aware of their "locatedness" in space and time and the relativity of their own viewpoints (69). Bordo believes this shift parallels a developmental stage in children in which they become increasingly aware of their own boundaries and their essential separation from their mothers. This growing awareness of the mother as a separate being corresponds to both increased anxiety in her absence and a compensating move toward independence (Bordo 107). Descartes's move toward separation of mind and body and utter reliance on rational thought divorced from sensory experience is, in Bordo's view, a defense mechanism of the same kind, "a reaction-formation to the loss of 'being-one-with-the-world' brought about by the disintegration of the organic, centered, female cosmos of the Middle Ages and Renaissance" (106). While many would argue that this disintegration had begun centuries earlier in ancient Greece, Bordo suggests that the seventeenth century dealt a particularly heavy blow to any remaining tendencies to feel at home in the material world as the realm of "Mother Nature." Scientific advances in anatomy and astronomy, in particular, had already resulted in a new vision of the "mechanical universe" for which Descartes supplied a coherent philosophical understanding based on a perceived split between inert matter (Latin *mater:* "mother") and the thinking mind observing it (102).

Thus, on a cultural level, epistemological uncertainty moved thinking yet more decisively from a "mother-centered" universe (rooted in the material, bodily world and a sense of unity with it) toward a "father-centered universe" (governed at a distance by God the father). In a mirroring of the patricentric Greek society that took the place of the earlier matricentric culture, the dynamic of hostility and distrust of nature plays out once again in the seventeenth century.

In this scenario, the mind is continually attempting to assert control and look for solid ground in a world in which "the final authority" no longer seems fixed. The search for truth becomes almost an obsession. Women are perceived as being more mired in bodily functions (through giving birth and associated processes) than men; thus, the revulsion of a mind that felt betrayed by the senses and no longer sure it could trust personal experience found a scapegoat in women. Women and nature were a kind of labyrinth *en malo*—full of snares and treachery. No wonder the straight and narrow path to God through reason was favored over the entanglements of the sensory world, passions, and the material body.

Bordo compares the "characteristic" thinking of the Middle Ages and Renaissance to that of a child still young enough to enjoy immersion in immediate experience and a permeable boundary between herself and the world. It is unlikely that such a total "mythic" immersion still existed so long after Plato had turned the labyrinth into a metaphor and championed philosophy over myth, but certainly the "split" became more pronounced in the seventeenth century. Medieval Christianity was strongly Neoplatonic (and Aristotelian), and the pursuit of science throughout the Middle Ages and the Renaissance would not have been possible without a capacity for abstract thinking. Thus it is unlikely that the mind/body split associated with Descartes can be isolated as neatly to the seventeenth century as Bordo claims. The medieval mind was already caught between Neoplatonic Idealism and Aristotelian empiricism, with the latter gradually gaining ground. The Catholic Church was no champion of the material world, since its brand of spirituality emphasized the next world over and above this one (and devalued the passions, as Hatab points out). Its church labyrinths were not for pleasure but rather for guidance and the avoidance of eternal damnation, a preoccupation shared by seventeenth-century religious minds.

A retreat into the mind makes a sensuous immediacy problematic, since objectivity calls for analysis and logical thinking, not immersion in lived experience. The world becomes increasingly inert and lifeless as the observer withdraws from it, which likely accounts for some of the cheerlessness in *The Pilgrims Progress* as a spiritual guide to the labyrinth of the world.

During the Enlightenment, the unicursal labyrinth thus became a metaphor for a disembodied journey devoid of any physical dimension. While the mazelike world itself is perceived as treacherous, offering sensory experience that is untrustworthy, there is a longing for certainty (along with considerable doubt that it can be obtained) provided by the mind alone. Hence, the seriousness with which discrimination and personal choices are viewed by Cervantes, Bunyan, and other writers of the period is understandable.

Labyrinths Made of Letters

If the world was untrustworthy, there was still the possibility of exerting control through the intellect; the intellectual challenge posed by word puzzles thus explains their popularity in the seventeenth century. The use of calligrams and cryptographs was common, especially in Germany, Spain, and Portugal. They often represented an approach to hidden spiritual knowledge contained not only in the content but also in the labyrinthine arrangement of the writing (the letters and words themselves). A poem might have several centers, for example, or be designed so that it could be read in many different ways, depending on the point at which one entered the puzzle. Word puzzles were not new to the Baroque and Enlightenment; they had been around for centuries (Peyronie, "The Labyrinth" 701). What was new was the alacrity with which poets and puzzle designers took up the labyrinth and began to use it overtly as a test of spiritual and intellectual acumen. The variety of ways in which the puzzles could be read also points to a growing awareness of the difficulty of ascertaining a final "truth," although the desire for it was greater than ever.

The days of leisurely wending one's way through the tangled pathways of box hedge and buckthorn were passing; getting lost was no longer in vogue. As mazes outgrew their popularity in the late eighteenth century, the forms of the labyrinth grew more abstract. The emphasis tilted toward the challenge to the mind and spiritual fortitude, and the labyrinth's physical dimension slowly vanished into thin air—literally. It reappeared in one of the least tangible art forms, that of music.

The Wall of Sound, Labyrinth-Style

Musical labyrinths can be labyrinthine by virtue of a retrograde melody (proceeding in one direction and then in reverse), tonal complexity, unexpected combinations of notes, dissonance, the appearance and reappearance of intertwined musical motifs, or the psychological state they induce in the listener (Wright 233-35, 253-55). Some musical labyrinths addressed themselves specifically to the legend of Ariadne, Theseus, and the Minotaur, expressing the story in music. Besides Johann Sebastian Bach and Wolfgang Amadeus Mozart, other composers such as Antonio Caldara (1670-1736), Johann Fischer (1670-1746), George Frederick Handel (1685-

1759), Pietro Locatelli (1695-1764), and Peter Winter (1754-1825) also created musical labyrinths.

Musical motifs based on the "journey and return" theme in the labyrinth went back as far as the Middle Ages. A musical motif called "retrograde motion" was often used by composers to suggest a journey and return such as one would experience by following the path of a church labyrinth into the center and out again. The labyrinth represented the going in and returning of Christ on three different occasions: his descent from heaven to earth and back again; his journey from life to death and back to life; and his journey into hell to liberate the souls languishing there before returning with them to heaven (Wright 106-11). An example of retrograde motion in action is the well-known musical theme built on the motif of a warrior-like Christ called "The Armed Man" (Wright 175). This melody appeared in numerous Masses in the Middle Ages and carried out the theme of "turn and return" in the arrangement of the notes, which were sung in one direction and then reversed. The symbolism of the music was obvious to the medieval listener, who readily equated it to the theme of the labyrinth with the victorious Christ as Theseus (Wright 166-74). (An example of this tune adapted from a Renaissance version appears on The Christmas Revels's *Sing We Now of Christmas* as "L'Homme Armé.")

Another simple form of musical labyrinth is the type based on the *tonus peregrinus* ("wandering tone"), a melody that may have originated in ancient Palestine in the time of King David. It made its way into Byzantine liturgy and from there into the Roman Catholic Church, which featured it in liturgical music at least as far back as the ninth century (Wright 234-35). It was the customary musical accompaniment to Psalm 114, which tells of the wandering of the Jews in the desert after leaving Egypt. The melody does not have a clear tonal "base," and because of this the tune seems to wander, creating a sense of uncertainty in the listener that parallels the experience of the wandering Jews. This song was sung by medieval clerics as they crossed the church labyrinths during Easter celebrations; it is the same song, as Wright points out, that is sung by the souls approaching the shore of Mount Purgatory in *The Divine Comedy*: " '*In exitu Isräel de Aegypto*' " (*Purg.* 2.46).

Musical tastes changed with the coming of the Renaissance. Music began to reflect emotions and themes "realistically" rather than "symbolically," with melodies, volume, and rhythm all communicating joy, sorrow, turmoil, or whatever the occasion called for (Wright 160). This monumental shift in the history of Western music coincided with the "secularization" of the labyrinth, so that beginning in the sixteenth century, not only did garden mazes, puzzles, board games, and textual labyrinths become popular as amusements, but musical labyrinths appeared that were no longer tied to the Mass or sacred liturgy (following on the heels of a few musical "labyrinths of love" from the medieval period). From relatively

182

simple beginnings in sacred music, the creation of musical labyrinths took on bolder and more complex forms.

Unusual Musical Excursions

By the seventeenth and eighteenth centuries, the musical theme of the labyrinth was carried out in increasingly esoteric and technical ways. In the *El Carlos* canon (written for King Charles II of Spain), composer Juan del Vado included eighty-two shorter pieces within a larger, circular canon; the challenge was to find them all. Del Vado also included a Mass to accompany this canon called *El Laberintho* (Wright 248).

Another musician, Wolfgang Caspar Printz (1641-1717), created retrograde motion in a canon that was very challenging to perform, so that the musician who completed it could be likened to Theseus; the feat involved mastering a section in which one violin was forced to play eleven measures backwards. As for the symbolism of this extreme exercise in musicianship, Wright says there is none: "there is no symbolism, just process. This maze is a brain-teaser designed to test the powers of concentration of the [violinist]" (Wright 254).

As the eighteenth century wore on, the concept of a "maze" in musical compositions took on the spirit of a joke or riddle to be solved by a clever musical insider. Even a new form of scale, nearly complete by Bach's time, used the labyrinth metaphor as its symbol (Wright 255). A number of composers incorporated a labyrinth into their compositions by using elaborate successions through keys.

J. S. Bach (1685-1750) wrote his 1705 composition, *Kleines Harmonisches Labyrinth* ("Little Harmonic Labyrinth"), as a piece with three sections: Introitus, Centrum, and Exitus. Both Introitus and Exitus feature a great deal of dissonance, which is absent in the Centrum, thus recapitulating the psychological dimensions of a labyrinth (Kern 244-45; Wright 261-62). Wright adds that because of its three-part structure imitating the nature of a maze, Bach's work is the mostly truly labyrinthine musical composition of the time. In addition to this piece, he also wrote other pieces that qualify as musical labyrinths because of their elaborate progressions of key: *The Well-Tempered Keyboard* (1722 and 1742) and the *Canon per tonos* from *The Musical Offering* (1747). Both works begin and end in the key of C after an exhaustive progress through the chromatic scale (Wright 260-61).

Mozart's *The Magic Flute* was based on knowledge of the Freemasons, of which Mozart was a member, and used the initiation rite of that society as the basis of its plot, in which a hero must face diabolical enemies in order to become king. Wright points out the similarity of this story to other myths of kings undergoing an underworld experience— Gilgamesh, Theseus, and even Jesus (266). After Mozart's death, his librettist, Emanuel Schikaneder, decided to write a follow-up to *The Magic*

Flute called *The Labyrinth* (1798). This piece, with music by Peter Winter, used the plot from *The Magic Flute* to create a sequel in which the lovers, Tamino and Pamina, are forced to undergo the terrors of a labyrinth in order to triumph over it.

The Labyrinth Goes Underground

Wright states that musical labyrinths, along with their cousins the church labyrinths and garden mazes, lost popularity in the nineteenth century and vanished from view (270). Perhaps they were not always referenced explicitly, but labyrinths as symbols were far from invisible. Although the labyrinth made fewer overt appearances in the nineteenth century, it did not disappear. Banished, due to different fashions in landscape design, the labyrinth no longer appeared in gardens and parks. However, it was still evident as metaphor in the twists and turns of the new detective stories written by Edgar Allen Poe and in the Gothic adventures of such novelists as Charlotte Brontë (Peyronie, "The Labyrinth" 702, 706).

In the eighteenth century, the maze had become increasingly abstract as it was transformed into a mental game or puzzle. The nineteenth century was a different story. There the labyrinth came to symbolize the struggle between the known and the unknown and the successive shedding of narrative mysteries as one crept closer to a central truth or moment of recognition. *Moby-Dick*, the great American novel from this time period, offers a plot full of whirlpools, knots, and hazards at sea that demonstrates how the theme of individuation, demonstrated in Ishmael's struggle to confront his own (and his society's) shadow, appears in connection with the labyrinth. In the detective story or Gothic novel, a labyrinth is a devious mystery with many twists that requires mental agility to be solved; it is frequently the labyrinth *en malo* that a protagonist tries to escape by means of perseverance and intelligence. The reasons for this shift to the labyrinth as plot and their ramifications for the history of epistemology are the subject of Chapter 5.

Chapter 5
God Has Left the Building

And now Gringolet stood groomed, and girt with a saddle
gleaming right gaily with many gold fringes,
and all newly for the nonce nailed at all points;
adorned with bars was the bridle, with bright gold banded;
the apparelling proud of poitrel and of skirts,
and the crupper and caparison accorded with the
saddlebows:
all was arrayed in red with rich gold studded,
so that it glittered and glinted as a gleam of the sun.

— J. R. R. Tolkien, *Sir Gawain and the Green Knight*

One stiff blind horse, his every bone a-stare,
Stood stupefied, however he came there:
    Thrust out past service from the devil's stud!

Alive? he might be dead for aught I know,
    With that red gaunt and colloped neck a-strain,
    And shut eyes underneath the rusty mane;
Seldom went such grotesqueness with such woe;
I never saw a brute I hated so;
    He must be wicked to deserve such pain.

— Robert Browning, "Childe Roland to the Dark Tower
Came"

The Disappearing Labyrinth?

Commentators such as Craig Wright believe that the labyrinth

disappeared from view in the eighteenth century and did not emerge again

until the 1990s at the beginning of the labyrinth revival (Wright 271). This

might be a valid assessment if we are considering only structural labyrinths,

such as hedge mazes, but the archetype of the labyrinth lived on through

the nineteenth and early twentieth centuries as a literary motif, sometimes

187

invoked specifically and other times hidden in a labyrinthine plot or setting. Moreover, according to André Peyronie, the nineteenth century yielded the most important development in labyrinth literature apart from the Renaissance. Whereas the Renaissance labyrinth broke with the spiritual, mythical, unicursal labyrinth, the nineteenth century broke with the very notion of the center being the goal (719). (That break is still significant in postmodern treatments of the labyrinth, which often replace the quest for the center with the search for the way out. In postmodern treatments of the labyrinth, a way out is sometimes possible, although at times the attempt is futile.)

In nineteenth-century literature, the labyrinth often appears in a negative light, as a prison or a trap from which it seems there is no escape. In Romantic literature, the labyrinth frequently takes the form of a castle or a forbidding Gothic mansion (as in *Jane Eyre*); elaborate underground passages, however, eclipse the aboveground structure as a symbol for what is hidden by surface appearances. Novels in which sewers or catacombs appear as labyrinths were one stage of this kind of treatment, as in Victor Hugo's novels of Paris (Peyronie, "The Labyrinth" 703). Dreams as labyrinths were also a common device, used to foreshadow or mirror the other actions of the novel. The city as labyrinth emerged as another common theme, whether explicitly stated or not. Detective stories (beginning with Poe in 1842) featured labyrinth-like mysteries that could be solved by the detective hero; despite their grim and sometimes lurid tales of crime and passion, treatments of this type were sometimes more "optimistic" than more modern appearances of the literary labyrinth because they championed reasoning and deduction as effective keys to solving or finding a way out of the puzzle (Peyronie, "The Labyrinth" 703-06).

Some modern critics question the authenticity of "labyrinths" when they consist of plots or settings whose features merely suggest a labyrinth: many twists and turns, complexity, periods of darkness and great peril, a difficult journey to a decisive goal, and a return. Some would argue that it is too easy to see labyrinths everywhere when one applies the term to structures or motifs that are merely "labyrinth-like." However, we have seen that even in classical and medieval times the concept of the labyrinth was well established as a literary and metaphysical concept, sometimes specifically named and sometimes only inferred. The labyrinth is at the same time a *nekyia*, an adventure, an initiation, a night-sea journey, a wasteland, a hero's journey, and (from a design perspective) a mandala. It corresponds to Campbell's outline of the hero's journey, pervasive in mythic material of all kinds, as a departure, road of trials, initiation, and return (*Hero* 245-46).

While we have been examining the labyrinth as a model for approaches to knowledge that define each successive age, it has a timelessness and archetypal integrity that make it recognizable in the different guises it assumes across the ages. It need not be a horizontal structure, as we have seen, but may easily exist in a vertical plane. It may be the scene of a ritual observance or the setting for frivolity and pleasure; it may be admired or feared. It may exist as a physical structure, or it may be invisible to the naked eye, known only by its effects on those wandering within it. It may be a forest, a palace, a wasteland, an underground passage, or a sea journey. In the end, what defines a labyrinth is the experience it engenders, the complexity of the path, the roundabout way to the goal, the feeling of frustration (or exhilaration, depending on the labyrinth). While it is sometimes a trap, it is frequently the way to freedom, whether this lies in finding the center or is accomplished by returning to the starting point. In a labyrinth, the way is winding and deceptive, and disorientation occurs time and again; another constant associated with the literary labyrinth is the expectation that the labyrinth, if not fatal, changes the individual who journeys through it. A person is not the same on the other side of a labyrinth as she was before venturing in, and the changes may be quite profound, as literary examples demonstrate.

Worlds Apart

The contrasting worlds illustrated by *Sir Gawain and the Green Knight* in the fourteenth century and Robert Browning's "Childe Roland to the Dark Tower Came" (1855) in the nineteenth century reveal very clearly the difference between a labyrinth experienced by an individual immersed in Christian myth and one who has experienced the loss of that myth. By Browning's time, the world of faith in Western Europe had been severely shaken by scientific discovery, industrialization, and the loss of traditional religious values. Childe Roland wanders in a wasteland that offers no end except death; while the trappings of old myths appear (the knight, the quest, and the wasteland), they have been rendered meaningless by the emerging "secular" myth. Loss of faith robs the symbols of their numinous power, and they now stand silent and empty—"the tower," for example, is dark, with no beckoning light.

Sir Gawain, on one hand, cheerfully wends his way through a luminous world of fearsome but magnificent green knights, magical beheadings, holiday feasts, heroic quests, mysterious castles, and amorous ladies with a sense that although his peril is great, succor is always near. Danger is given meaning and is encompassed by the greater spiritual powers that support and surround the world Gawain moves in. For this reason, he makes his way towards an apparent appointment with death with bells on his harness, fine apparel, and a sense of adventure. The presence of unseen support is always with him.

Childe Roland, on the other hand, stumbles through his quest in a twisted and charmless wasteland. There is certain peril ahead, but its form, as well as the point of the entire exercise, is only vaguely imagined. The landscape is tedious and ugly. Childe Roland retains the wit to mock himself and his circumstances and makes a brave stand, but his action is more like bravado than triumph. He will go down swinging, but he's not even sure why he's fighting. He lives in a world in which the empty shells of former myths loom like haunted ruins; the new myth posits a hostile universe that offers no answers or possibility of understanding. Roland is much like Descartes at the time of his "bad dreams." He is unable to find a strong center or anything that holds firm. His plight is similar to that of another nineteenth-century man, Matthew Arnold, who laments in "Dover Beach": "we are here as on a darkling plain / Swept with confused alarms of struggle and flight, / Where ignorant armies clash by night" (lines 35-37).

In "Childe Roland," we witness the specter of an ashen and unforgiving labyrinthine world. This dark and apocalyptic vision of a wasteland is the mirror opposite of the medieval Grail Quest and the Adventure of the Green Knight, in which meaning is not only profoundly spiritual but taken for granted. Roland stumbles through a stunted landscape in which even purported "guides" are suspect, motivation is muddied, and the goal, when reached, offers ambiguity rather than resolution. Like Sir Gawain, Roland finds himself on a quest he cannot avoid, for reasons that are inscrutable, and whose ending appears to offer nothing but bitterness. But unlike Gawain, whose adventure takes place against the backdrop of brilliant jewel tones during a merry Christmastide, and the Grail knights, who encounter supernatural visions and mysterious helpers at every turn, Roland struggles alone in a dim, rusty, and menacing landscape whose loneliness is exceeded only by its utter lack of charm.

Roland mentions that the road from which he departs is a "safe road," but it is one that apparently leads nowhere in particular. Its main virtue seems to be its predictability and the ease with which it is followed. This part of his journey resembles a unicursal labyrinth of unthinking allegiance to the old but worn-out verities that still govern the unexamined lives of many of his fellow men. Roland chooses to leave this path to step into the trackless waste. He is in a maze as soon as he leaves the road, having decided that to face his fate, even if death it must be, is more desirable than a meaningless round of existence:

> Nor hope rekindling at the end descried,
> So much as gladness that some end might be.
>
> For, what with my whole world-wide wandering,
> What with my search drawn out through years, my hope
> Dwindled into a ghost not fit to cope. (Browning 17-21)

Roland symbolizes the truth of Jung's assertion, in "Psychology and Religion," that liberation from common wisdom and striking out on one's own is, while potentially rewarding, also extremely hazardous and difficult (*CW* 11: 144-45). In Browning's poem, the protagonist finds himself on a thankless errand. The reminders of lost faith mock him, and unlike the knights on the Grail Quest, he is without a clear purpose. Roland's uncertain way takes him through a wasteland whose ugliness mirrors his alienation, a condition that is the lot of all his fellows as well, whether they know it or not.

Browning's saga of Victorian doubt and hopelessness reflects an age when the loss of religious certainty and the rise of science as a godless replacement created an attitude of nostalgia for a receding past no longer in reach. In his introduction to *The Major Victorian Poets: Tennyson, Browning, Arnold*, William Buckler writes that the Victorians "were acutely aware that they had inherited a psychologically and spiritually dismembered world . . . They knew intensely, soulfully, that some force had been set in motion that had shattered into a million atoms the coherence of the Christian era" (xi). The impetus to which Buckler refers was the Renaissance, with its humanism and emphasis on science and the inquiring mind.

It is ironic to consider that what began with an explosion of new ideas, a spirit of discovery, and a flowering of creativity inspired by the legacy of ancient Greece spelled the beginning of the end for a sense of unified purpose and meaning in Western civilization. While the Renaissance is rich in artistic images inspired by Greek and Roman mythology— celebrated in paintings, sculpture, architecture, and literature—the same exuberant spirit of humanism that characterized these artistic productions eventually led humanity (at least in the West) to see the limitations of the myths it had been living by. In Arnold's terms, the Victorians had a "sense of want of correspondence between the forms of modern Europe and its spirit, between the new wine of the eighteenth and nineteenth centuries, and the old bottles of the eleventh and twelfth centuries, or even of the sixteenth and seventeenth" (qtd. in Buckler xi). The heady Enlightenment period led to a cultural inflation and identification with the gods that was followed inevitably, as Edinger tells us, by a period of alienation as the gods (or God) lost their power and the West lost its connection to a sense of something greater than itself (*Ego* 52). Rick Tarnas describes the situation this way:

> in the aftermath of the Enlightenment, the modern understanding is gradually so transformed that the world is no longer seen as a locus of pregiven meanings and purposes, as had been true not only in the immemorial primal vision but also for the ancient Greeks, medieval Scholastics, and Renaissance Humanists. With the full ascension of the modern mind, the world is no longer informed by numinous powers, gods and goddesses, archetypal Ideas, or sacred ends. It no longer embodies a cosmic order of meanings and purposes with which the human self seeks to be aligned. (20)

Rather than leading man to God, the unicursal labyrinth of early Christian and medieval philosophy now came to be seen as a trap that led to an empty center. The gods had fled, and there was, with the rise of the "godlike" individual and the spirit of inquiry fueled by many scientists and thinkers working independently, a growing sense that a shared spiritual reality was a thing of the past. The great thinkers and philosophers tested and argued their own theories, institutionalized existential loneliness, and fractured the monolithic structure that had been Christianity.

From this standpoint, Roland's cheerless wasteland can be seen as the somber successor, centuries later, of the sureties of the world of *Queste del Saint Graal, Sir Gawain and the Green Knight*, and other Arthurian tales in which Christian (and non-Christian) images swirl together in a rich and numinous tapestry of meaning. Christian and pagan myths support, challenge, and interpenetrate one another in the Arthurian landscape, creating an enchanted world with multiple layers of significance. Roland, by contrast, faces a struggle unto death that he fears may have no meaning at all.

Thus, Gawain rides "bewildering ways" (Tolkien stanza 29) to seek the Green Knight, but he moves with greater clarity of purpose through his labyrinth than does Roland. His handsome and gaily appointed horse Gringolet carries him faithfully, representing support from sources other than Gawain's own ego. The horse Roland encounters in his wanderings, on the other hand, is sad and paltry, its thinness making Roland want to lash out at it, certain that "He must be wicked to deserve such pain" (line 84), a highly uncharitable view of things that reveals Roland's tortured state of mind, projected onto the animal. This horse symbolizes the weak psychic resources of a warrior bereft of a sustaining myth. Gawain, on the other hand, calls freely on Christ and the Virgin Mary for support. Fear he is familiar with, but not hopelessness. Indeed, we are told that he rides "merrily," even to his appointment with death. It is the lack of similar aid and the coldness of a hostile universe that crushes Roland's spirit and makes his ordeal so dreadful.

Riding Into the Labyrinth

Both Roland and Gawain cross the river of death, the symbol of an underworld journey, for a showdown with dark forces. Indeed, Gawain's fate initially seems more certain, since, by the law of knightly honor, he must accept the blow of the redoubtable Green Knight with no chance to defend himself (Tolkien stanza 20). Nevertheless, Gawain's situation, though perilous, never seems as terrifying as Roland's because the magical atmosphere in which Gawain moves suggests that he is not alone, that forces other than his own will are at work. Roland, by contrast, faces an unknown menace in a world seemingly bereft of purpose. He is a broken and stumbling hero who must make his stand alone, except for the silent presence of ghosts seen "in a sheet of flame" (line 201) and the mocking witness of an ominous black bird Browning calls "Apollyon's bosom-friend" (line 160).

The contrasting poems offer two final actions with two different outcomes: Roland holds his slug-horn to his lips, and Gawain bears his neck. One act is defiant, the other passive and humble. Gawain acts out the scene that has been set for him, while Roland (almost like a modern jazz musician) appears to improvise. As Joseph Campbell suggests in *Occidental*

Mythology, an age that has lost its gods and its certitudes forces an individual to find his own meaning—and in that very act, heroism lies (4).

Gawain's trial takes the form of a game, begun at Arthur's court, continued at Bertilak's hall, and finished at the tryst at the Green Chapel. "Game" in *Sir Gawain* could be another word for "labyrinth," with its "bewildering ways" and sudden reversals; it is, however, a game with clear (if unyielding) rules that Gawain is clearly able to discern. Roland, on the other hand, is forced to stumble blindly, unsure of what the rules are or even if any exist. Gawain's labyrinth has a structure, and if the path is confusing, he at least has signposts and guidance; Roland has none.

Browning invokes the mythologies of the past in the labyrinthine journey of his poem, using many of the same symbols that appear in Arthurian tales: the hero, the horse, the threshold, the wasteland, the river, and the tower. He simultaneously implies the inadequacy of the old symbols while subtly invoking their archetypal qualities. The wasteland is a potent image of modern alienation and the sterility of life divorced from mythic sensibility, later used to great effect by T. S. Eliot in *The Waste Land*. Whereas the Grail hero initially encounters the wasteland as a maze hiding the key to salvation, Roland encounters an endless nonentity, a sprawling and inexplicable no-man's land that captures the emptiness and squalor of the new industrial age. The symbols of the past are present, but they are now ominously silent.

At the center of all is the Dark Tower. The tower traditionally symbolizes vertical aspiration, the Christian movement toward transcendence and spirituality, the axis mundi connecting heaven and earth, which we saw previously in Dante. It is a symbol for the hero's journey, an "ascensional myth" that includes a return. But Roland's tower is dark, indicating that the lights have all gone out on the Christian myth. There is no connection to divinity or anything larger than a hardscrabble struggle, and what remains is a confrontation with the unknown. Roland's friends have preceded him in this same battle and failed to make the best of it; like the Athenian youths preceding Theseus, they have been devoured by the Minotaur (though in "Childe Roland" the identity of the antagonist is hidden).

Gawain and Roland are at different points on the same historical continuum. Gawain is protected by the myths he lives by. Roland's task is harder—his struggle is the inevitable result of moving out of a dying cultural myth on the way to a new one not yet established. Whatever symbols still exist are merely a mocking commentary on the emptiness of the old myth and offer little to sustain hope. The period is haunted by a dispiriting belief in nothingness born of the collapse of the previous system. Browning intimates that a newer and better myth may never be established, that all myth and illusion are at an end.

At the climactic opening of the battle, we wait to see what Roland will do in the encounter. At the last moment, there seems a sudden possibility that *he* will be the knight to redeem the wasteland. Mario D'Avanzo believes that "Childe Roland attains a nobility in just such a final act of dauntless defiance and triumph over evil, fate, and despair. His resistance makes him a Prometheus" (699). Does the final meaning of Roland's act lie in just that same defiance of a cold, dark universe? There is a kind of beauty in the jaunty attitude Roland's gesture exemplifies at this climax. Is it nothing more than bravado, or is the wasteland of modernity waiting to be revivified by the outcome of this battle? If so, what form will this rejuvenation take?

The poem stops shy of answering these questions, drawing the curtain on Roland and his defiant horn. Roland has reached the center of his labyrinth and found his Minotaur (unseen to us and therefore more unsettling), but whether he will survive the encounter or not is in doubt. There is no promise of a return journey for Roland once the battle is over. In this modern take on the labyrinth, the hero finds his own way through a sinister maze, without any ready guideposts, and success is very uncertain. Browning seems to believe there is no real freedom to refuse this quest unless one is to continue in ignorance of his true situation, that the journey is the unavoidable fate of humanity in the existential hell that constitutes the universe. One is reminded of Borges's "The Library of Babel," in which the universe extends endlessly and monotonously in all directions, full of portents but no real answers (51-58). While in a certain sense, there is a similarity between Browning's wasteland, Borges's library, and Herman Melville's open sea in *Moby-Dick*, Melville's vision is less despairing because it offers a spiritual dimension to the visible universe, an undercurrent of meaning that lies beneath the waves and within the heart.

The Labyrinthine Sea

Moby-Dick, first published in 1851, specifically invokes the labyrinth of Theseus and the Minotaur, in a passing but nonetheless portentous image. Ishmael, who has just received a terrible fright when he discovers that his roommate at the Spouter-Inn is a cannibal, has had the presence of mind to judge his new companion as a good man, appearances to the contrary.

Concluding that it is better to "sleep with a sober cannibal than a drunken Christian" (Melville 36), Ishmael has been rewarded with the soundest sleep of his life. Chapter 4, entitled "The Counterpane," reveals that on awaking the following morning, Ishmael is surprised to find that Queequeg's arm is stretched over him "in the most loving and affectionate manner."

> You had almost thought I had been his wife. The counterpane was of patchwork, full of odd little parti-colored squares and triangles; and this arm of his tattooed all over with an interminable Cretan labyrinth of a figure, no two parts of which were of one precise shade—owing I

suppose to his keeping his arm at sea unmethodically in
sun and shade, his shirt sleeves irregularly rolled up at
various times—this same arm of his, I say, looked for all
the world like a strip of that same patchwork quilt. Indeed,
partly lying on it as the arm did when I first awoke, I could
hardly tell it from the quilt, they so blended their hues
together; and it was only by the sense of weight and
pressure that I could tell that Queequeg was hugging me.
(Melville 36-37)

Ishmael says that this episode reminds him of another one that occurred

much earlier in life and left a lasting impression. As a child, banished early

to his room for a minor infraction, he suffered the discomforts of an active

child forced to endure many daylight hours in bed. Having passed the

greater part of his imprisonment in sulky resentment, he has fallen into an

uneasy sleep, only to awaken in darkness to a terrifying sensation:

Instantly I felt a shock running through all my frame;
nothing was to be seen, and nothing was to be heard; but a
supernatural hand seemed placed in mine. My arm hung
over the counterpane, and the nameless, unimaginable,
silent form or phantom, to which the hand belonged,
seemed closely seated by my bedside. For what seemed
ages piled on ages, I lay there, frozen with the most awful
fears, not daring to drag away my hand; yet ever thinking
that if I could but stir it one single inch, the horrid spell
would be broken. I knew not how this consciousness at
last glided away from me; but waking in the morning, I
shudderingly remembered it all, and for days and weeks
and months afterwards I lost myself in confounding
attempts to explain the mystery. Nay, to this very hour, I
often puzzle myself with it. (Melville 37-38)

What is too frightening for a child's psyche to comprehend takes on a

different complexion for an adult. Ishmael goes on to say that, taking away

the fearful, supernatural aspect of his childhood experience, the effect of

Queequeg's arm over his on the counterpane has a similar, though more benign, strangeness. As the two events are strongly linked in Ishmael's mind, we conclude that the earlier experience—hallucination, dream, or vision—prefigured the later event. The almost instantaneous friendship and connection the two men feel for one another and the strange way in which Queequeg eventually saves Ishmael's life have the character almost of fate.

Ishmael's problem, suggested by a few lines describing a difficult early life, originates in his life as an orphan, cut off from his roots. For him, rescue begins with Queequeg, who becomes his roommate and then his friend and close companion. Initially, he is frightened and repulsed by this outlandish figure from another world—quite naturally, since Queequeg represents his shadow, the free, nature-loving, primordial man that Ishmael as a "civilized man" has repressed. Queequeg is the Minotaur inside the labyrinth. Because he is already on the fringes of society, Ishmael is perhaps more open to Queequeg than he would be if he himself were an accepted, fully integrated member. His journey through the labyrinth takes him back to nature, saving him from the alienation that wreaks so much havoc for Ahab. As Merton M. Sealts, Jr., says of Ishmael, "we learn with him how Captain Ahab had projected his rage and hate upon one particular White Whale, and we begin to understand as well how Ishmael came first to share and later to distance himself from Ahab's obsession" (65).

Ishmael's education starts early in the novel, before the sea voyage even begins. He starts out with no ties and no connections. His voyage is psychological as well as physical, since he comes to know himself through his connection with Queequeg and the larger society of the ship. He learns to see his own humanity reflected in the Other and gradually enlarges his sense of self to take in the primitive, uncivilized, but natural qualities therein. He comes to know and face down his own savagery and finds a way to salvation by opening himself to nature in a way that Ahab cannot.

Paul Brodtkorb, Jr., describes our perceptions of Queequeg, the other harpooners, and Fedallah as men of nature, spontaneous and unconscious, based on our observation that they are unhampered by the thinking that comes between natural, spontaneous action and civilized, overly refined man. In situations of mortal peril, where others are paralyzed, they are able to act quickly and appropriately, in part because, as natural men, they do not fear death as others do. "For Queequeg, it is no more than a trifle, to be accepted if it is convenient and rejected if it is not" (Brodtkorb 670). Brodtkorb observes that while men such as Queequeg and Fedallah are not at all feminine in aspect or bearing they have qualities of subtle understanding and intuitive awareness that are as close to being feminine as men can be. "Their natural grace allows them to seem part of the rhythms of nature, but it is also a sign of their distance from us [civilized people]," Brodtkorb contends, adding, "They are always outside of us; as Queequeg's hieroglyphics, and Queequeg himself, remain" (670).

This may be true for the observer who does not enter into Ishmael's view of things, but as for Ishmael himself, his close connection to Queequeg bridges the gap that Brodtkorb finds insurmountable. Queequeg is explicitly associated with nature, the female, and the labyrinth, even by a commentator who doubts our ability to get beyond an external view of the unknowable Other. Brodtkorb does not identify these reactions as projections, seeming instead to believe these others are too different from us to ever be known as anything besides "bits of animate nature . . . forbiddingly of a piece" (670).

The closeness between Queequeg and Ishmael and the yin-yang nature of their friendship is indicated not only by the terms in which Ishmael describes their physical closeness at the Spouter-Inn ("You had almost thought I had been his wife") but also in a passage in Chapter 72 ("The Monkey-rope"). Ishmael describes the tricky and highly dangerous business of cutting up and bringing in the whale, which befalls Queequeg, as harpooner, to carry out, while balancing on the whale's back in the water. His lifeline is Ishmael, standing on the deck of the ship, to whom he is connected by the "monkey-rope" attached at either end to the belts of the two men:

> So that for better or for worse, we two, for the time, were
> wedded; and should poor Queequeg sink to rise no more,
> then both usage and honor demanded, that instead of

cutting the cord, it should drag me down in his wake. So, then, an elongated Siamese ligature united us. Queequeg was my own inseparable twin brother; nor could I any way get rid of the dangerous liabilities which the hempen bond entailed. (Melville 255)

The umbilical thread that connects Queequeg to safety on the ship is the same thread that could pull Ishmael to his death. In reflecting further on this circumstance, Ishmael understands that it is not only Queequeg to whom he is connected in this way, but to every other human in a vast net of mutual dependency and need. No longer the lone wolf, Ishmael has enlarged his view of himself to include relationships that extend outward in various directions. He is now caught in a web of relations, a web that resembles a labyrinth. This passage foreshadows the connection that ultimately leads to a descent into the whirlpool by both men, followed by Ishmael's "rebirth."

Forms of the Labyrinth in Moby-Dick

Very noticeable in Melville's work is the preponderance of spirals, coils, and circles, appearing everywhere from Queequeg's tattooed skin, to coils of rope, to whirlpools, to Ahab's doubloon, to the zigzag nature of the sea voyage itself. A description of Queequeg hard at work on his erstwhile coffin (which becomes his sea-chest) connects the intricate designs Queequeg engraves on its surface with the labyrinthine designs tattooed on his skin. At this late juncture of the novel (the description appears in Chapter 110, "Queequeg in his Coffin"), Melville poetically reveals the

origin and meaning of the elaborate tattoo Queequeg received at the hands
of an artist from his native island, who included in the design:

> a complete theory of the heavens and the earth, and a
> mystical treatise on the art of attaining truth; so that
> Queequeg in his own proper person was a riddle to unfold;
> a wondrous work in one volume; but whose mysteries not
> even himself could read, though his own live heart beat
> against them; and these mysteries were therefore destined
> in the end to moulder away with the living parchment
> whereon they were inscribed, and so be unsolved to the
> last. (Melville 366-67)

At the end of this description, Melville has Ahab stare in frustration at
Queequeg's tattooed person, as if he realizes its profound significance but is
completely unable to read it. Melville might have added that although
Queequeg does indeed perish, and though the markings on his sea-chest
may not replicate exactly those on his skin (as no work of art can perhaps
ever duplicate in full the complex windings of the human soul), his riddles
have not gone completely unread. Just as it is Queequeg's sea-chest that
ultimately saves Ishmael's life during the sinking of the Pequod, it is
Queequeg's humanity that has communicated itself to Ishmael and remains
inscribed on his heart. Unlike Ahab, a "grey-headed, ungodly old man,
chasing with curses a Job's whale round the world" (Melville 158), a man
whose obsession with vengeance distorts his view of things, Ishmael
manages to cling to his humanity.

Starbuck, similarly imbued with a sense of the holiness of life and
the futility of Ahab's quest, is not as lucky as Ishmael in escaping with his

life. So although it is tempting to equate Ishmael's salvation with his moral and psychological growth (and in some sense, this is true), the loss of Starbuck and the courageous Queequeg are reminders that the mystery of life and death is not reducible to questions of who is deserving and who is not. Ahab is predictably destroyed by his obsession, but he takes the entire crew of the Pequod (save one) along with him. In Chapter 52, "The Albatross," Melville explicitly invokes the character of the labyrinth in describing the sea voyage, which is also the voyage of life:

> Round the world! There is much in that sound to inspire proud feelings; but whereto does all that circumnavigation conduct? Only through numberless perils to the very point whence we started, where those that we left behind secure, were all the time before us.
> Were this world an endless plain, and by sailing eastward we could for ever reach new distances, and discover sights more sweet and strange than any Cyclades or Islands of King Solomon, then there were promise in the voyage. But in pursuit of those far mysteries we dream of, or in tormented chase of that demon phantom that, some time or other, swims before all human hearts; while chasing such over this round globe, they either lead us on in barren mazes or midway leave us whelmed. (195-96)

With *Moby-Dick*, we are reminded that water, fluid and changeable as it is, can support a labyrinthine journey. (If we did not know this already, we need only consider the voyage of Odysseus, the "man of many turns," pushed and pulled in various directions on his long way home, never farther away from Ithaca than when he seems closest.) Melville hints that mazes may ultimately lead to nothing but bewilderment or worse, or, in the best case, take us back to where we started. But as Ishmael demonstrates, not every voyage need be as profitless as that. If a journey proves to be meaningless for some voyagers, it is only because they have their eyes closed.

Bainard Cowan points out that Melville was quite conscious of the symbolism of diving, of going "deep into the sources of the soul [to] face them" (226). Ishmael sees Queequeg dive from the ship to save someone else's life long before he takes his final, fatal plunge. In this, Queequeg prefigures the soul-searching task Ishmael must take on. Melville's first chapter suggests that the sea fascinates because it is the origin of life, and a sea journey takes us back to our source, both biologically and psychically. Ishmael recognizes this when he speaks of the almost universal desire to go to sea and the "mystical vibration" (Melville 19) most voyagers feel on first losing sight of land. "[Like Narcissus] we ourselves see in all rivers and oceans," he says (20). Whether life began in the oceans or not, to plunge into the depths is to plunge symbolically toward beginnings, back to the level of instincts and the unconscious. Entering this labyrinth means leaving land behind, moving away from civilization and back in time to a place where humans have not yet separated themselves from nature. If culture and civilization are humanity's highest achievements, they also involve a split from the natural world and in some ways a protection (at least in our minds) against its power. Out on the open sea, however, this protection shrinks to the flimsy confines of the Pequod, a bit of floating civilization that is "rather small if anything," in Ishmael's estimation (Melville 69).

The leviathan, Moby Dick, *is* nature. And though *Moby-Dick* is framed as a story of conflict between man and nature, one is struck by repeated references to the whale's wrinkled brow (Melville 138) and the wrinkled brow of Ahab (166), which come to be associated with one another in their implacability. Though Ahab believes he is struggling against an uncaring God and the cruelty of nature, his struggle is against a creature whose face in some way resembles his own. Outer reality and internal psychological truth parallel one another in *Moby-Dick*.

The Labyrinth Beyond the Mirror

In the first chapter of *Moby-Dick*, Ishmael speaks of the thrill one feels on leaving the sight of land for the first time. It is not only sailors, he says, but all humankind who experience the mystic pull of the ocean. He asks what accounts for the lure of the sea and goes on to observe that we see ourselves reflected in all bodies of water, as Narcissus did, seeing an image that is "the ungraspable phantom of life" and "the key to it all" (Melville 20).

The title of *Moby-Dick*'s first chapter is "Loomings," a nautical term referring to objects such as ships or land masses that are discernable—even though they are still beyond the horizon—under certain atmospheric conditions (Melville 18). This image of something barely glimpsed, seen by reflection and not in actuality, is another metaphor for the face seen in the water. To reach the land or ship whose image is seen, one must go beyond the place where the reflection first appears. To encounter reality is to take a radical journey beyond appearances, plunging below the surface, "beyond the looking glass," to the deep world of primordial truth. Even then, Melville implies, a person can never truly touch bottom and know everything there is to know (a point with which Jung would concur). Human beginnings and endings are both lost in obscurity. In Melville's labyrinth, one begins at the center, circles out on the voyage of life, and returns to the center at death, as in the sinking of the Pequod in the maelstrom.

Ishmael and the rest of the crew enter the labyrinth as hands aboard a whaling ship embarked on what would seem to be a routine journey were it not for the premonitions and strange warnings Ishmael receives ahead of time. The crew does not know it is bound for an extraordinary encounter, and Ishmael is unaware of the education that awaits him on Ahab's ship. Ishmael is certainly wiser by the novel's end, and his wisdom is the result of a very physical adventure that leaves him battered and bruised (wounding in a physical *and* psychic sense is a powerful teacher in *Moby-Dick*).

In classical times, the labyrinth was the measure of the hero's worth (as well as the measure of his shadow); in the Middle Ages, the labyrinth pointed the way to God (or to damnation); in the Renaissance, the labyrinth opened up to reveal a whole world awaiting exploration and human advancement in the arts and sciences; in the Enlightenment, it became increasingly mathematical and abstract in an age impatient with the myths of the past. In the nineteenth century, a time of growing religious uncertainty, the labyrinth reflects humanity's attempt to understand its own place in a world that might or might not be bereft of God. Moby Dick is the Minotaur in Melville's labyrinth, as elusive as the Holy Grail and as final as death. The ultimate question to be answered on this journey concerns the nature of the white whale, which is also the answer to the age's great existential question: is Moby Dick simply nature, is he the face of God, or is he humankind reflected back to itself—or is he all of these at once?

The spiral is conspicuously present in *Moby-Dick* in coils of rope, circling whales, and the climactic whirlpool that swallows the mariners of the Pequod. Tellingly, Moby Dick himself carries the image of a spiral in his flesh as the harpoons embedded there have the twisted pattern of a corkscrew (Melville 138). Edinger examines the spiral as a metaphor for the encounter with the unconscious that takes on the character of the final frontier in *Moby-Dick* (*Melville's* Moby-Dick 138-39). If the nineteenth

212

century was preoccupied with taking back its projections and discovering the extent to which its gods lived within, the unconscious (even before it had a name) was its natural hunting ground. The great whale himself represents both the possible origins of humankind in the sea and the end to which it returns in death (literally, in the case of the Pequod's crew).

Melville describes the breathing apparatus of the sperm whale as consisting of "a remarkable involved Cretan labyrinth of vermicelli-like vessels" (290); Ishmael later recounts wandering through the skeleton of a beached whale, which islanders have turned into a temple, in the manner of Theseus: "with a ball of Arsacidean twine, [I] wandered, eddied long amid its many winding, shaded colonnades and arbors. But soon my line was out; and following it back, I emerged from the opening where I entered" (346). Moby Dick's complexity as a symbol is echoed in these comparisons to the labyrinth, in which the whale is simultaneously the goal of the journey and a metaphor for the journey itself. Christopher Sten argues that Moby Dick, source of the precious oil for which the whales are hunted, represents the totality of God, "the inner source of light available to all. *This* is the ultimate boon, the discovery that the light of the soul, of truth, is within oneself, that the hero and the Father are one. Sun, whale oil, soul, and God—all are variations of the same principle of light and life" (417). This creature of the sea (the ancient home of life on earth?) carries within its body the same light we have associated with the Minotaur in its character as a primordial sun god.

Moby-Dick plays with images of the journey to consciousness as a maze. The Pequod weaves backwards and forwards, proceeding in anything but a straight line; it gets lost and goes off course in a wayward voyage that reflects the unpredictable process of exploring the unconscious. The labyrinth's Minotaur corresponds to the Other, the nonhuman world represented by the whale. And if the adventures of the Pequod's crew are mazelike in their overall form, they also involve the mandala, the circle of the globe crisscrossed by the ship that resembles the overall design of a labyrinth. The voyage creates a type of "Leonardo's knot," a mandala form that Purce describes as "manifold and complex" and "apparently baffling but made up of a single thread," so that "when unravelled it leads us, like the thread of Ariadne, to the heart of our nature" (plate 27).

The labyrinth as a mandala is related to the symbolism of the maze as a journey; it symbolizes roundness and totality and hence the Self. Edinger likens the alternating storms of alienation and inflation in the basic psychological process of growth to the image of the spiral in its repeated movement toward the center and out again (*Ego* 5). As one of humanity's oldest and most enduring symbols (first appearing in Neolithic cave drawings), the spiral carries intimations of eternity, birth, death, rebirth, and the inward journey toward consciousness and psychological development.

Queequeg, Starbuck, and Ishmael are in the whaleboat that sails to the center of the circling whale herd (Chapter 87, "The Grand Armada"), where they witness the wonders in the depths. The way in to the center is chaotic and dangerous; the men are threatened by panicked, churning whales on every side with nothing but a flimsy whaleboat and a few weapons standing between them and extinction. The clearness and stillness of the water at the center of the herd lets the men see what lies below— whales giving birth and about to give birth, a newborn whale still attached to the long thread of its mother's umbilical cord, and the amorous pursuits that will lead to yet more births. The creative urge toward new life is at the still-point, and Melville describes an amorous "dance" of the whales:

> And thus, though surrounded by circle upon circle of consternations and affrights, did these inscrutable creatures at the centre freely and fearlessly indulge in all peaceful concernments; yea, serenely revelled in dalliance and delight. But even so, amid the tornadoed Atlantic of my being, do I myself still for ever centrally disport in mute calm; and while ponderous planets of unwaning woe revolve round me, deep down and deep inland there I still bathe me in eternal mildness of joy. (303)

The witnesses of this circle of life are Ishmael, Queequeg, and Starbuck, the three men most likely to appreciate it: Queequeg because of his instinctive and natural openness, Starbuck because of his reverence for life, and Ishmael because of his willingness to learn. Nature responds with a transcendent glimpse of life-affirming beauty. If death is at the center of the whirlpool, so is life.

For Melville, epistemology is two-pronged: it is knowledge of oneself (growth in consciousness) and knowledge of one's place in nature. In the nineteenth century, a growing feeling of existential loneliness forced Western humanity to look within for answers. Unlike Browning, who seems to have concluded that the human race, for all its struggles, is ultimately alone in a wasteland that amounts to a cruel joke, Melville is more spiritual. *Moby-Dick* is a morality tale warning of the dangers of too much hubris: playing God is ultimately self-destructive, as Ahab finds out. There is something larger than any single man and larger than the human world as a whole.

Before Jung wrote about individuation, alienation, and inflation, Melville described these processes in *Moby-Dick*. In a world in which the old gods seem to be dead or dying, man comes face to face with himself as he confronts the need to take back his projections, come to know his own limits, and understand his relationship to whatever force encompasses his world—call it Nature, God, the Self, or the Other. Although Christianity may no longer hold the answers, Melville maintains a mystical sense of holiness and a reverence for nature, which he seems to believe is alive, if not with meaning, at least with a beauty that balances out its terrors. If nature is not the product of a transcendent God, it may still be godlike, and if its mysteries are beyond the ability of man to comprehend, they are nonetheless real and profound. Just as humanity sees itself mirrored in rivers and oceans, the human mind shares the characteristics of the ocean depths teeming with rich but unseen life. For Melville, the labyrinth of life is a rich, rewarding, but hazardous journey (for those alive to its meaning) toward knowledge of the self and Other (the nonhuman world).

Epistemological Quandaries

At this stage in the modern period, we discern three different attitudes toward what can be known. Browning's version, which despairs of being able to know anything at all, presents an image of profound existential anguish. While Matthew Arnold's "Dover Beach" (1867) presents a similarly despairing image of a "darkling plain" where "ignorant armies clash by night," in which there is no way of recapturing certainties formerly taken for granted, Arnold holds out hope that love can provide at least some solace for the loss of all else. In "Childe Roland," all is tragedy; even Roland's friends have all preceded him in death and offer nothing more to him during his hour of trial than their unseen presence. For both Browning and Arnold, the inability to know—to rely on certain knowledge—is a major cause of suffering. For Melville, there are necessary limits to what can be understood, but within such limitations there is all of nature to be explored. One's relationship to nature and one's place in the world are meaningful avenues of inquiry. Melville sounds very much like an environmentalist (before there was such a word) in his insistence that nature is to be respected, not subdued. While he maintains a belief in nature's unforgiving ferocity and a certain inscrutability, he also believes there is much beauty in the world and, even more importantly, that nature has its own laws and patterns. While the mystery of being may remain forever enigmatic, humanity has the ability, the right, and the duty to explore and come to terms with its place in this larger world.

While Melville explored the twin labyrinths of nature and the human psyche, other nineteenth-century writers treated the labyrinth differently, depicting it as a trap created by human agency. Rather than mystical/spiritual labyrinths, they imagined dark labyrinthine plots that required intelligence and fortitude of their protagonists, whose task was to solve the twisted puzzles created by other people. Here the labyrinth is composed of devious actions and motivations that entrap the innocent in a net of moral and/or physical danger.

Dark Labyrinth—The Spell of the Gothic

Another literary form in which the labyrinth emerged in the late eighteenth and the nineteenth centuries was that of the Gothic novel. This genre, satirized by Jane Austen in *Northanger Abbey* (1817), featured such conventions as a young and vulnerable heroine, a sinister mansion, a dark and brooding male protagonist, overtones of the supernatural, and an air of mystery. *Jane Eyre* (1847) is an exemplar of this type of novel; the plot is full of twists and turns whose contours, if diagrammed, would form a maze of gigantic proportions. Even when Jane triumphs at the novel's end, a price has been paid for her freedom; she does not escape the labyrinth unscathed, and even a happy ending is tempered by a bittersweet remembrance of darkness narrowly (and perhaps never completely) escaped. This type of ending is also found in Wilkie Collins's *The Woman in White*, whose protagonists endure a hellish series of abuses in a tangled web woven of the hidden motives and dark designs of other people.

Another type of labyrinthine novel, similar in some ways to the Gothic novel, is the detective story, whose invention (in short story form) is usually attributed to Edgar Allen Poe (Peyronie, "The Labyrinth" 706). Whereas the Gothic heroine relies on her wits and "spunk" to survive, the protagonist of the detective novel (often male) is primarily a logician whose application of reasoning supplies the thread that both guides him and serves to unravel the mystery. The work of Wilkie Collins spans both genres, serving as an early example of the detective novel and including a strong overlay of the Gothic mood. In *The Woman in White* (1859-60), Collins creates a heroine assisted by a male protagonist in the uncovering of a breathtakingly devious plot whose authors are evil and unscrupulous. Like *Jane Eyre*, the novel finishes on a note of sorrow co-mingled with a satisfying resolution and a righting of wrongs (with, however, the strong implication that some wrongs can never be made wholly right). The sense of wounding familiar to us from *Moby-Dick*, in which individuation and maturity are purchased at the price of scarring, is strongly present in Collins's story.

The opening lines of *The Woman in White* sum up the tale: "This is the story of what a Woman's patience can endure, and what a Man's resolution can achieve" (Collins 1). We are introduced to Walter Hartright, a young drawing-master who is caught up in events beyond his imagining when a friend helps him obtain a position in a wealthy household in Cumberland, near the Scottish border and far from Hartright's London home. At twenty-eight, Hartright is not in the first blush of youth, but he is unmarried and close to his mother and sister, whom he frequently visits. The novel opens on an ominous note, with Hartright describing a sullen and gloomy summer's end in London, his own low spirits and ill health, and financial straits that have forced him to curtail his usual holiday plans.

The kindness of his friend brings the unexpected windfall—Hartright is recommended for an enviable position as a restorer of drawings and a drawing-master to two young ladies at the distant estate of Limmeridge. In a bit of foreshadowing, presented ironically in the speeches of Hartright's friend Professor Pesca, the fateful opportunity enters the story just when Pesca is engaged in teaching the puzzled and uncomprehending daughters of his employer the intricacies of Dante's *Inferno*:

"We are all four of us down together in the Hell of Dante.
At the Seventh Circle—but no matter for that: all the
Circles are alike to the three young Misses, fair and fat, —
at the Seventh Circle, nevertheless, my pupils are sticking
fast; and I, to set them going again, recite, explain, and
blow myself up red-hot with useless enthusiasm, when—a
creak of boots in the passage outside, and in comes the
Golden Papa, the mighty merchant with the naked head
and the two chins." (Collins 7)

The Seventh Circle appears in Canto 12 of *Inferno* and is the abode of the

violent (and the place where Dante encounters the Minotaur). So

charmingly does Pesca skewer the characters of his employer and pupils

that the point is almost lost in the comedy. It is only with hindsight that the

reader understands the irony of this passage. The stolid, pampered pupils

are light years removed from any experience that could teach them the

horror of the Seventh Circle. At this stage, Hartright is as innocent in his

own way as the girls and their father; he is as much a stranger as they are to

the dark places Dante maps so vividly in *Inferno*. Yet it is a "round-about

way" of "winding paths" (Collins 12) that Hartright takes on his last

evening walk in the stifling London heat that leads him, in search of cooler

air, to an encounter with the woman in white whose story is the heart of the

mystery. Their meeting takes place near a crossroads, with the mysterious

stranger asking Hartright for directions. She is already lost in the labyrinth

that now begins to enfold Walter as well.

When Pesca enthusiastically mentions the name of his friend Hartright as the man for the drawing-master's job, he describes him as a genius. The papa immediately retorts, " 'Never mind about his genius, Mr. Pesca. We don't want genius in this country, unless it is accompanied by respectability . . . Can your friend produce testimonials . . . ?' " (Collins 8). In this passage, the gentleman puts his finger on the crux of the problem in the novel. A respectable exterior, connections, rank, and a good name are all perceived in English society as more desirable than personal merit. They are considered so important in themselves that a person possessing them needs no other passport in the eyes of society; these conditions are the equivalent of (or an adequate substitute for) character. In the events that follow, we see how the "rank," good breeding, social ease, and personal charm of Sir Percival Glyde blind most of his acquaintances to something troubling in his manners and behavior and the tragic consequences that follow on his ability to hide behind his name and position. In contrast, Walter Hartright (whose name is the first clue to his character) has all the imagination, artistic sensitivity, innate kindness, tact, courage, and strength of character that Glyde lacks but is held in little worth in the eyes of English society because he is not a nobleman.

Sir Percival has inherited the name of one of the worthiest of the Arthurian knights (in some versions of the Grail cycle, Perceval is *the* Grail

Knight, pure and unstained in every particular). In *The Woman in White*, Collins uses the name of the storied knight to chilling effect in connection with the character of Percival Glyde. From one perspective, the name is an ironic commentary on the failure of so many around him to "pierce the veil" of the mask he wears to hide his evil doing. In addition, the name— with its storied associations—being connected so ironically with a scoundrel points to the failures of the English class system. It is Walter Hartright, an innocent, who, like Sir Galahad in the tales of old, has just recently left his mother's society and embarked on a quest that will test him to the limits, who resembles the Desired Knight, not Sir Percival.

The class system is another of the certitudes the nineteenth century found shifting beneath its feet, a circumstance that left a society already reeling from the effects of scientific discoveries (Charles Darwin's *On the Origin of Species* had been published in 1858) and the loss of religious cohesion in a state of uncertainty. The atmosphere of the novel is not one of triumph over evil and a return to security but rather of melancholy and a sense of disaster narrowly averted by the determination of two people in the face of an uncaring world. Walter says at one point, "I thought I had my hand on the clue. How little I knew, then, of the windings of the labyrinth which were still to mislead me!" (Collins 372) and "I began to doubt whether the clue that I thought I had found was really leading me to the central mystery of the labyrinth, after all" (373). Later, he says of two of the conspirators, "Out of the dark byways of villainy and deceit, they had crawled across our path—into the same byways they crawled back secretly and were lost" (493). Walter and Marian escape the horrors of the maze that threatens to destroy them and their beloved Laura, but in the end that is their only triumph. The maze has nothing to offer them save a solution to the mystery and the rescue of their loved one from the insane asylum where she has been hidden. In a callous world, in which survival of the fittest seems to be the order of the day, Marian and Hartright outwit the villains and free Laura but do not succeed in regaining her stolen fortune (eventually she inherits Limmeridge when her uncle dies). The tone of the novel is not unlike that of Arnold's "Dover Beach." The speaker in that poem sadly concludes:

> Ah, love, let us be true
> To one another! for the world, which seems
> To lie before us like a land of dreams,
> So various, so beautiful, so new,
> Hath really neither joy, nor love, nor light,
> Nor certitude, nor peace, nor help for pain;
> And we are here as on a darkling plain
> Swept with confused alarms of struggle and flight,
> Where ignorant armies clash by night. (29-37)

The world has become a dark labyrinth beyond the hope of redemption in Arnold's viewpoint and perhaps in that of Collins as well. Unlike Browning, however, Collins and Arnold at least hold onto the power of love to cast a light on the darkness, as does the author of one of the most celebrated novels in Romantic literature, *Jane Eyre*.

While Arnold and Collins hold on to the hope that love can justify

existence (or at least provide solace in a darkened world), Charlotte Brontë

insists on it, creating an elaborate and thoroughly Gothic labyrinth of love

in *Jane Eyre* (1847). In this novel, love is all: the heroine negotiates the

twisting corridors of a brooding mansion much as she navigates the

corridors of her own heart and her troubled relationship with Edward

Rochester. As Naomi Schor describes the novel, it is a showcase of the

Gothic labyrinth:

> A poor, plain, but modest and plucky young orphan
> arrives before a sort of castle ruled by a master richly
> endowed with charm and power. In this castle, a veritable
> labyrinth full of traps, the young woman must face a series
> of trials and endure all manner of moral and physical
> suffering. . . . At one point, worn down by her suffering,
> the young woman leaves this damned and fascinating place
> for a sort of exile in the wilderness. In the end she returns
> to the castle and, having resisted the master's advances,
> ends up mastering him and becoming the mistress of the
> castle. (Schor 149)

In *Jane Eyre*, we meet one of the most memorable heroines in all of fiction.

Jane's intelligence is equal to that of any man (if not superior), but she is

also passionate, headstrong, and sensitive. She is the Ariadne to Rochester's

Theseus; literally, at the end of the novel, she leads the blinded Rochester

around his own garden. Unlike Ariadne, she has woven the thread herself,

using her own resources to find her way through the complications

provided by the existence of Rochester's first wife—the madwoman in the

225

attic—and a formidable romantic rival in the aristocratic Blanche Ingram. Even the name of Rochester's mansion, Thornfield Hall, suggests a tangled hedge of thorns from which escape is difficult. Thornfield is no delicately clipped allée of love, but rather a knot of trials and snares.

In the novel's opening lines, Jane describes "wandering" in the shrubbery outside her aunt's home on a cold, blustery day (Brontë 9), a beginning that suggests the labyrinth *en malo* and her own forlorn state as an unloved child. She fares no better indoors, and the lines she reads in Bewick's *History of British Birds* contain a quotation from the poet James Thomson—"Where the Northern Ocean, in vast whirls, / Boils round the naked, melancholy isles"—that echoes Jane's condition and suggests the inescapable vortex that threatens to swamp her (Brontë 10). Jane needs all of the resources at her disposal; as an orphan, she is abused and traumatized, surviving on strength of will and an inner refusal to be defeated. Later, as a young woman entering service as a governess at Thornfield Hall, Jane's quiet demeanor belies the fierceness and strength of character attained by surviving her ghastly childhood. Jane is penniless and nearly friendless but has great self-command and a heart that, despite its many sorrows, remains open. Her plain clothes and composed exterior disguise steely reserves of character.

Jane's first meeting with her new employer reveals much about the personalities of both Jane and Rochester. As Jane enjoys the country in the vicinity of Thornfield on foot, she encounters an apparition materializing out of the dusk. Horse and rider have passed her by when a patch of ice topples the steed and its rider onto the road. A brusque and irritated Rochester is forced to ask her for assistance in regaining control of his horse. In the end, Rochester must lean on Jane's shoulder while she leads him. In time, Jane's good sense and loving heart become the lifeline that helps Rochester escape the trap of his past. If Jane is Ariadne, holder of the guiding thread, she is also Theseus. Eventually penetrating the mystery of Thornfield Hall and finding the Minotaur at its center (which turns out to be the madwoman in the attic, Edward's wife), she escapes the dangerous maze of love only to return later, on her own terms. She leads Rochester, blinded and crippled, out of the labyrinth of his wrecked marriage and into a new life.

Even the joyful ending, in which Jane and Rochester are married, has a somber quality because of the losses both Jane and Rochester have suffered. Nevertheless, it is a happy ending, with Jane independently wealthy, Rochester partially recovering his sight, and the couple rejoicing over the birth of their first child. As in *The Woman in White*, a terrible struggle precedes the final happiness, a struggle motivated by love and rewarded in the end by the lovers' reunion and marriage.

What is remarkable about *Jane Eyre* is the strength of its protagonist, who proves to be a match for every labyrinth that entangles her. She refuses to stay with Rochester under any terms but honorable marriage, leaving Thornfield as penniless as she came to it. She avoids a loveless marriage with her cousin St. John Rivers, who presses her to accompany him on his missionary trip to India. She not only finds her way out of this entrapment, presented in the strongest terms by St. John as a Christian duty, but by rescuing herself, rescues Rochester also. Returning to him after the death of his wife, the ruin of Thornfield Hall, and his own disfigurement, she secures at last the loving marriage and fulfillment of her hopes. The labyrinth of love in this novel is a much darker one than the playful labyrinths in the European gardens of the Renaissance, but it, too, takes its place in the long history of the labyrinth as an erotic/sexual motif. When Jane determines to follow her heart instead of answering the cold sense of "duty" urged on her by St. John, her search for Edward takes her to his new manse deep in the woods, about which nature has fashioned a forbidding maze. It is Jane's final test:

> Even when within a very short distance of the manor-house, you could see nothing of it . . . Iron gates between granite pillars showed me where to enter, and passing through them, I found myself at once in the twilight of close-ranked trees. There was a grass-grown track descending the forest aisle between hoar and knotty shafts and under branched arches. I followed it, expecting soon to reach the dwelling; but it stretched on and on, it wound far and farther . . .
>
> I thought I had taken a wrong direction and lost my way. . . . I looked round in search of another road. There was none: all was interwoven stem, columnar trunk, dense summer foliage—no opening anywhere.

> I proceeded: at last my way opened, the trees thinned a
> little; presently I beheld a railing, then the house. (Brontë
> 431)

The novel ends with a description of the birth of Jane and Edward's first child and an account of the happy marriages of Jane's cousins Diana and Mary. In contrast, Jane's final description of her cousin St. John's single-minded devotion to his mission work drives home the contrast between the earnest Christian labyrinth chosen by him ("his is the sternness of the warrior Greatheart, who guards his pilgrim convoy from the onslaught of Apollyon" [Brontë 453]), a pilgrim's progress indeed—compared with the luxuriant labyrinth of love, passion, sentiment, marriage, and children Jane has chosen for herself.

As the nineteenth century gives way to the twentieth, the labyrinth continues to appear as a symbol for a confusing world with many possible choices. It eventually becomes an exemplar of the postmodern search for truth (or more precisely, *truths*) as an open-ended, multi-faceted, and contentious enterprise. It also continues to appear in the context of the labyrinth of love and even, at the end of the twentieth century, takes a surprising turn back toward the medieval tradition of church labyrinths, with a new, modern interpretation and use. Most of these variations of the labyrinth, along with their significance, will be explored in Chapter 6.

Chapter 6
Are We Having Fun Yet?

> That's just where it happened, in that last lighted room:
> Peter and Magda found the right exit; he found one that
> you weren't supposed to find and strayed off into the
> works somewhere. In a perfect funhouse you'd be able to
> go only one way, like the divers off the highboard; getting
> lost would be impossible; the doors and halls would work
> like minnow traps or the valves in veins.

> — John Barth, "Lost in the Funhouse"

The Search for Certainty

Each succeeding age formulates its characteristic concerns but may

at the same time continue to explore the preoccupations of previous times,

as Peyronie points out ("The Labyrinth" 686). Each of the eras we have

investigated thus far presents a different philosophical stance, but each one

exists, like an embryo waiting for its own time to be born, in the womb of

the preceding age. Peyronie understands the transformations of the

labyrinth as corresponding to changes in thought as the Western mind

moved out of the mythic and into the humanistic age. Until the

Renaissance, he believes, the labyrinth was perceived as an external object

or a place. With the movement "away" from myth, according to Peyronie,

the labyrinth is understood to exist within the mind of the individual ("The

Labyrinth" 719).

Whether we have truly moved away from myth as Peyronie

suggests is doubtful. New myths constantly arise without announcing

231

themselves as myths; "secular" myths are just as potent as religious ones. The importance of mythic themes and images never subsides, although the images themselves are in constant flux. The changing appearance of the labyrinth over time, from multicursal to unicursal and back again, from ritual, to structure, to artistic design, to plot device, to lived experience, demonstrates that the archetype endures. With a Hermetic fluidity, it is always finding new forms in which to appear, and the hero, the guide, the monster, and the maze live on, regardless of whether we name them as such.

If a mythology serves all of Campbell's four functions of myth—acknowledging a sense of the mystery of being, providing a coherent cosmology, structuring a social or cultural system, and providing a guide for psychological and spiritual well-being (*Masks of God: Occidental Mythology* 519-21)—it may live in the hearts and minds of a group of people for many years. But once it no longer serves all of these functions, cracks begin to appear in the edifice. Writing in the early twentieth century, Jung discussed the burden placed on the psyche as soon as former religious certitudes are shaken. Though himself a scientist and a product of the same Enlightenment that spawned Descartes, he turned his scientific scrutiny to the very topic the Enlightenment had done so much to discredit—religious belief. He took the reality of religious experience seriously and noted the predicament of modern man and woman, whose unacknowledged gods "have become diseases" ("Commentary on 'The Secret of the Golden Flower' " *CW* 13: 54). While a modern scientist—like one of Jung's patients, troubled by a series of dreams—fears or discredits uncanny experiences, human beings in an earlier time, immersed in the mythic world, took such experiences for granted. Moreover, Jung says, "Our modern attitude looks back arrogantly upon the mists of superstition and of medieval or primitive credulity, entirely forgetting that we carry the whole living past in the lower storeys of the skyscraper of rational consciousness. Without the lower storeys our mind is suspended in mid air" ("Psychology and Religion" *CW* 11: 56).

A basic issue here is the banishment of imagination as an honored presence. In place of imagination is the disembodied mind, suspended, as Jung says, and seemingly secure in its rational processes but in reality cut off from the stratum of life that birthed it, estranged from the phenomenal world of experience. There may be no demons to fear, but there are no angels to bless us, either. The sense of a living God (or gods) creates a very different experience of the world than does a godless universe. Whether we speak of monotheism, with its transcendent God, or pantheism, or polytheism, in which the gods, as James Hillman describes them in *Re-Visioning Psychology*, live in the processes and patterns of nature and human experience, a spiritual world is a qualitatively different world.

It was in response to rationalism that first Edmund Husserl and
then Maurice Merleau-Ponty, Martin Heidegger, and the existential
philosophers sought a way out of the trap created by the mind/matter split
that became a philosophical commonplace in the wake of Descartes's
"Cogito ergo sum." For these philosophers, the way out was, we might say,
down: down into the world of lived experience that is the original ground
of all other systems of thought and abstraction that have developed from it.

"Prior to all our verbal reflections, at the level of our spontaneous,
sensorial engagement with the world around us, we are *all* animists,"
phenomenologist David Abram declares (57). Furthermore, he reminds us
that it is not we alone who perceive the world and the other creatures in it:
we are also perceived by them in a kind of duet of interdependent
awareness that in essence calls forth the "sensible" (read: "sense-able")
qualities of each animal, plant, cloud, rock, and human being. Every
phenomenon in nature, including the human animal, is involved in this
interplay, which, far from confirming a determinate, mechanistic view of
things, reveals that careful attention (a receptive attitude toward the
experiences of the senses) not only opens up but actually *calls forth* the
qualities of the things we sense. The act of perception, in other words, has a
profound creative effect on what is perceived, and vice versa. A mythic
imagination is alive to this interplay and fosters it.

While the logical positivism of modernity (still influential among those who believe that if something cannot be measured it does not exist) and the relativism of postmodernity would seem to have stifled the old myths, it is only a matter of time before the myths hiding within *these* habits of thought are recognized and acknowledged as such. At present, it seems that the myth of Prometheus, the Titan most concerned with human affairs, has become the hero of the modern scientists and technological innovators, followed closely by Theseus, the hero capable of piercing the heart of the most confounding mysteries (while remaining somewhat blind to the whole picture).

The Rise of the Postmodern Labyrinth

After the appearance of the Gothic and detective novels, in which a sober psychological view of the labyrinth prevailed, an even darker turn pervaded appearances of the labyrinth in literature. While a sense of darkness clung to some of the nineteenth-century labyrinthine adventures that never entirely dissipated, the labyrinths themselves were not always inextricable if approached by literary protagonists with intelligence and resolve. In the early twentieth century—in anticipation of the shifting sands of postmodernism that followed World War II—literary works of a psychological or existentialist bent were frequently more pessimistic, as the works of Franz Kafka and Jean-Paul Sartre prove. Some literary labyrinths are presented as a writer's attempt to solve the mystery of his own

235

existence, as in Proust's *The Remembrance of Things Past* (1913-27) or Joyce's *A Portrait of the Artist as a Young Man* (1916) (Peyronie, "The Labyrinth" 707-09). Later on, postmodern literary labyrinths play with the nature of narrative itself, revealing that the illusion of a single story hides the possibility of multiple stories and multiple outcomes, as in Borges's "The Garden of Forking Paths" (1941) and John Barth's "Lost in the Funhouse" (1967). Borges is a central figure in the postmodern literature of the labyrinth, as is Umberto Eco, whose *The Name of the Rose* (1980) is a curiosity, a novel about a mazy labyrinth set in medieval times, centuries before the first multicursal labyrinth (as maze) was ever constructed.

The Anachronistic Labyrinth

Eco's *The Name of the Rose* takes place in a fourteenth-century Italian monastery, somewhere in the northern mountains. The novel is preoccupied with labyrinths of an announced and unannounced variety. The prologue to the book, an account by an unnamed narrator purporting to explain the "discovery" and "history" of the manuscript that tells the main plot, is rambling and filled with historical and literary minutiae. The introduction to the novel tells us that Eco was initially advised to condense the first one hundred pages, including this backstory, but that he refused, saying that the navigation of these pages served as an initiation to the rest of the novel (Lodge xiii-xiv). Thus, a preliminary labyrinth tests the mettle of the reader in advance of the even more convoluted labyrinth that challenges the wits of the "detective" monks in the narrative of Adso of Melk.

Eco's protagonist, William of Baskerville, is a learned Franciscan monk of about fifty years of age who has been charged with a diplomatic mission that takes him to a wealthy Benedictine abbey at a time of great political turmoil within the Church and the region. With William is a young Benedictine novice, Adso, who is serving as his assistant and scribe. Eco makes an allusion in William's name to a certain resemblance his character holds to Sherlock Holmes, Arthur Conan Doyle's resourceful and observant detective, who put his genius for reasoning to the test in "The Hound of the Baskervilles," among other adventures. Adso, the eager and devoted companion, bears some resemblance to the loyal Dr. Watson, who accompanies Holmes on most of his detecting triumphs.

The original purpose of William's visit is soon overshadowed by a series of murders at the monastery. As William tries to fulfill his diplomatic obligations while attempting to solve the crimes that begin to pile one on top of another, Adso gets a chance to observe his mentor's methods of reasoning close up. William is a firm believer in the power of rational philosophy and logic, and his ability to tease out implications from facts is dazzling. It is apparent, however, that someone is staying several steps ahead of William to cover up the crimes. At the heart of the abbey (and the heart of the mystery) lies the abbey's magnificent library, a beacon of scholarship and learning that houses a dangerous secret. The library is in the form of a maze, with a bewildering series of interlocking rooms to which few have access. The presence of this maze in a fourteenth-century monastery is one of Eco's historical jokes—no mazes existed at that time in Europe, when the first hedge mazes had yet to be built and the unicursal labyrinth was the emblem of Christian teachings. Eco has planted a very modern symbol of the search for truth in the midst of a medieval monastery that has its iron hand firmly locked on "truths" to be dispensed. The control of "truth," or whose version of truth prevails, is at the heart of the political and social turmoil that constitutes the background of the plot and brings William and Adso to the abbey in the first place.

The abbey's blind "unofficial" librarian, Jorge of Burgos, along with head librarian Malachi and his assistant Berengar, are the keepers of the secret of the labyrinth, which William is expressly forbidden by the abbot to visit, even though the first murder victim may have fallen from one of the library's windows. Jorge's name is another of Eco's literary jokes, as it refers to that other great twentieth-century explorer of literary labyrinths, Jorge Luis Borges. The abbot tells William at the outset that the library's design is intended to protect the unwary from dangerous knowledge that might ensnare them in heresy. In an ironical turn, this labyrinth does not represent heresy, as was often the case with medieval literary labyrinths; instead, it is a means of "locking down" heretical material and protecting the faithful from it. The idea of knowledge being kept under lock and key does not sit well with William's humanistic faith in learning, but the abbot is firm, as revealed in the following exchange:

> 'So in the library there are also books containing falsehoods. . . .'
>
> 'Monsters exist because they are part of the divine plan, and in the horrible features of those same monsters the power of the Creator is revealed. And by divine plan, too, there exist also books by wizards, the cabalas of the Jews, the fables of pagan poets, the lies of the infidels. . . . And therefore the library is a vessel of these, too. But for this very reason, you understand, it cannot be visited by just anyone. . . .'
>
> 'And so no one, except for two people, enters the top floor of the Aedificium. . . .'
>
> The abbot smiled. 'No one should. No one can. No one, even if he wished, would succeed. The library defends itself, immeasurable as the truth it houses, deceitful as the falsehood it preserves. A spiritual labyrinth, it is also a terrestrial labyrinth. You might enter and you might not emerge.' (Eco, *The Name of the Rose* 48)

This labyrinth is impenetrable to those without and inextricable to anyone who might manage to get in. It is no surprise that with cleverness and patience, William and Adso eventually do get in, discover the lost second book of Aristotle's *Poetics* (a treatise on comedy), uncover the reasons for Jorge's determination to hide the book, and learn the reasons for the murders. This knowledge is only obtained, however, at the cost of the library's destruction, more deaths, and William's disillusionment. As David Lodge points out in his introduction to the novel, *The Name of the Rose* breaks with the tradition of the detective novel in leading not to a resolution of difficulties and a righting of wrongs but instead to a tragic

conclusion. While the detective novel, as we have seen, relies on an

optimistic view of man's ability to reason, Eco reveals that William's

reliance on reasoning is the cause of his downfall and the destruction of

much that cannot be replaced:

> In the debate between Jorge and William, therefore, immutable dogma is opposed to open-minded enquiry, and fear to laughter. To prevent William, and posterity, from reading Aristotle's dangerous treatise on comedy, Jorge first attempts to eat it, then to burn it, and this action sets fire to the library, and eventually destroys the whole monastery. . . . William derives no satisfaction from solving the mystery of the murders, and in opposing the tyranny of prescriptive orthodoxy he finds himself questioning the existence of order in the universe, and therefore of God. Along with his anticipation of modern liberal values he encounters the philosophical downside of modernity—the possibility that there are no solid foundations for any belief. (Lodge xxii-xxiii)

In this postmodern work, a fourteenth-century Franciscan and admirer of

Aristotle is pitted against a hater of Aristotelian philosophy and humanism

who is willing to kill to keep the fear of God instilled in the populace. It

looks very much like a clash of Platonic and Aristotelian philosophies and

not the harmonious blending we saw in the Gothic cathedrals of the period.

The shattering of William's faith in reason is also the shattering of his faith

in God. Leaping forward across the centuries, William takes his place beside

modern humans searching for meaning in a world where old systems of belief no longer work and the tools of the intellect sometimes create tragic outcomes.

Although William, whose quick intellect shines a light on dark places throughout the novel, is the undisputed star of Eco's tale, his broken disillusionment at the end casts doubt on who really has the last word. Adso, as narrator, records William's bitter summing up of the adventures they have shared at the abbey: " 'I behaved stubbornly, pursuing a semblance of order, when I should have known well that there is no order in the universe' " (Eco, *The Name of the Rose* 550). William has realized that the "apocalyptic pattern" he descried in the series of murders (and which he used to solve them) was not the true one, but rather one that he imposed on events. Instead of providing a path to the truth (though it led him to Jorge it also led to the destruction of not only Aristotle's book but the entire abbey), it provided a thread for the diabolically clever Jorge to "string him along" and entrap him in his own mental labyrinth. When Adso questions William about his conclusions, asking if seeing chaos in the universe is not the same as admitting the absence of God, William has no reassuring answer. For William, the labyrinth has led to a conclusion he had not anticipated. The abbey falling to ruins around them echoes the effect of the implacable logic that has brought William to a loss of faith not only in God but also in his cherished tools of reasoning.

Adso is not William's intellectual equal. At the novel's end, he is an old man, remembering his youth and the time he spent with William as distant events. He once attempted to piece together his own version of truth by revisiting the ruined abbey and saving scraps and fragments of old books and manuscripts he managed to pull out of the debris. He tells of his eventual success in identifying some of the works by deciphering a sentence or two, and of seeking out the works he has identified so as to read them in their entirety. Although he says he has concluded that it was chance, not design, that led him to these works, he admits that they have been as precious to him as if they were "an oracle," without his understanding whether they truly have any significance other than what he has attributed to them:

> I have almost had the impression that what I have written on these pages, which you will now read, unknown reader, is only a cento, a figured hymn, an immense acrostic that says and repeats nothing but what those fragments have suggested to me, nor do I know whether thus far I have been speaking of them or they have spoken through my mouth. But whichever of the two possibilities may be correct, the more I repeat to myself the story that has emerged from them, the less I manage to understand whether in it there is a design that goes beyond the natural sequence of the events and the times that connect them. And it is a hard thing for this old monk, on the threshold of death, not to know whether the letter he has written contains some hidden meaning, or more than one, or many, or none at all. (Eco, *The Name of the Rose* 559)

Although Eco seems to leave Adso in the same ungrounded place William occupied after the abbey's destruction, Adso's stubborn clinging to the scraps of wisdom he has saved and his tendency (against his better judgment) to believe there is a kind of destiny in them leaves the door open to other conclusions. While reason alone has not been successful in leading William or Adso to satisfactory answers, the possibility remains that the last word is really hidden elsewhere in the novel, like a sacred word quietly contained in the acrostic Adso describes.

A Clue Hidden in Time

Some of the most beautiful language in the novel occurs in a much earlier chapter. Having previously penetrated the labyrinth in the library with William, Adso, out of curiosity, has gone back on his own to look at some of the books. Overwhelmed by what he sees in the books (in which he detects labyrinthine designs even in the illustrations), he is overcome by an increasing sense of mental confusion and disorientation. Adso stumbles out of the labyrinth and into the kitchen below to clear his head. He is surprised to discover that he is not alone there; an impoverished girl who has come to the kitchen for scraps of food is hiding there. Although Adso, in recalling the incident, couches it in terms of sin, a temptation he failed to avoid, it is obvious that at the time his experience of sex with the girl was a sacred experience; Lodge refers to the "ecstasy of erotic and romantic love" in the incident (xviii). Although Adso is almost immediately overcome with remorse and shame, he has been profoundly changed by the experience in ways that he does not seem to fully appreciate. He confesses to William, who advises him not to worry too much about what has happened. Freed from his anguish over the breaking of his vow by his confession, Adso begins to think of the incident in a different light. While he tells us that already the physical union has begun to fade in his memory, what he remembers is infinitely more vivid: "my soul had not forgotten her face, and could not manage to feel that this memory was perverse: rather, it throbbed as if in that face shone all the bliss of creation" (Eco, *The Name of the Rose* 313). The experience has transformed Adso and opened him to the beauty of life in a way none of his previous experience has managed to do. He discovers on looking around him that nature, too, has been transformed:

> I saw her in the branches of the bare tree that stirred
> lightly when a benumbed sparrow flew to seek refuge
> there; I saw her in the eyes of the heifers that came out of
> the barn, and I heard her in the bleating of the sheep that
> crossed my erratic path. It was as if all creation spoke to
> me of her . . . It was, now I am trying to understand, as
> if—just as the whole universe is surely like a book written
> by the finger of God, in which everything speaks to us of
> the immense goodness of its Creator, in which every
> creature is description and mirror of life and death, in
> which the humblest rose becomes a gloss of our terrestrial
> progress—everything, in other words, spoke to me only of
> the face I had hardly glimpsed in the aromatic shadows of
> the kitchen. (313-14)

The heightened language used here is unequalled in all the labyrinthine reaches of the novel. It is Adso's experience, not William's. It occurs in the middle of the action, and murders, political intrigue, plotting, injustice, fire, calamity, and madness are still to come. Adso himself, as an old man, has all but discounted his experience as morally wrong. It is not clear, however, whether Adso's re-interpretation of his experience is one we should accept. The incident shines with tenderness and an aching beauty that is unmatched by anything else Adso witnesses at the abbey. The Church to which he, at the end of his life, still gives his allegiance is the author of many of the horrors Adso chronicles, including the death of the innocent girl who made such an impression on him.

Adso stumbled out of the labyrinth in the Aedificium and into an encounter with the girl in the kitchen. The meeting is unexpected, and the timing of the incident, which goes unremarked by Adso, is passed over casually; and yet, one is struck by the confusion and terror that leads Adso to escape the library as a trap, in contrast to the quietly ecstatic vision with which he beholds his surroundings after his meeting with the girl. It is as if the real truth in the twists and turns of the monumental events is not to be found in the books, the political disputations, or even the beauty of philosophical argument. It takes a poetic eye and an open heart to catch a glimpse of this truth, the mysterious and "unlawful" power of love. Adso's path, while he daydreams of the girl, is "erratic"—he is caught in a labyrinth of love.

Adso's experience is similar to the experience of the three men in the whale boat—*Moby-Dick*'s Queequeg, Starbuck, and Ishmael—who are given a rare glimpse of beauty within the circle of whales that shelters

mothers giving birth and pairs of whales mating. In this vision, it is the

principle of creativity behind life that drives the cycle of mating, birth, and

death—and so it seems to be with Adso. In his own "erratic path" (Eco,

The Name of the Rose 313) he cannot escape the vision of Creation he has

been given and cannot avoid drawing a spiritual conclusion: "I said to

myself that the world was good and admirable" (319).

A Maze of One's Own

Lawrence Durrell's 1947 novel *The Dark Labyrinth* is one of the

most explicit postmodern treatments of the labyrinth story from the Greek

original. Durrell's story is placed in Cefalù on the island of Crete in the year

1947. A group of tourists on a cruise is offered an opportunity to explore a

recently opened cave purported to be the actual labyrinth of legend.

Although they are warned of the dangerous condition of the cave, which is

subject to rock falls, a group of them elects to take on the adventure; it is

also revealed in an aside that one character, Baird, who does not go on the

excursion, had operated a guerilla warfare operation out of the labyrinth

during World War II and knew parts of it well. The tourists are a disparate

group and include an English nobleman/poet, an eccentric medium, a

young convalescent woman, a married couple, an abrasive Christian

missionary, and a flamboyant, amoral artist. Rumors about a monstrous

beast and stories about the disappearance of previous expeditions do little to dampen the interest of the tourists, who are unaware that their own journey is fated to be disastrous.

Following on the heels of World War II, this story of a cross-section of English society brought together by fate to a holiday-turned-disaster has an archetypal quality that befits its setting. These survivors of a battered nation represent the condition of modern humanity adrift on a sea in which the truths of the past have been shaken loose by the calamities of two world wars, not to mention the revolutions (scientific, industrial, and social) of the preceding century. Viewing the labyrinth adventure as just an exciting addition to their holiday, the party is surprised to learn that the myths of the past still have power, manifested in unexpected ways. The very setting of the labyrinth in a cave connects the present to a prehistoric past in which the tradition of the labyrinth originated.

The lure of the labyrinth is described by the *Europa*'s purser as an almost universal attraction to the carnival-esque prospect of being lost in the dark for a short period of time:

> Death and holiday-cruises, he thought, were things that no amount of explaining could reconcile; and he remembered how nearly he himself had been tempted to join the party that had set off from the ship's side on that fine spring morning. The word "labyrinth" suggested something at once terrifying and enticing. What was it? At the old Wembley Fun Fair there had been a water-labyrinth. You sailed through the darkness in a small boat, passing at last through a corridor of mirrors and lighted panoramas. (Durrell 19-20)

When a rock fall kills the party's local guide, the labyrinth becomes just as much a psychological adventure as a physical one and turns into a different experience for each member of the party. In this postmodern (but still mythic) world, the labyrinth contains a multitude of narratives and is not bound by any one of them. Lord Graecen, who has come to Crete knowing he may have only three months to live, escapes the labyrinth with relative ease when he stumbles onto a fissure that opens out on a hillside above the home of his friend:

> he had blundered out on to the back of Cefalû, in full sight of the house he had come to die in. Graecen was trembling all over at the narrowness of his escape. He sat on a rock drinking in mouthfuls of the blue air, tasting the scent of the thyme, watching the blue race of the sea beneath the house. Never had the world seemed so desirable a thing. (Durrell 170)

Graecen, an expert in antiquities, has, ironically, come to the labyrinth in a professional guise to assess whether some statues and other remnants of the "City in the Rock" are genuine. He has just had time to examine them (seeing among them a statue of a winged man with a boy, suggesting Daedalus and Icarus) and determine that they are genuine when the cave-in separates him from the rest of the party. Knowing that he is fortunate in being closer to the entrance than the others, he is attempting to retrace his steps when he stumbles on the shortcut. His escape suggests two things. The labyrinth has released him because, with his own impending death, he is closer to penetrating its secrets than any of his companions. In addition,

248

while coming out of the labyrinth, he sees not only the house "he has come to die in" but also the beauty of the idyllic Greek landscape, bursting with life. In the face of his own death, he tastes life to the fullest.

In the labyrinth, Miss Dombey, the missionary, becomes the first of the tourists to die. Panicking over an unresponsive companion, whom she presumes dead, she is unable to form a plan of action. In her final hour, she thinks back over her life and can remember no redeeming episodes; when she attempts to pray, she realizes that she may never really have believed in God, though her life has been devoted to bringing others to the Christian faith. After hearing muffled sounds that the party had earlier attributed to "the Minotaur," she takes an overdose of sleeping pills. In a stream of memories that forms as her life is ebbing away, she remembers her father, a beloved figure who was as kind and wise as Miss Dombey is hostile and uncharitable. These memories reveal the secret tragedy of Miss Dombey's life: she never recovered from the long-ago loss of her cherished father. At the last moment, Miss Dombey realizes that in her mind "in some vague way the Second Coming had been designed as a plot to bring him back" (Durrell 189). Only in her final moments does Miss Dombey come to know herself. "It was in the shadow of this immense Imago that Miss Dombey fell asleep at last" (189). For Miss Dombey, the labyrinth leads inexorably to the one thing she had always avoided: self-knowledge.

The medium, Fearmax, comes to his senses shaken and confused but has the presence of mind to locate his torch and attempt to find a way out. As an intellectual, he is calmed by his thoughts, imagining the article he will write based on his experience in the labyrinth. Once a sought-after medium, he has lost contact with the spirit with whom he had the longest relationship. Like Miss Dombey, Fearmax is mourning a loss, and when he sees Miss Dombey's footprints in the tunnel, he attributes them not to the living woman but to his lost French Marie.

Fearmax has studied paranormal phenomena for years. His work has earned the respect of not only the public but other great minds of the day. He does not know himself, however, and all of his research simply leads to empty corridors, like the labyrinth he wanders in: "as the corridors multiplied and ramified, stretching away into infinity, he became despondent. How could one find anyone in this maze? It was possible, too, that he was only going in a circle" (Durrell 190).

Fearmax makes his way into a cavern open to the sky and realizes that it is only the lack of a rope that prevents him from escaping. He has no Ariadne's thread to guide him out of the labyrinth of his own mind, by which he is led deeper into the maze of mysticism instead of out of it. What began as an intellectual labyrinth is now an actual one with endless passages and tunnels. Fearmax becomes unhinged as his mind fills with thoughts of French Marie, the spirit wife, lover, (and mother?) that Fearmax has sought

250

for so long. When Fearmax takes the sinister, unpromising tunnel instead of the one leading to fresher air, it is as if he has surrendered to his own unconscious. His final fate is mysterious, since he seems to have descended into madness: he believes he is being carried off in a "soft wet mouth of enormous dimensions" (Durrell 197).

Virginia Dale and the artist, Campion, find a way out of the labyrinth to a place of apparent safety, which turns out to involve a difficult choice. They have climbed onto a rocky ledge from which there is no escape except by diving into the sea three hundred feet below. Campion and Miss Dale decide to take their chances after spending one night on the ledge. We are not privy to Virginia's thoughts, except in what she says to Campion, but, for all her simplicity, she seems to have a greater appetite for survival than the famous artist, who has spent most of his life escaping one domestic situation or relationship only to move on to another. When he teases Virginia about whether is it worth going back to their lives or not, she grows impatient with his cynicism: " 'I suppose you're afraid,' she said, and added hastily, 'I don't mean of the jump, but of the world. You oughtn't to be. A great artist should have some control over the world. Not be bowled over by small worries' " (Durrell 211).

Campion has come to understand himself as lacking a moral sense, searching selfishly and in vain for novel places, situations, and women. Miss Dale, who has already suffered the loss of her fiancé in the war and the breakdown of her own health, knows more about true suffering than the artist and also has a greater will to live. After the jump, it is revealed that Miss Dale survives with a broken leg. She is rescued by monks who saw her fall from the sky, in a comic scene that turns the tables on the myth of Daedalus and Icarus. Campion has not been found by the end of the story.

The final members of the party, the Trumans, discover the surprising identity of the Minotaur. Hearing the noise of a large creature moving near them, they prepare to confront it with weapons only to realize it is a terrified cow, lost in the labyrinth just as they are. Following it down a tunnel, they emerge with it into the blinding light of day and find themselves in an Edenic paradise of meadows, fruit trees, blue sky, and towering mountains.

They eventually discover that while they are truly in paradise, it is an inescapable Eden: they are surrounded by sheer cliffs. And they are not alone: a previous survivor of the labyrinth has been living there alone since the loss of her companions. While stunned by the beauty of their surroundings, the Trumans have an initial difficulty in accepting their predicament.

Unlike most of their fellow tourists, the Trumans are self contained and intent on enjoying life, despite their personal sorrows. Having a readiness to embrace life, they adjust to their situation, finding an amiable companion in their new friend. They have slipped through a crack into another myth, that of the Garden of Eden. Their companion puts into

words the reason for her contentment in this unlooked-for situation:

> "Man as a person looking for what I think I've found. The
> search throws up bright bits of gold and information
> which catch his attention and prevent him from looking
> deeper into himself. . . . And yet every activity leading back
> like an arrow on the map to central metaphysical problems
> of the self. The wars of factories, of diplomats, of
> concepts—all hopelessly entangled in the opposites that
> created them." (Durrell 250-51)

The Trumans embark on an adventure in which getting to know themselves

on a basic human level seems not a regression but rather the possibility of a

better future. A lost wisdom rooted in nature appears as an unexpected

possibility in a century rocked by world wars and other calamities of

modern life.

A Postmodern Labyrinth Master

A very different postmodern take on labyrinths—as infinite,

inextricable, and often meaningless—is espoused by Jorge Luis Borges. In

Labyrinths: Selected Stories & Other Writings (1962), Borges explores labyrinths

from a number of perspectives that often, in their very openness, lead by a

kind of trick into a feeling of limitation and entrapment—the labyrinth *en*

malo. Of particular interest in this context are three short stories: "The

Garden of Forking Paths," "The Library of Babel," and "The House of

Asterion." The first of the three is one of Borges's better known works, a

meditation on metaphysics, parallel realities, and despair, in which a

German spy, Yu Tsun, murders Sinologist Stephen Albert in order to communicate in code the name of the city the Germans are to attack. Far from being an enemy of Yu Tsun, Albert is actually a stranger, though by a strange twist of fate, he is the translator of Yu Tsun's ancestor's mysterious and illustrious work, "The Garden of Forking Paths." Rather than being an actual labyrinth, like the path Tsun takes to Albert's home, in which turning left repeatedly is the way to the goal, the labyrinth turns out to be a book. Albert has penetrated its secret after years of study, revealing that the obscure and unreadable manuscript is the author's attempt to illustrate the truth of parallel realities such that all outcomes are possible. In one version a man dies; in another, he lives; in another, he never existed. Albert explains this to Tsun, who is stunned by the revelation that not only is Albert an expert on the work of his great-grandfather but that he alone has penetrated its secret and revealed its true audacity and brilliance. Thus Tsun is caught in a remarkable trap of his own making; in the very hour that he meets the erudite professor and learns the secret of his ancestor's genius, he kills Stephen Albert in order to relay a message to the government in Germany, a country he despises. Tsun thereby seals not only Albert's fate but his own, a certain outcome of death. The labyrinth of knowledge opens and closes immediately on Tsun, who discovers that knowing the truth is no salvation from it.

In "The Library of Babel," Borges presents a universe arranged as an unending series of hexagonal rooms in a vast library. One can neither escape this library nor find the solution to the secret of the universe in it. Though infinite, it offers no meaning. Any book that is possible has already been written. One can neither decipher the relation of one book to another nor divine his own reason for existing among all of these books. There is "knowledge" in abundance, but all of it is useless. Borges envisions a special cadre of librarians called "inquisitors," roaming the hexagons and looking for a truth they are doomed never to find:

> it was also hoped that a clarification of humanity's basic mysteries—the origin of the Library and of time—might be found. It is verisimilar that these grave mysteries could be explained in words: if the language of philosophers is not sufficient, the multiform Library will have produced the unprecedented language required, with its vocabularies and grammars. For four centuries now men have exhausted the hexagons . . . There are official searchers, *inquisitors*. I have seen them in the performance of their function: they always arrive extremely tired from their journeys; they speak of a broken stairway which almost killed them; they talk with the librarian of galleries and stairs; sometimes they pick up the nearest volume and leaf through it, looking for infamous words. Obviously, no one expects to discover anything. (Borges 55)

Borges adds, almost unnecessarily, that their lack of success has led to depression and despair.

In his most direct approach to the Greek myth, "The House of Asterion," Borges tells the story of the labyrinth from the viewpoint of an unlikely character—the Minotaur, who is revealed to be both lonely and bored. He dreams of hosting another Minotaur, another Asterion, so that he can show him the multitude of rooms and galleries that form his house—which is not, like the Library of Babel, an inextricable affair, merely one that is large and complicated. Shy about his appearance, Asterion rarely ventures into the world outside, though he insists that his palace is not a prison. He is simply disturbed by the fear his appearance arouses in outsiders.

Asterion is illiterate but intelligent. He longs to be relieved of his huge palace of rooms, which he describes as "the same size as the world." He describes the coming of the Athenian contingent every nine years as his occasion to "deliver them from all evil." Apparently, they die of fright at the very sight of him, "without my having to bloody my hands." One of these visitors informed the Minotaur that a redeemer would one day come to him, which gave the Minotaur hope that he might at last be taken to a more comfortable abode with fewer rooms and doors. As it happens, that redeemer does come and is revealed to be Theseus, who remarks to Ariadne at the story's end that he found it strange that the Minotaur hardly defended himself.

In this postmodern take on the Minotaur, the monster suffers from boredom and near madness, knowing that, despite being the son of a queen, he is quite alone in the world. The Minotaur remains baffled by his fate. Borges hints that the death of the Minotaur, who is associated with the

256

sun and perhaps even "created the stars and the sun and this enormous house" (Borges 140), is the passing of an old god and the beginning of a new dynasty. Although the defeat is a triumph for Theseus, the death of the Minotaur seems tragic, as his true identity has gone unrecognized and his loneliness has been mistaken for wickedness. In typical fashion, however, Borges creates an ambiguous ending, writing, "The morning sun reverberated from the bronze sword" (140). Is the choice of the word "redeemer," then, more literal than ironic? Has the Minotaur been freed from his exile and returned to his place as a sun god?

The Narrative Labyrinth

Contemporary literary critics such as J. Hillis Miller have analyzed story itself as a kind of labyrinth negotiated with the aid of story line, character, figure, and other elements of fiction, which together create the narrative thread. In *Ariadne's Thread: Story Lines* (1992) Miller concludes that each of these elements, though initially promising to lead to the heart of the narrative, in fact leads to a dead end, "the tropological name for which is *catachresis*" (Miller 224). In fact, the promise of the labyrinth "leading to something" is a lie:

> Each figure is a mask that deforms what it covers. Behind each disfiguring mask only another mask can be uncovered. The reader is always left face to face with what Henry James, in a splendid phrase in *The Golden Bowl*, calls a "figured void," though whether or not the apparent void is really empty is not certain. Narration and criticism disfigure what the tracks or traces of the story reveal. They

do this in putting forth words that seem devoted to tracking the quarry down, tracing out the meaning the figures reveal. But these words create new patterns of their own, covering the tracks they would elucidate, as a detective may make tracks of his or her own obliterating the tracks of the criminal. (256)

Here Miller describes exactly the same predicament Eco created for his detective-monk William of Baskerville, whose logical framework is turned against him by the murderer. Meanwhile, the murderer's true rationale remains hidden! Miller articulates one of the epistemological problems of postmodernity, which is the absence of a solid ground, in fiction, on which any certainty can be founded behind the figures and the forms of writing. Miller concludes, "it is also always possible to go beyond any apparent stopping place or ultimate point in a reading, even one that seems to be a culmination in some elegantly formulated and hermetically sealed aporia. The good reader will learn to distrust interpretations that claim to give reliable knowledge, even bracingly negative knowledge" (242).

The Funhouse and Narrative Uncertainty

In "Lost in the Funhouse" (1967), John Barth experiments with the narrative form Miller has called "unreliable" and reveals the ways in which a narrative can jump off the tracks, confounding our expectations of what a story is and should be. Wallace Martin asserts that Barth's narrative innovations belong to a group of literary works that changed the rules for discussion of narrative in advance of the critics, noting that, "While critics debate about theories, creative writers may produce new literary works that alter the very ground of the debate" (28). Anticipating Miller, Barth has his narrator stop and self-consciously analyze what he has just said, questioning throughout not only the overall direction of the story but even more microscopic elements such as timing, phrasing, and word choice. He sometimes leaves sentences unfinished so that they trail off into nothingness. He critiques his technique in mid-stream, bemoaning lack of detail here and questioning psychological realism there. He self-consciously "frets" over the inclusion of so much detail on the character's state of mind; in a move worthy of Eco, he includes an elaborate backstory that derails the forward movement of the plot by continuing to point backwards at an event that took place outside the frame of the story. The irony is that by breaking the narrative "rules," and throwing the Freytag's Triangle of exposition, rising action, climax, and denouement to the winds, Barth still creates a recognizable story, a "figure in the carpet," that emerges from the stops, starts, hesitations, interruptions, and backtracking of his narrative experiment. It is overtly mazelike in its many dead ends and unexpected turns and creates a sort of vertigo in the reader, who suddenly finds himself farther along than he realized he was.

By the end of the story, Ambrose seems still to be lost in the funhouse, writing his way toward possible endings that he has not yet reached. He inhabits the never-never land Miller delineates in Borges's short story, "Death and the Compass," in which the main character solves a knotty mystery only to bring about his own death, a death that is imminent but never quite happens. Miller asserts, "This perpetual intervention of yet another delay is like the first paradox of Zeno" (252). Borges comments on the nature of time according to the Greek philosopher Zeno in his essay, "Avatars of the Tortoise." In Borges's own words, quoted by Miller, "Movement is impossible (argues Zeno) for the moving object must cover half of the distance in order to reach its destination, and before reaching the half, half of the half, and before half of the half, half of the half of the half, and before . . ." (Borges 203).

Barth's narrator alludes to this same predicament several times, saying at one point, "At this rate our hero, at this rate our protagonist will remain in the funhouse forever" (723-24). And again: "We should be much farther along than we are; something has gone wrong; not much of this preliminary rambling seems relevant. Yet everyone begins in the same place; how is it that most go along without difficulty but a few lose their way?" (724). Again: "There's no point in going farther; this isn't getting anybody anywhere; they haven't even come to the funhouse yet" (727). Time seems to roll forward and backward, and even to be suspended, at the narrator's will. And yet the closing paragraphs of the story reveal an Ambrose looking back from somewhere in the future, understanding how his fate as a storyteller came to resemble the labyrinth in which he stumbled as a precocious thirteen-year-old: "He wishes he had never entered the funhouse. But he has. Then he wishes he were dead. But he's not. Therefore he will construct funhouses for others and be their secret operator—though he would rather be among the lovers for whom funhouses are designed" (738).

Despite its lack of conventional coherence, the story creates a memorably awkward and endearing narrator and captures the poignancy not only of adolescent confusion and yearning but the loneliness of the creative life, which Ambrose both anticipates and epitomizes. "Lost in the Funhouse" openly invokes the theme of the labyrinth, which the narrator mentions over and over. For Barth it is the metaphor for a postmodern narrative shattered into many possible alternatives, underlining the fact that any particular story is only one among many that could have been told. It is also a symbol for consciousness, which does not proceed smoothly and in a straight line but constantly changes direction, giving the narrative a "stream of consciousness" quality. The labyrinth is also the image of the ever-changing emotional and psychological landscape of adolescence, which leads to the labyrinthine mental and emotional landscape of the adult artist. Importantly, it is a metaphor for sexuality, both experienced and imagined. It is also a symbol for the life of the narrator, in all its frustrating perplexity, unexplained blind alleys, loneliness, and sense of being on a separate and little-traveled path. Lastly, it is the symbol for modern life in a non-religious age, when long-standing myths of the past have lost much of their power to guide us and a void seems to yawn in their place.

Ambrose comments on the way in which transportation to Ocean City, where he is headed with his family for their holiday, has changed. Previously, the trip was accomplished by train, which was not as fast or as convenient but featured more camaraderie as a large group of strangers journeyed together to the same place. Now, Ambrose travels with his family in their car; there is still, on the surface, the sense of a shared trip, although Ambrose's alienation reveals that in many ways he feels alone even in proximity to his family and the girl of his fantasies. Nevertheless, he is participating in an established family ritual with its own conventions and sense of shared expectations. Finally, Ambrose wanders completely "off the track," getting lost not just in the funhouse proper but in an obscure section not meant to be accessed by visitors. Separated from his brother and Magda, he occasionally hears people on the other side of the wall but is unable to reach them.

This progression is parallel to the one we have been examining in the march from premodernism to postmodernism. There is the initial shared journey, in which everyone gets to the same place at the same time, following an established route from which there is no deviating. Next, there is a small group, bound by family ties, venturing to the same destination, but on their own, a small microcosm, sharing their established ritual but feeling nostalgic for the camaraderie of the bigger group. Finally, Ambrose is on his own, wandering in the coils of the backside of the funhouse labyrinth, struggling not to panic and attempting to create order from his experience—a very postmodern predicament. "Even the designer and operator have forgotten this other part," Ambrose says, "that winds around on itself like a whelk shell. That winds around the right part like the snakes on Mercury's caduceus" (Barth 727). This labyrinth is reminiscent of the tightening maze of rooms in *The Name of the Rose*. Gaston Bachelard says that the curve "warms" but that angles "trap" and "detain" (144). If the "angle is masculine and the curve feminine" (Bachelard 146), Ambrose appears to be lost in the space between them. His labyrinth is a spiral broken up by false turns and dead ends so that instead of a rebirth, Ambrose experiences a suspension in time. He is always detained at the "half of the half of the half."

Ambrose notices the general decrepitude of the amusement park, a place that has fallen from its former glory. Even the silver gilding on the handles of the fortune-telling machine has disappeared: "the glass windows around the dummy were cracked and taped, her kerchiefs and silks long-faded" (Barth 728). He describes "the *vertigo attendant on his recognition* that Ocean City was worn out, the place of fathers and grandfathers, straw-boatered men and parasoled ladies survived by their amusements" (731). In his description of the funhouse, aside from noting that its makers have

263

forgotten about all of its lost corners (much as Daedalus was unable to remember all the complexities of his labyrinth), Ambrose mentions seeing the operator through the chink between two panels:

> a small old man, *in appearance not unlike* the photographs at home of Ambrose's late grandfather, nodding upon a stool beneath a bare, speckled bulb. A crude panel of toggle- and knife-switches hung beside the open fuse box near his head; elsewhere in the little room were wooden levers and ropes belayed to boat cleats. At the time, Ambrose wasn't lost enough to rap or call; later he couldn't find that crack. Now it seemed to him that he'd possibly dozed off for a few minutes somewhere along the way . . . he couldn't be sure he hadn't dreamed part or all of the sight. (730)

Ambrose has witnessed the god of the works sleeping behind the scenes of the funhouse, his hand no longer on the controls. This leads Ambrose to imagine himself as the master of the labyrinth, building a far superior one to the ramshackle version in which he finds himself. Though he wonders whether funhouses might not be out of date by the time he gets around to designing his, he brushes the thought aside as fantasies of building a better labyrinth come to the fore. In this funhouse, order will be exerted from an efficient control room, with Ambrose himself at the controls: "panel lights would show what was up in every cranny of its cunning of its multifarious vastness; a switch-flick would ease this fellow's way, complicate that's, to balance things out" (738). Even as Ambrose imagines himself as the omnipotent and benevolent designer of this labyrinth, he loses the thread of his thought and discovers himself still lost in the labyrinth he did not create.

264

In one comical scene, Ambrose comments on the diving of the other boys at the amusement park pool. He declines to participate, preferring to watch Peter and the other divers from the side of the pool, along with Magda. Ambrose describes the antics of the boys and young men, largely calculated to elicit attention and admiration from the girls nearby, but he is also struck by the repetitive, ritualistic, circular movement of the line of divers, up the ladder, onto the board, into the water, and back again. The only thing that distinguishes one diver from another is the execution of the dive, which each tries to make as daring, comical, or athletic as possible, and Ambrose notes that with each repetition of the circuit, it becomes more difficult to make one's dive new and exciting. In addition, the long build-up for one's turn on the board is followed by a disappointingly quick moment in the spotlight—and yet the divers stand in line again and again for another chance to dive.

Ambrose is aware that the diving makes a good literary device. It is easy to see diving as a metaphor for an individual life, in which one strives to carve out his place in the midst of stultifying routine and an endless round of days. The climactic dive itself is reminiscent of Childe Roland's defiant trumpet call, his moment of bravado in a spotlight about to go out, perhaps permanently. It is not surprising that Ambrose finds the repetitiveness boring, since he dreams of building funhouse mazes, despite his own inability to navigate them successfully. Peter, on the other hand, as Ambrose tells Magda, "in feigned admiration," is an excellent diver. " 'You really have to slave away at it to get that good' " (727). Conventional, unimaginative, happy-go-lucky Peter successfully competes at diving and, unlike Ambrose, has little trouble negotiating the funhouse. Unlike Ambrose, he does not get lost—even in the funhouse, he sticks to the beaten track, flirts with Magda, and makes it through without trauma or ever once stopping to consider the meaning of it all. On the diving board, he is one of many, distinguished only by his greater skill. "Spring, pose, splash. Spring, neat-o, splash," as Ambrose wryly sums up the experience (727). In the funhouse, Peter enjoys himself, "hollering joyously," tripping Magda and hitting her backside, and letting Magda chase him into the mirror maze. Ambrose, on the other hand, tries to explain the workings of the funhouse to Magda, "misses the point" of the tumbling barrel at the entrance, and is convinced (rightly) that the others are having more fun than he is. He hears Peter and Magda, who have gone ahead of him into the mirror maze, laughing together, and is poignantly aware of his singularity:

> "Here!" "No, here!" they shouted to each other; Peter said, "Where's Amby?" Magda murmured. "Amb?" Peter called. In a pleased, friendly voice. He didn't reply. The truth was, his brother was a *happy-go-lucky youngster* who'd've been better off with a regular brother of his own, but who seldom complained of his lot and was generally cordial. Ambrose's throat ached; there aren't enough different ways to say that. He stood quietly while the two young people giggled and thumped through the glittering maze,

266

hurrah'd their discovery of its exit, cried out in joyful alarm
at what next beset them. Then he set his mouth and
followed after, as he supposed, took a wrong turn, strayed
into the pass *wherein he lingers yet*. (Barth 735-36)

It is tempting to see Ambrose the same way Ambrose sees himself and to

equate him with the adventurous Grail Knight, striking off on his own to

enter the woods where it seems best to him. From this perspective,

Ambrose is the maze walker and Peter the walker of the unicursal labyrinth,

content to follow the established path and do things the conventional way.

The circular image of the diving ritual encourages this interpretation; Peter

excels at diving and doesn't mind waiting in line over and over again.

Ambrose refuses to participate and only pretends to be interested to

impress Magda; inwardly, he is bored. And yet in the passage quoted above,

we see Peter and Magda enjoying the experience of being lost in the maze.

The disorientation and confusion are temporary for them, a challenge to be

enjoyed and then left behind. Ambrose, the Daedalus of the story and a

would-be fabricator of labyrinths, is caught up in the labyrinth *en malo*. For

him, the labyrinth is both a permanent state of dislocation and a mental

challenge to be analyzed. He does not experience the bodily joy of either

diving or moving confidently through the labyrinth; Peter experiences both.

Who, then, is right? Possibly the one who navigates successfully (if

unthinkingly), who understands "what the labyrinth is for," and who comes

through the experience happy and unscathed. Peter is like the labyrinth dancers of the Renaissance (and perhaps the original labyrinth dancers, who participated in the dance as a fertility ritual), knowing the steps and performing them skillfully. Ambrose makes the labyrinth an intellectual experience, substituting his imaginings for the joyous, bodily experience he is unable to achieve. Immediately after he hears Peter and Magda having fun in the maze without him, he starts to follow them, somehow getting into a part of the labyrinth that most visitors never see. He imagines himself as a latter-day Ulysses, finding his way through the labyrinth with a blind girl who is also lost. Instead of staying onstage with the other players, Ambrose has wandered backstage into the props and cables. Since he is seeing what others do not even realize is there, it looks as if he is more knowledgeable than they are. If, however, he is unable to extricate himself from the labyrinth, what does his superior knowledge consist of? Ambrose resembles Socrates in Plato's dialogue, with the distinction that he is not able to end up back where he started but remains lost in the middle. His labyrinth is an intellectual one.

Ambrose revels in his intellectual superiority to his brother and excels at breaking experiences down into their constituent components and analyzing them, revealing the temperament of an engineer. He is clever with words, able to render his experiences into a narrative, and able to delve into the inner workings of his own emotions and perceptions (though perhaps no one else's). He is a Daedalus rather than a Theseus, but he longs to be both. Barth has painted a portrait not just of a precocious adolescent boy but of a modern individual trapped in the habit of intellectualizing.

Sexual Imagery and the Funhouse

The prevalence of sex, with everything else "as build-up," is impressed on Ambrose's mind most forcefully as he considers his surroundings at the amusement park. He observes that:

> In the tumbling-barrel, too, just inside the Devil's-mouth entrance to the funhouse, the girls were upended and their boyfriends and others could see up their dresses if they cared to. Which was the whole point, Ambrose realized. Of the entire funhouse! If you looked around, you noticed that almost all the people on the boardwalk were paired off into couples except the small children; in a way, that was the whole point of Ocean City! If you had X-ray eyes and could see everything going on at that instant under the boardwalk and in all the hotel rooms and cars and alleyways, you'd realize that all that normally *showed*, like restaurants and dance halls and clothing and test-your-strength machines, was merely preparation and intermission. (Barth 731-32)

Ambrose realizes this self-consciously and intellectually. His uncle is surprised when Ambrose declares his wish to enter the funhouse because, as Ambrose realizes, he does not think Ambrose knows what the purpose of the funhouse is. What others take for granted, Ambrose discovers with his intellect.

Though only a teenager, Ambrose typifies in his precocious way the predicament of the modern human. The myths of former years have faded and no longer hold power; even a child can see how old-fashioned

269

and out-of-date Ocean City is. Since he sees *through* everything, Ambrose is left with a feeling of loneliness and alienation. He imagines he is smarter, more loving, and more deserving of love than his brother, but he loses himself in the funhouse just at the moment he could have been found. He is reduced to making up a friend to share the journey with him, and it is unclear at the end how or with whom he has escaped the labyrinth. He speaks of the family in the car on the way home from Ocean City, and his uncle teasing him about the blind girl who became his companion in the funhouse. Whether or not she is real, her blindness seems to mirror a limitation in Ambrose's own outlook that affects his ability to navigate the maze.

Ambrose is a maze walker who would rather find a simpler path. Like the speaker in "Dover Beach," he has lost a living connection with the symbols of previous generations and has yet to find new ones. He sees and understands clearly what is happening but secretly wishes to be like his brother; he longs for a unicursal solution.

Miller's "Interrelations" and Ambrose's "Genealogy"

The "end" of the story reminds us of the truth we have been aware of all along: the narrative is a creation with stops, starts, "false turns," and "hesitations" on display. In the thick of the narrative, we become so caught up in the conventions of fiction (and our own desire for coherence) that we lose sight of the fact that the telling is at the narrator's whim. Choices have been made that eliminated other possibilities. The blind Negro girl may or may not have "been" there; the entire story is an artifice. The "unreliable" narrative is similar to that of Ian McEwan's *Atonement*, in which we are made aware of the motives of our narrator, who may have chosen an ending to satisfy her emotional needs (and ours). Both stories are postmodern commentaries on the arbitrary nature of storytelling and the possibility of many truths in any given situation. Multivocality is a possibility even for a single writer.

Miller's observation that all literary devices that appear to give coherence and solidity to narrative are merely threads that come unraveled the more closely we look at them is amply illustrated by Barth's story. Ambrose questions his ability to know himself, consistently loses the thread of his narrative, changes outcomes, then attempts to fix himself in space and time by imagining his genealogy, back to the time of Lord Baltimore and Charles I. Doing so only creates a sense of disorientation and is accompanied by thoughts of dirt and trash. *Anastomosis* is the revelation of the linkage of all human beings in a vast genealogical map that extends like a labyrinth all the way back to Eve (Miller 157). In this linkage, the self is lost in a network of sexual relationships. No wonder Ambrose feels dizzy.

Chapter 7
Plus Ça Change

The house is haunted and the ride gets rough
And you've got to learn to live with what you can't rise
above.

— Bruce Springsteen, "Tunnel of Love"

Archetypal images decide the fate of man.

— C. G. Jung, *The Tavistock Lectures*

The Labyrinth as Structure in the Contemporary World

The labyrinth continues to be a popular motif in literature and film, and in addition, a new fascination for both unicursal labyrinths and multicursal mazes as built structures has blossomed into an enterprise, particularly in North America and Europe. Mazes can be found everywhere from Africa to Australia, and building materials range from wood and wattle to mirrors and plastic. There are flat mazes (cut into turf, outlined on canvas, or designed with tiles and bricks) as well as vertical mazes (with walls of natural or man-made materials, such as willow or Lego bricks). Garden mazes are most often found in Great Britain, where the tradition of maze building has grown into a creative industry going well beyond hedge mazes in design ingenuity and innovative use of materials. In the United States, it is difficult to find hedge mazes outside of a few formal gardens, such as the Missouri Botanical Garden in St. Louis or the Magnolia Plantation Gardens in Charleston, South Carolina—except in autumn,

273

when corn mazes are a common sight.

The first corn maze was created in 1993 in Annville, Pennsylvania, a collaboration between theatre producer Don Frantz and leading maze designer Adrian Fisher. As Fisher tells it, Frantz was inspired by the popularity of the film *Field of Dreams* (1989) (in which a baseball field with supernatural power was created in a corn field) to envision an attraction built amid rows of corn (Fisher 127). As All-American as the image was, it also tapped into a more ancient association of maize with the life cycle. In the Navajo creation myth, the first human beings were made of corn; for many other Native Americans, corn was a deity or represented the life-giving properties of the gods. These traditions are similar to the association of Ceres or Demeter with grain as a symbol of fertility and the harvest—which brings us back to the labyrinth's ties to ancient fertility rites.

Usually, none of this is stated explicitly, although corn (or wheat) mazes are a common feature of fall festivals and harvest celebrations across the United States and in Britain. As temporary attractions, American corn mazes are often designed with a historic theme, seasonal motif, or "local color" in mind. For instance, the design may feature the face of a well-known person or the outline of a local landmark. The overall design of the maze is easily discerned when viewed from above (a view not available to the maze walker but often shown in advertising for the maze). An advantage for the proprietor is the ability to mow the maze down at the end of the season and create a completely different design the next year. One of

the hallmarks (and sources of fascination) of corn mazes is their complexity;

they may be ten acres or more in size and nearly impossible to complete

without recourse to a map. In the fall of 2011, one seven-acre maze in

Danvers, Massachusetts, made the news when an anxious family called 911

after being lost in the maze until darkness fell. Steve Inskeep of National

Public Radio reported that—ironically—the family was only twenty-five

feet from the street when they made the emergency call ("Corn Maze

Baffles Family of Four"). This family's experience pinpoints the problem

with a maze: it stops being fun when it becomes too complicated. The

mother told the dispatcher: "We thought this would be fun. Instead it's a

nightmare. I don't know what made us do this. . . . Never again" (" 'I Am

Really Scared': Family Lost in Corn Maze Calls 911 for Help").

The Labyrinth of Consciousness in Inception

A much talked about film, *Inception* (2010), carried the concept of

the labyrinth to yet another level of complexity in its depiction of a group

of experts probing the architecture of consciousness. This group of

specialists uses the ability to implant pre-designed structures in the dreams

of subjects as a way to manipulate outcomes and achieve certain results

(one of the team members is a young woman named Ariadne who is

discovered to have a talent for creating these structures). The viewer

experiences a dizzying and disorienting plunge through the multiple layers of consciousness and reality experienced by the characters, who must rely on certain clues, such as the behavior of a spinning top, to recognize base-level waking consciousness.

The end of the film generated heated discussion, on the Internet and elsewhere, as filmgoers attempted to establish whether the main character was "awake" or lost in a dream at the end of story. There was no clear consensus, even as fans analyzed the minutest of clues and endlessly debated the film's subtlest nuances. Filmgoers were divided among those who thought the protagonist was awake, those who thought him still asleep, and those who insisted that the ending was purposely ambiguous. The disquieting possibility of the protagonist being forever lost in his dream, which was suggested in the final frames of the film, sent a seismic tremor throughout the movie's vast audience. The viewer suddenly became aware that, if he accepted the film's premises, he could no longer be sure whether the "reality" presented was "real" or "manufactured." This predicament was a true maze indeed, one that was possibly without an exit.

The Labyrinth Revival

Aside from these developments, the last twenty years have witnessed a revived interest in unicursal labyrinths based on the medieval design. This phenomenon is largely due to the efforts of Lauren Artress, a canon at Grace Cathedral in San Francisco, who began discussing the spiritual and meditative possibilities of the labyrinth with audiences across the country after herself walking the still extant labyrinth in Chartres Cathedral. In *The Sacred Path Companion: A Guide to Walking the Labyrinth to Heal and Transform*, Artress reminds readers that there is much we do not know about the way medieval worshippers used the labyrinths (xii). Artress was moved by her own experiences and her observations of others walking a newly installed labyrinth in Grace Cathedral to develop guidelines for approaching the labyrinth as a spiritual practice. Her guidelines are based on her knowledge of both modern and historical labyrinths but largely grow out of contemporary practice and experience, not attempts to re-create what was done in the past.

Labyrinths and Meditation

The instructions provided for most labyrinths generally follow the pattern developed by Artress, which she calls either the Three Rs ("releasing, receiving, and returning," the summation of her earlier work on the labyrinth) or the Four Rs (an expanded version of the Three Rs that is more explicitly spiritual). Artress's Four Rs are "remembering, releasing, receiving, and resolving" (*Sacred Path Companion* 39-41). Most labyrinth guidelines include a statement that assures the visitor that there is no right or wrong way to approach the labyrinth. Although the unicursal labyrinth might appear to be self-explanatory, the fact that it is not is revealed by the number of people who ask what "the right way" to walk a labyrinth is. Although to some people the way in and out seems obvious, this is not true of everyone. (Author's note: I was once asked by a friend who encountered a labyrinth in a parking lot whether it was all right to walk across the circuits instead of through them to get to the middle. Although I repeated the advice that there is "no right or wrong way," it had not occurred to me that someone would consider walking across the circuits.) In our contemporary culture, it seems that even an ancient symbol may be interpreted in unimagined ways; what was once a "single path to truth" may now look like an invitation to "jump the fences."

The next bit of guideline lore is usually some form of the following advice: on walking into the labyrinth, the visitor is asked to think of a problem or a question that he or she is deeply concerned about. The walker is asked to meditate on that issue (or "ask for guidance") while walking into the labyrinth. On reaching the center, the visitor is asked to pause in an attitude of "receptivity" to see if an answer or suggested action presents itself. While walking out, the visitor is asked to concentrate on the ways in which he or she can act on any insight gained. Thus the labyrinth offers a type of walking meditation similar to that practiced by Zen Buddhists, although the labyrinth fosters a more guided meditation.

Artress recognizes the association of the labyrinth with "feminine" qualities of imagination and intuition that are often denigrated in our rational, male-dominated culture (*Walking a Sacred Path* 14). In her conception of labyrinth meditation, the center of the labyrinth can be a place for the walker, male or female, to practice "receptivity." The association of the center of the labyrinth with a source of inspiration and the conception of new ideas echoes the ancient connection of the labyrinth with birth and rebirth, physical and spiritual. Although Artress uses the image of the medieval Christian labyrinth, her interpretation of the symbolism reaches much farther back in time to encompass pre-Christian meanings.

Where the Labyrinths Are

Today's Chartres-inspired labyrinths are most frequently encountered in or near churches, although public parks, hospitals, retreat centers, and even cemeteries also host them. Occasionally, a labyrinth uses the Cretan pattern on which the medieval symbol was based, creating a much simpler design, although its meaning and uses are usually identical to those connected with the Chartres design. Although the modern labyrinth revival is connected with the Episcopal Church (of which Grace Cathedral is a member), the movement is ecumenical and also includes many non-religious labyrinth installations. A city, a non-profit organization, or a business might construct a labyrinth in a public or a private place. If a church hosts a labyrinth, the institution may be Episcopalian, Lutheran, Presbyterian, Methodist, Baptist, Catholic, Unitarian, or nearly any other denomination. Labyrinths may be painted, outlined with rocks, cut into a lawn, or laid out in marble or paving stones. The Robert Irwin-designed labyrinth (1997) in the garden of the Getty Museum in Los Angeles features azalea shrubs set in planters amidst a large fountain to form a "floating" water labyrinth meant to be viewed from above (Fisher 217).

Most but not all contemporary labyrinths are based on the "classical" eleven-circuit design of the labyrinth at Chartres, although it is not unusual for an installation to have fewer circuits or to employ an alternative design, such as the "Cretan" style. A common feature is the presence of markers or printed material with suggestions for the visitor on how to walk the labyrinth; this is especially true in religious and/or meditative settings. A non-religious setting may let the labyrinth stand on its own. An instance of the latter is the pavement labyrinth (2010) at the Seattle Center in Seattle, Washington. It is one of an eclectic group of attractions at the Seattle Center that includes the Space Needle, several museums, a sculpture garden, and a nearby pavement maze.

In this latter instance, the juxtaposition of the two labyrinths is readily visible from the viewing platform at the top of the Space Needle. The proximity of the two (labyrinth and maze) might have created a more striking contrast if the designers had made the two more equal in size and provided a stronger visual link between them. According to an article by Susan Gilmore in *The Seattle Times*, the maze was built primarily for children, and the labyrinth for adults. Gilmore quotes Debra Daoust, spokeswoman for the Seattle Center, as saying, "Our mission statement was to inspire the human spirit and we were looking for something that would appeal to adults. Labyrinths are trendy" ("Center Square Steps Into Fun Forest's Former Footprint"). Intriguingly, in this showcase of cutting-edge architecture (the Frank Gehry-designed Experience Music Project is adjacent to the labyrinth) and Space Age technology, the labyrinth is larger and more prominent than the maze. Their presentation is so entirely without fanfare that there are likely many visitors who only become aware of them when looking down at the plaza from the Space Needle (a testament to the persistent but sometimes unrecognized appearance of ancient symbols in the modern world).

The Carnival Labyrinth

Labyrinths in a somewhat disguised form have long been a feature of amusement park attractions. The "funhouse" (which we examined in Chapter 6), the tunnel of love, and the mirror maze are three examples. The "tunnel of love" is a modern form of the labyrinths of love that first appeared in the Middle Ages, using water and boats instead of shrubbery and walkways as the medium. In the presence of this attraction and its cousins, the funhouse and the mirror maze, one senses the faint echo of ancient fertility rites, the same association Ambrose discovers with such poignancy in "Lost in the Funhouse" (Barth 732).

Proving that this association is still alive and laden with modern complications, Bruce Springsteen's song "Tunnel of Love" captures the fear and uncertainty of the labyrinth of love as a literal structure and as it unfolds in the emotional complexities of a relationship. On the same album, *Tunnel of Love*, on which the title song appears, another song dealing with the uncertainties of a romance in which two people have lost their way is entitled "One Step Up (Two Steps Back)." As a kind of riff on Dante's *terza rima* (one step forward, one step back, then forward again) in *The Divine Comedy*, this song describes the maze of a troubled love affair in which the progress is, instead of haltingly forward, dismayingly retrograde. In another song, "Brilliant Disguise," the bewildered lover describes himself as a "lonely pilgrim" who is "lost in the darkness of our love." On this album, which *Rolling Stone* selected as number 25 of the "100 Best Albums of the Eighties" (1989) and number 475 of the "500 Greatest Albums of All Time" (2003), the tunnel of love is a leitmotif for the emotional darkness of a faltering romance. According to Jon Pareles, writing in *The New York Times*, Springsteen's songs on *Tunnel of Love* explore the darker byways of a relationship by "turning inward" and "pondering" ("His Kind of Heroes, His Kind of Songs"). The labyrinth of love here is intensely introspective as well as erotic.

Closed and Open-Ended Labyrinths

While we have considered the maze as a more fitting symbol of postmodern epistemology than the one-way labyrinth, the evident popularity of the unicursal labyrinth and the fact that it is a more prominent

282

fixture in most American communities brings up an interesting question: why is the unicursal eleven-circuit labyrinth, enduring symbol of Christian spirituality in the Middle Ages, found in so many modern settings in exactly the same form familiar to medieval Christians? It is true that many people attracted to the challenges and complications (without religious associations) of mazes have little interest in unicursal labyrinths, which are often steeped in spiritual correlations. By the same token, some people who do not enjoy mazes do like unicursal labyrinths; one woman quoted by Artress in her earlier book, *Walking a Sacred Path*, described the "stress" involved in trying to think one's way out of a maze in comparison with the relaxing predictability of a unicursal labyrinth (51-52). Some people enjoy both types. At the same time, it is common for people to associate the word "labyrinth" exclusively with a maze, especially if they have never seen a Chartres-style labyrinth; this is in spite of the widespread nature of the "labyrinth revival."

While the ties the unicursal labyrinth has to religion explain why people with no religious convictions may have little interest in "church" labyrinths, they do not explain the symbol's ubiquity in communities large and small, in varied settings and circumstances, across the United States. Artress ascribes the popularity of the labyrinth to its appeal, in the midst of a world of difficult choices, to a psyche hungry for centering symbols. She writes, "It invites our intuitive, pattern-seeking, symbolic mind to come forth. It presents us with only one, but profound, choice. To enter a labyrinth is to choose to walk a spiritual path" (*Walking a Sacred Path* 52). This spiritual path is not a dogmatic, religious path, but rather a personal one.

A Symbol Across Time

We have watched the symbolism of the literary maze take root and flourish, becoming increasingly open-ended (and non-centered) with the rise of postmodernism; we have interpreted its presence as a metaphor for an increasingly fragmented and complicated world. Then, at the end of the twentieth century, we have seen the unicursal labyrinth as a structure begin to appear once more, materializing everywhere from art museums to small-town churchyards. Is its appearance a symptom of a post-postmodernism that begins to conflate the emphasis on multiple, individual truths with an answering need to recover some firmly established common ground? Wendy Doniger points out the consequences of pluralism carried to its extreme conclusion. She writes, "The emphasis on individual cultures [or individual truths] . . . may lead to problems of infinite regress . . . This emphasis tends to generate a smaller and smaller focus until it is impossible to generalize even from one moment to the next" (67). Doniger goes on to remind us that any comparison of differences starts with an assumption of an underlying similarity. We are back once again in the territory of the Idealists and the Realists, attempting to "keep an exquisite balance between the Platonist drive to unity and the nominalist drive to the irreducibly particular. If we go to bed with Plato, we might better wake up with Aristotle" (Ralph Williams, qtd. in Doniger 67-68). One is reminded of the disorienting conclusion of *Inception*, in which the protagonist seems to suffer from a problem of infinite regress, not knowing which of his splintered selves is the true one.

In other words, denying commonalities in variant approaches to truth is as problematic as overemphasizing the similarities. Too much insistence on absolute difference makes it impossible to compare things—if they have *nothing* in common, one is left with a heap of disparate ideas and stories and no way to make sense of them. The stress of this situation, of living in a chaotic library of competing truths (as in *Inception*, "Lost in the Funhouse," or "The Library of Babel"), appears to call out a balancing image in response (Jung, "The Practical Use of Dream-Analysis" *CW* 16: 330). The unicursal labyrinth, with its roots in prehistory, brings us back to the common ground of human, biologically based experience buried under multiple layers of history, belief, and culture.

The unicursal labyrinth, while looking the same as it did a thousand years ago, has become a symbol that encompasses both the universal human experience of truth seeking and a very private and individual way of receiving that truth. Labyrinth walkers are not advised to meditate on the image of Jesus (or Buddha or Krishna); they are asked to look inside themselves for questions and answers that are highly idiosyncratic and personal. The universal aspect of the experience comes from the expectation that wisdom is available, and that answers exist, although the means for accessing them may lie in a faculty other than logical problem solving. The practice of walking a labyrinth suggests an opening to intuition, inspiration, universal wisdom, or whatever name the person gives to his or her individual experience of truth. Just as the traditional maze actually contains a hidden one-way path (so that the appearance of multiple avenues is an illusion and a solution is possible), the symbol of the unicursal labyrinth contains, paradoxically, room enough for an infinity of individual paths. What looks like a single path becomes a different road each time it is walked, even by the same person. The yearning for individuality and the experience of the universal are combined in a single symbol.

The labyrinth, which began in ancient times as a ritual, has become, for many, a ritual once again. It now facilitates a meditative state in which the bodily experience of walking unblocks habitual thought patterns and creates an opening for intuition or other forms of insight. In the modern world, having experienced the dizzying possibilities of competing truths, we are drawn not to deny the authenticity of multiple voices and points of view, but to search out an accompanying common ground. We enjoy the challenge of discovering our own path through life, or our own path through the corn maze at the local farm; our rational minds enjoy the task of solving the puzzle, though we may be put off by a maze that seems to entrap us. At the same time, in an age without a single guiding religious or philosophical truth, we seem to be drawn by an impulse like the one that touched our ancestors eons ago. The labyrinth attracts us as a path to our own "center," where we can contact a source of wisdom rooted in our psychosomatic nature, the nature that we all share as humans. Ariadne's thread is the umbilical cord that leads us back to a primordial state of unity with nature, where divisions, boundaries, and differences dissolve.

Works Cited

Abram, David. *The Spell of the Sensuous: Perception and Language in a More-Than-Human World.* New York: Vintage-Random, 1997.

Allums, Larry. "Dante's Transformation of Epic." *The Epic Cosmos.* Ed. Allums. Dallas: Dallas Institute, 1992. 157-84.

Arnold, Matthew. "Dover Beach." *The Major Victorian Poets: Tennyson, Browning, Arnold.* Ed. William E. Buckler. Boston: Houghton, 1973. 617-18.

Artress, Lauren. *The Sacred Path Companion: A Guide to Walking the Labyrinth to Heal and Transform.* New York: Riverhead, 2006.

---. *Walking a Sacred Path: Rediscovering the Labyrinth as a Spiritual Practice.* Revised ed. New York: Riverhead, 2006.

Attali, Jacques. *The Labyrinth in Culture and Society: Pathways to Wisdom.* Trans. Joseph Rowe. Berkeley: North Atlantic, 1999.

Bach, Johann Sebastian. BWV 591 *Kleines harmonisches Labyrinth.* 1717. Leipzig: Edition Peters, 1940.

Bachelard, Gaston. *The Poetics of Space.* Trans. Maria Jolas. Boston: Beacon, 1994.

Barth, John. "Lost in the Funhouse." *The Heath Introduction to Fiction.* Ed. John J. Clayton. Lexington: D. C. Heath, 1977. 719-38.

Becker, Ernest. *The Denial of Death.* New York: Free-Macmillan, 1973.

Bordo, Susan. *The Flight to Objectivity: Essays on Cartesianism and Culture.* Albany: State U of New York P, 1987.

Borges, Jorge Luis. *Labyrinths: Selected Stories & Other Writings.* Ed. Donald A. Yates and James E. Irby. New York: New Directions, 1964.

Brodtkorb, Paul, Jr. ["Selfhood and Others"]. *Moby-Dick.* By Herman Melville. Ed. Hershel Parker and Harrison Hayford. 2nd ed. New York: Norton, 2002. 669-74. Excerpt from *Ishmael's White World: A Phenomenological Reading of "Moby-Dick."* New Haven: Yale UP, 1965.

Brohi, Allahbakhsh K. "The Spiritual Significance of the Quran." *Islamic Spirituality: Foundations*. Ed. Seyyed Hossein Nasr. New York: Crossroad, 1987. 11-23. World Spirituality: An Encyclopedic History of the Religious Quest 19.

Brontë, Charlotte. *Jane Eyre*. New York: Penguin, 2009.

Browning, Robert. "Childe Roland to the Dark Tower Came." *The Norton Anthology of Western Literature*. Ed. Sarah Lawall. 8th ed. Vol. 2. New York: Norton, 2006. 850-56.

Brunel, Pierre, ed. *Companion to Literary Myths, Heroes and Archetypes*. Trans. Wendy Allatson, Judith Hayward, and Trista Selous. London: Routledge, 1992.

Buckler, William E. Introduction. *The Major Victorian Poets: Tennyson, Browning, Arnold*. Ed. Buckler. Boston: Houghton, 1973. x-xxiv.

Bunyan, John. *The Pilgrims Progress: From This World to That Which Is to Come*. Illus. Gertrude Demain Hammond. London: A & C Black, 1921.

Bushe, Vera. "Cycles of Becoming." *The Long Journey Home: Re-visioning the Myth of Demeter and Persephone for Our Time*. Ed. Christine Downing. Boston: Shambhala, 1994. 173-85.

Campbell, Joseph. *The Hero With a Thousand Faces*. 2nd ed. Princeton: Princeton UP, 1968. Bollingen Ser. XVII.

---. *The Masks of God: Occidental Mythology*. New York: Penguin Compass, 1976.

---. *Thou Art That: Transforming Religious Metaphor*. Ed. Eugene Kennedy. Novato: New World, 2001.

Chevalier, Jean, and Alain Gheerbrant, eds. *A Dictionary of Symbols*. Trans. John Buchanan-Brown. London: Penguin, 1996.

The Christmas Revels. "L'Homme Armé." By Josquin des Près. *Sing We Now of Christmas*. Revels, 1991. CD.

Cohen, Sarah R. *Art, Dance, and the Body in French Culture of the Ancien Régime*. Cambridge: Cambridge UP, 2000.

Collins, Wilkie. *The Woman in White*. Ed. T. N. R. Rogers. Mineola: Dover, 2005.

"Corn Maze Baffles Family of Four." Narr. Steve Inskeep. *Morning Edition*. Natl. Public Radio. WUKY, Lexington, 12 Oct. 2011. Radio.

Cornish, Alison. Introduction. *Reading Dante's Stars*. By Cornish. New Haven: Yale UP, 2000.

Cowan, Bainard. "America Between Two Myths: *Moby-Dick* as Epic." *The Epic Cosmos*. Ed. Larry Allums. Dallas: Dallas Institute, 1992. 217-46.

Dante Alighieri. *The Divine Comedy*. Trans. Allen Mandelbaum. New York: Everyman's-Knopf, 1995.

D'Avanzo, Mario L. " 'Childe Roland to the Dark Tower Came': The Shelleyan and Shakespearean Context." *Studies in English Literature (Rice)* 17.4 (1977): 695-708.

Doczi, György. *The Power of Limits: Proportional Harmonies in Nature, Art, and Architecture*. Boston: Shambhala, 2005.

Doniger, Wendy. *The Implied Spider: Politics & Theology in Myth*. New York: Columbia UP, 1998. Amer. Lectures on the Hist. of Religions. Amer. Acad. of Religion New Ser. 16.

Doob, Penelope Reed. *The Idea of the Labyrinth: From Classical Antiquity Through the Middle Ages*. Ithaca: Cornell UP, 1990.

Doran, Madeleine. Introduction. *A Midsummer Night's Dream. William Shakespeare: The Complete Works*. Ed. Alfred Harbage. New York: Viking, 1977. 146-49.

Downing, Christine. *The Goddess: Mythological Images of the Feminine*. New York: Authors Choice-iUniverse, 2007.

Dreyfus, Hubert, and Sean Dorrance Kelly. *All Things Shining: Reading the Western Classics to Find Meaning in a Secular Age*. New York: Free Press, 2011.

Durrell, Lawrence. *The Dark Labyrinth*. New York: Penguin, 1978.

Eco, Umberto. "Borges and My Anxiety of Influence." *On Literature*. Trans. Martin McLaughlin. Orlando: Harvest-Harcourt, 2005. 118-35.

---. *The Name of the Rose*. Trans. William Weaver. New York: Everyman's-Knopf, 2006.

Edinger, Edward F. *Ego & Archetype: Individuation and the Religious Function of the Psyche*. Boston: Shambhala, 1992.

---. *Melville's* Moby-Dick: *A Jungian Commentary*. New York: New Directions, 1978.

---. *The Psyche in Antiquity: Book Two, Gnosticism and Early Christianity—From Paul of Tarsus to Augustine*. Ed. Deborah A. Wesley. Toronto: Inner City, 1999. Studies in Jungian Psychology by Jungian Analysts 86.

Fisher, Adrian. *The Amazing Book of Mazes*. New York: Abrams-Harry N. Abrams, 2006.

"500 Greatest Albums of All Time." *Rolling Stone*. 2003: n. pag. *Rolling Stone*. Web. 27 Mar. 2012.

Freitas, Lima de. "Labyrinth." *Encyclopedia of Religion*. Ed. Lindsay Jones. 2nd ed. Vol. 8. Detroit: Macmillan Reference USA-Gale, 2005. 5273-79. *Gale Virtual Reference Lib*. Web. 27 Mar. 2012.

Freud, Sigmund. *Beyond the Pleasure Principle*. Trans. C. J. M. Hubback. London: International Psycho-Analytic, 1922. International Psycho-Analytic Lib. 4.

Gilmore, Susan. "Center Square Steps Into Fun Forest's Former Footprint." *Seattle Times* 22 May 2010: n. pag. *Seattle Times*. Web. 27 Mar. 2012.

Greene, Thomas M. "Labyrinth Dances in the French and English Renaissance." *Renaissance Quarterly*. 54.4 (2001): 1403-66.

Harrison, Robert Pogue. *Forests: The Shadow of Civilization*. Chicago: U of Chicago P, 1993.

Hatab, Lawrence J. *Myth and Philosophy: A Contest of Truths*. Chicago: Open Court, 1990.

Hesiod. *The Works and Days. Theogony. The Shield of Herakles.* Trans. Richmond Lattimore. Illus. Richard Wilt. Ann Arbor: Ann Arbor Paperbacks-U of Michigan P, 1991.

Hillman, James. *Re-Visioning Psychology.* New York: HarperPerennial, 1992.

Homer. *The Iliad.* Trans. E. V. Rieu. Rev. Peter Jones and D. C. H. Rieu. Ed. Jones. London: Penguin, 2003.

Hunt, Winifred. "On Even Ground: A Note on the Extramundane Location of Hell in *Paradise Lost.*" *Modern Language Quarterly* 23.1 (1962): 17-19.

" 'I Am Really Scared': Family Lost in Corn Maze Calls 911 for Help." *Msnbc.com.* Msnbc Digital Network, 12 Oct. 2011. Web. 27 Mar. 2012.

Inception. Dir. Christopher Nolan. Perf. Leonardo DiCaprio, Ken Watanabe, Joseph Gordon-Levitt, Marion Cotillard, and Ellen Page. Warner Bros. Pictures, 2010. Film.

Irwin, John T. *The Mystery to a Solution: Poe, Borges, and the Analytic Detective Story.* Baltimore: Johns Hopkins UP, 1996.

Jung, C. G. "Commentary on 'The Secret of the Golden Flower.' " *The Collected Works of C. G. Jung.* Vol. 13. Ed. Herbert Read, Michael Fordham, Gerhard Adler, and William McGuire. Trans. R. F. C. Hull. Princeton: Princeton UP, 1967. Bollingen Ser. XX.

---. "Conscious, Unconscious, and Individuation." *The Collected Works of C. G. Jung.* Vol. 9i. Ed. Herbert Read, Michael Fordham, and Gerhard Adler. Trans. R. F. C. Hull. New York: Pantheon, 1959. Bollingen Ser. XX.

---. "The Practical Use of Dream-Analysis." *The Collected Works of C. G. Jung.* Vol. 16. Ed. Herbert Read, Michael Fordham, and Gerhard Adler. Trans. R. F. C. Hull. New York: Pantheon, 1954. Bollingen Ser. XX.

---. "Psychology and Religion." *The Collected Works of C. G. Jung.* Vol. 11. Ed. Herbert Read, Michael Fordham, and Gerhard Adler. Trans. R. F. C. Hull. New York: Pantheon, 1958. Bollingen Ser. XX.

Jung, Emma, and Marie-Louise von Franz. *The Grail Legend*. Trans. Andrea Dykes. 2nd ed. Princeton: Princeton UP, 1998. Mythos.

Kanekar, Aarati. "From Building to Poem and Back: The Danteum as a Study in the Projection of Meaning Across Symbolic Forms." *The Journal of Architecture* 10.2 (2005): 135-59.

Kerényi, Carl. *Dionysos: Archetypal Image of Indestructible Life*. Trans. Ralph Manheim. Princeton: Princeton UP, 1976. Bollingen Ser. LXV.2. Mythos.

---. *The Gods of the Greeks*. New York: Thames, 1980.

---. "Kore." *Essays on a Science of Mythology: The Myth of the Divine Child and the Mysteries of Eleusis*. By C. G. Jung and C. Kerényi. Trans. R. F. C. Hull. Princeton: Princeton UP, 1969. 101-55. Bollingen Ser. XXII.

Kern, Hermann. *Through the Labyrinth: Designs and Meanings Over 5,000 Years*. Ed. Robert Ferré and Jeff Saward. Trans. Abigail H. Clay, Sandra Burns Thomson, and Kathrin A. Velder. Munich: Prestel, 2000.

Leyerle, John. "The Rose-Wheel Design and Dante's *Paradiso*." *University of Toronto Quarterly* 46.3 (1977): 280-308.

Lincoln, Bruce. "The Rape of Persephone." *The Long Journey Home: Re-Visioning the Myth of Demeter and Persephone for Our Time*. Ed. Christine Downing. Boston: Shambhala, 1994. 166-72. Excerpt from *Emerging From the Chrysalis: Studies of Rituals of Women's Initiation*. By Lincoln. Cambridge: Harvard UP, 1981. 72-90.

Lodge, David. Introduction. *The Name of the Rose*. By Umberto Eco. Trans. William Weaver. New York: Everyman's-Knopf, 2006. vii-xxiv.

Luke, Helen M. *Dark Wood to White Rose: Journey and Transformation in Dante's Divine Comedy*. New York: Parabola, 1993.

Mandelbaum, Allen, trans. *The Aeneid of Virgil*. New York: Bantam, 1972.

---. *The Metamorphoses of Ovid*. San Diego: Harvest-Harcourt, 1995.

Martin, Wallace. *Recent Theories of Narrative*. Ithaca: Cornell UP, 1986.

Matarasso, P. M., trans. *The Quest of the Holy Grail*. London: Penguin, 1969.

Matthews, W. H. *Mazes and Labyrinths: A General Account of Their History and Development*. 1922. Charleston: Forgotten Books, 2008.

Melville, Herman. *Moby-Dick*. Ed. Hershel Parker and Harrison Hayford. 2nd ed. New York: Norton, 2002.

Merleau-Ponty, Maurice. Preface. *Phenomenology of Perception*. By Merleau-Ponty. Trans. Colin Smith. London: Routledge, 2002.

Miller, J. Hillis. *Ariadne's Thread: Story Lines*. New Haven: Yale UP, 1992.

Mills, Sophie. *Theseus, Tragedy and the Athenian Empire*. New York: Oxford UP, 1997. Oxford Classical Monographs.

Milton, John. *Paradise Lost. Samson Agonistes. Lycidas*. Ed. Edward Le Comte. New York: Mentor-New American, 1961.

Morford, Mark P. O., and Robert J. Lenardon. *Classical Mythology*. 8th ed. New York: Oxford UP, 2007.

Nietzsche, Friedrich. *The Birth of Tragedy and Other Writings*. Ed. Raymond Geuss and Ronald Speirs. Trans. Speirs. Cambridge: Cambridge UP, 1999. Cambridge Texts in the Hist. of Philos.

"100 Best Albums of the Eighties." *Rolling Stone*. 16 Nov. 1989: n. pag. *Rolling Stone*. Web. 27 Mar. 2012.

Panofsky, Erwin. *Gothic Architecture and Scholasticism*. Cleveland: Meridian-World, 1957.

Pareles, Jon. "His Kind of Heroes, His Kind of Songs." *New York Times*. 14 July 2002: n. pag. *NYTimes.com*. Web. 27 Mar. 2012.

Parker, Hershel, and Harrison Hayford. Preface. *Moby-Dick*. By Herman Melville. Ed. Parker and Hayford. 2nd ed. New York: Norton, 2002. ix-xiv.

Peyronie, André. "The Labyrinth." *Companion to Literary Myths, Heroes and Archetypes*. Ed. Pierre Brunel. Trans. Wendy Allatson, Judith Hayward, and Trista Selous. London: Routledge, 1992. 685-719.

---. "The Minotaur." *Companion to Literary Myths, Heroes and Archetypes*. Ed. Pierre Brunel. Trans. Wendy Allatson, Judith Hayward, and Trista Selous. London: Routledge, 1992. 814-21.

Plato. *Euthydemus*. *Plato in Twelve Volumes: Laches. Protagoras. Meno. Euthydemus*. Trans. W. R. M. Lamb. Vol. 2. Cambridge: Harvard UP, 1924. Loeb Classical Lib. 165.

Plutarch. *Lives: Theseus and Romulus. Lycurgus and Numa. Solon and Publicola*. Trans. Bernadotte Perrin. Vol. 1. Cambridge: Harvard UP, 1914. Loeb Classical Lib. 46.

Purce, Jill. *The Mystic Spiral: Journey of the Soul*. New York: Thames, 1980. Art and Imagination.

Rabel, Robert J. *Plot and Point of View in the* Iliad. Ann Arbor: U of Michigan P, 1997.

Radding, Charles M., and William W. Clark. *Medieval Architecture, Medieval Learning: Builders and Masters in the Age of Romanesque and Gothic*. New Haven: Yale UP, 1992.

Reeve, Matthew M. Introduction. *Reading Gothic Architecture*. Ed. Reeve. Turnhout: Brepols, 2008. 1-10. Studies in the Visual Cultures of the Middle Ages 1.

Saward, Jeff. *Labyrinths & Mazes: A Complete Guide to Magical Paths of the World*. New York: Lark-Sterling, 2003.

Schimmel, Annemarie. *Mystical Dimensions of Islam*. Chapel Hill: U of North Carolina P, 1975.

Schor, Naomi. "Before the Castle: Women, Commodities, and Modernity in *Au Bonheur des Dames*." *Bad Objects: Essays Popular and Unpopular*. By Schor. Durham: Duke UP, 1995. 149-55. Trans. of "Devant le château: Femmes, Marchandises et Modernité dans *Au Bonheur des Dames*." *Mimésis et Semiosis: Littérature et Représentation*. Ed. Philippe Hamon and Jean-Pierre Leduc Adine. Paris: Nathan, 1992. 179-87.

Sealts, Merton M., Jr. "Whose Book Is *Moby-Dick*?" *Melville's Evermoving Dawn: Centennial Essays*. Ed. John Bryant and Robert Milder. Kent: Kent State UP, 1997. 58-74.

Segal, Charles. *Language and Desire in Seneca's* Phaedra. Princeton: Princeton UP, 1986.

Shakespeare, William. *A Midsummer Night's Dream*. Ed. Madeleine Doran. *William Shakespeare: The Complete Works*. Ed. Alfred Harbage. New York: Viking, 1977. 150-74.

Slattery, Dennis Patrick. "Dante's Image of Hope in *Paradiso*." *Renascence* 33.1 (1980): 24-35.

---. "Dante's Terza Rima in *The Divine Comedy*: The Road of Therapy." *The International Journal of Transpersonal Studies* 27 (2008): 80-90.

Springsteen, Bruce. *Tunnel of Love*. Columbia Records, 1987. CD.

Sten, Christopher. "Threading the Labyrinth: *Moby-Dick* as Hybrid Epic." *A Companion to Herman Melville*. Ed. Wyn Kelley. Malden: Blackwell, 2006. 408-22. Blackwell Companions to Lit. and Culture 41.

Tarnas, Richard. *Cosmos and Psyche: Intimations of a New World View*. New York: Plume-Penguin, 2007.

Taylor, Charles. *A Secular Age*. Cambridge: Belknap-Harvard UP, 2007.

Taylor, Mark C. *Erring: A Postmodern A/theology*. Chicago: U of Chicago P, 1987.

---. "Refiguring Religion." *Journal of the American Academy of Religion*. 77.1 (2009): 105-19.

Tolkien, J. R. R., trans. *Sir Gawain and the Green Knight, Pearl, and Sir Orfeo*. New York: Ballantine-Random, 1980.

Van Gennep, Arnold. *The Rites of Passage*. Trans. Monika B. Vizedom and Gabrielle L. Caffee. Chicago: U of Chicago P, 1960.

Wright, Craig. *The Maze and the Warrior: Symbols in Architecture, Theology, and Music*. Cambridge: Harvard UP, 2004.

ABOUT THE AUTHOR

Mary Hackworth has a Ph.D. and an M.A. in myth studies from Pacifica Graduate Institute along with an M.S. in Library Science, an M.A. in English, and a B.A. in Psychology from the University of Kentucky. She is a former librarian, copywriter, and editorial assistant and lives in Lexington, Kentucky, where she blogs on mythology, writing, and everyday life.

Made in the USA
Charleston, SC
08 August 2016